Dallapiccola on Opera

Dallapiccola on Opera

Selected Writings of Luigi Dallapiccola

Volume One

Translated and Edited by
Rudy Shackelford

Foreword by
Antal Doráti

Musicians on Music
No. 4

**TOCCATA
PRESS**

First published in English by Toccata Press, 1987
© Il Saggiatore, Milan, 1980.
Translation © Rudy Shackelford, 1987
Music examples by Barry Ould.

British Library Cataloguing in Publication Data

Dallapiccola, Luigi
   Dallapiccola on opera : selected writings of
   Luigi Dallapiccola.—(Musicians on music,
   ISSN 0264–6889; no. 4)
   1. Opera
   I. Title   II. Shackelford, Rudy   III.Parole e
   musica. *English. Selections.*   IV. Series
   782.1   ML1700

   ISBN 0–907689–09–4 (cased)
   ISBN 0–907689–10–8 (paperback)

Set in 11 on 12pt Baskerville
by Alan Sutton Publishing, Gloucester.
Printed and bound by Short Run Press Ltd, Exeter.

Contents

		Page
Foreword	*Antal Doráti*	9
Overture	*Rudy Shackelford*	13
Acknowledgements		27
Publisher's Note		31

PART I
SONGS OF IMPRISONMENT,
SONGS OF LIBERATION
(PIECES OF A LIFE)

The Genesis of *Canti di Prigionia* and *Il Prigioniero*	35
Job, a Mystery Play	61
Pages from a Diary: Alexander Moissi	70
Two Encounters with Antoine de Saint-Exupéry	74
For the Première of *Volo di Notte*	79

PART II
FROM MALIPIERO TO MOZART:
COMMENTS AND COMMUNICATIONS

Comments on Contemporary Opera	99
Further Comments on Opera	107
In Memoriam Gian Francesco Malipiero	109
L'Enfant et les Sortilèges	117
Pages from a Diary: *Salome*	126
Letter to Léonide Massine	129
Letter to Wolfgang Wagner	131
Words and Music in 19th-Century Italian Opera	133
Pages from a Diary: *Rigoletto*	164
Reflections on *Simon Boccanegra*	172
Thoughts on a Passage in *Falstaff*	182
Notes on the Statue Scene in *Don Giovanni*	186

PART III
THE ULYSSES THEME
(PIECES OF A MYTH)

Monteverdi's *Il Ritorno di Ulisse in Patria*   215

Birth of a Libretto   232

Ulisse at La Scala   263

Three Scenes from *Ulisse*   267

Index   280

List of Illustrations

	Page
Dallapiccola with Roger Sessions around 1960	15
Il Prigioniero: The Prisoner sees the stars	56
Job: Job demands an answer	66
Volo di Notte: Fabien's last message	88–89
From the manuscript of '*Parole e Musica nel Melodramma*'	157
Figure 1: the terzetto from *Un Ballo in Maschera*, Act II	158–159
Figure 2: the structure of *Don Giovanni*	196
Fernando Farulli's designs for the première of *Ulisse*	241, 245, 249, 252, 269, 271, 277
Figure 3: the structure of the libretto of *Ulisse*	255
Ulisse: Ulysses contemplates the stars	278

Foreword
Antal Doráti

Reading these extremely intriguing, stimulating writings of Luigi Dallapiccola, I felt as if I were sitting with him in his study, or in mine, discussing the same subjects with him, passionately, at considerable length, way into the small hours of the night.

As it happened, I was at his home in Florence only once and he never in mine; we met at other people's lodgings, in hotels and opera houses. But those extended discussions did take place – sometimes, I believe, to the discomfort of our fellow humans, whose own conversations or rest might easily have been disturbed by the noise we made, for our voices were anything but restrained.

The thermometer of passion rose parallel with our agreement on one point or another. When we disagreed, we were polite and matter-of-fact; but when we had the same or similar views, then – oh! then we went 'to town', 'to the world', even 'to the universe' (mostly the last), wherever our point of departure had sent us.

Our main contacts were centred around various productions of his *Il Prigioniero*, which I had the pleasure of conducting often and which is particularly near to my heart. The presence of composers at rehearsals is not always an asset to the work of preparation. Dallapiccola's presence always was; his comments were lucid, constructive, interesting. He did not have stifled, fixed opinions of his works and of the way they were to be reproduced. He felt the independent life-pulse of his music and was not only open to new approaches to it, but encouraged them, kindled them – often provoked them.

That was long ago – and we were young then.

Today Luigi Dallapiccola is firmly established as one of the most significant composers of our time. (I avoid the word 'great', for it is used – and misused – too often nowadays. I shall be ready to employ it again if and when it loses its currently somewhat embarrassing connotations.) This book, to which I have the pleasure and honour to supply these introductory words, is a mile-stone – as are quite a number of publications by now – establishing him a decade or two later as an extremely fine and important writer. With this I refer not only to his profundity and sincerity, to the merciless sharpness of his logic as well as of his conscience, or the 'Sardanapalian riches' of his knowledge and culture (an expression with which he once decorated a colleague; I now borrow it to describe him); but also – and in the context of these essays perhaps mainly, for it is the word that makes the writer, and vice versa – to his exceptional, creative command of language.

This command is so strong that it is clearly felt even in translation, but it shines out, of course, in its full splendour in the noblest use of his native tongue, in which he was well nigh unsurpassable, even in his most casual conversation. One should have heard him.

One should, indeed, have heard him – not reading a paper in public (I didn't know him as lecturer, although I presume that he must have been very eloquent), but speaking in private. His voice was clear and ringing, in the range of baritone, his articulation as precise as one can imagine and his manner convincing to the border of demagogy. Yet he never fell into rhetoric – he was basically uninterested in it – and always remained within the realm of conversation.

In fact – and here comes the actual message of this short preamble, that I think the readers of this volume should and might like to know before embarking on their reading – Dallapiccola was, to me and, I am certain, to all who knew him, one of the last masters of that sublime art which in our own days has (alas!) dwindled near to complete extinction: the art of human dialogue, of conversation.

Perhaps I might be permitted to stray from my subject for a moment with the melancholy thought that if today the wish for and the satisfaction derived from the art of dialogue really did exist, many grave problems and sorrows of our age would look more hopeful than they do; and also that so far, possibly, the real warriors for human peace are the creative conversationalists, dialoguists, the Dallapiccolas, their ancestors and – if they come forth – their descendants.

I began by saying that I felt I was talking with Luigi Dallapiccola when I read his writings. For me it was easy to recreate him in my fantasy. For someone who did not know him, who never met him in the flesh, had never seen that proud bearing of his head (he looked much taller than he actually was), never heard his precise, intense voice, never watched his mind working behind his face – it was actually 'visible' – it will not be so simple to conjure up his presence.

Nevertheless, let me remind the reader: what you have before you are, in essence, not monologues but dialogues, in which the author speaks not *to* but *with* you. You should therefore not just 'read' these essays, sketches, letters, but allow their writer to reach you through them and *answer him*: agree, disagree, probe, question, bring forth new ideas – keep him company.

And he will continue to talk with you, long after you have turned the last page.

Overture

Rudy Shackelford

'The theatre has always had a charm for me,' Luigi Dallapiccola remarked, 'that I could find in no other medium, be it orchestral or chamber music.'[1] The manifold sources and resources of that charm are explored in this book, gathering the most significant writings on opera from the thirty-five-year period, 1938–73, that spans his entire career as 'a man of the theatre'.

Dallapiccola's characteristic method of investigation, both of self and the world, was a *recherche du temps perdu* understood not as passive 'remembrance' but as an active, relentless *search*. I have therefore arranged the texts in a broadly anti-chronological sequence according to subject, starting around 1950 and tracing a retrospective arc of slightly longer than three hundred years. The first half of the present century is most densely populated, with such figures as Strauss and Busoni, Schoenberg and Berg, Debussy, Ravel, and Malipiero; while Wagner and, above all, Verdi represent the 19th century, Mozart the 18th. The deepest stratum penetrated by this descent into 'the well of the past' is the earlier 17th century of the first great opera composer, Claudio Monteverdi.[2]

The Ulysses theme of Monteverdi's *Il Ritorno di Ulisse in*

---

[1] 'Luigi Dallapiccola: Fragments from Conversations', presented by Hans Nathan, *The Music Review*, Vol. XXVII, No. 4, Cambridge (UK), November 1966, p. 307.

[2] 'Perhaps it is not far-fetched to suggest that Dallapiccola is in fact, both technically and spiritually, in Monteverdi's direct line. Monteverdi's pre-occupation with vocal line, his amazing sense of timbre, his daring in the treatment of affective harmony, are all found in Dallapiccola.'
Richard F. Goldman, 'Current Chronicle: New York', *The Musical Quarterly*, Vol. XXXVII, No. 3, New York, July 1951, p. 406.

Patria provides, via Dallapiccola's tercentenary 'practical edition' of that opera (1941–42) and his own stupendous *Ulisse* (1960–68), both a point of return to the later 20th century – 'a time of doubt, of perennial inquiry' – and a glance into an even more profound abyss of history – the Greek myth, and of memory – a 1911 film of *The Odyssey*. The eloquent, pathetic silence of that Homeric travesty, which so indelibly touched the eight-year-old boy, is broken, finally, more than half a century later, in the Epilogue of his last opera (see page 276). Here occurs the revelation that at once solves the riddle posed by the Prisoner at the end of *Il Prigioniero* (1944–48) and resolves the quest begun by the composer himself *Nel mezzo del cammin*[3]. . . .

Like Dante, his polestar, Dallapiccola was an intensely autobiographical – not to say confessional – writer. 'For the composer who writes criticism,' he observed apropos of the centenary of Schoenberg's birth, 'every sentence may offer a clue for the investigation of his personal problems.'[4] Roger Sessions, another artist endowed with this double perspective, cogently articulated its extents and limits in 1939, the tragically eventful year that saw the completion of Dallapiccola's first opera, *Volo di Notte*:

> Many composers have been active as critics and theorists, and in fact it is to composers that we owe a tremendous proportion of what has been most illuminating and most enduring in these fields. The composer's point of departure, however, is entirely different from – perhaps is even opposed to – that of

---

[3] 'Alone on the same metaphysical sea where Melville's "Rachel", searching for her missing children, was to find only the orphan Ishmael, Ulysses discovers his Father in a heaven unknown to Homer. The veiled B major triad which had previously tempted him with dreams of immortality is now, beneath the night stars, heard with new ears. It is the promise of another kind of victory over death, and the antithesis of that flawed B minor triad which in *Il Prigioniero* had offered false hope as the ultimate torture'.

David Drew, 'Dallapiccola's Odyssey', *The Listener*,
LXXX, London, 17 October 1968, p. 514.

[4] Luigi Dallapiccola, '*Arnold Schoenberg. "Premessa a un Centenario"*', *Parole e Musica*, ed. Fiamma Nicolodi, Il Saggiatore, Milan, 1980, p. 247.

*Dallapiccola with Roger Sessions in New York, around 1960
(photograph courtesy of BMI, New York).*

the scientific scholar or thinker. It is based not on careful analysis, weighing, and comparison of facts, but at best on an insight, born of intense and active experience, into the nature of the materials and the creative processes of his art.[5]

After developing this antithesis further, Sessions concedes that 'such distinctions can never be absolute; not only do pure types scarcely ever exist, but it is certainly not desirable that they should'. Thus the composer who calmly affirms his intention to exhaust all the possibilities of the

---

[5] Roger Sessions, 'The Composer and His Message', *Roger Sessions on Music: Collected Essays*, ed. Edward T. Cone, Princeton University Press, Princeton, 1979, p. 4; subsequent quotation from p. 5.

twelve-tone system 'by means of *sensibility rather than theory*'[6] can submit the Act II terzetto of *Un Ballo in Maschera* to the most minute, 'scientific' scrutiny, with the defence that 'analysis can neither detract from what is aesthetically perfect nor add to what is artistically worthless' (see pp. 154–163). And the analyst astonished by Verdi's intuitive 'miracle of proportions' can comment, on his own un-planned, ingenuously planted symmetries:

> I believe that the dance of Apollo in *Marsia* is so singularly effective because it occurs in the arithmetically exact middle of the ballet. Indeed, when Apollo reverses his lyre (a gesture of the highest dramatic significance – in ballets, as is well known, one hears with the eyes), the sixteenth minute has arrived, and the work lasts thirty-two minutes. This fact I did not know before Milloss discovered it when he staged *Marsia*.[7]

Sessions alludes also to certain 'limitations of personality' that condition the composer's insight. Such limitations – or eccentricities – of vision may be manifested in those uncon-scious *misreadings* of the world or self that often give an artist his first vital impulse. Perceiving the Statue scene in *Don Giovanni* as a foreglimpse of 20th-century expressionism, Dallapiccola overlooks the precedents for the Commendato-re's tenths. Vocal intervals larger than the octave were, in fact, common property of *opera seria* from the time of Handel. And the language of 19th-century librettos, which strikes Dallapiccola as 'surrealistic', is really only the idiom of Italian tragic drama from Alfieri to Manzoni and beyond.[8]

[6] Luigi Dallapiccola, '*Testimonianza sulla Dodecafonia*', *Parole e Musica*, p. 465, italics added. *Cf.* Josef Rufer, *Composition with Twelve Notes*, transl. Humphrey Searle, Macmillan, New York, 1954, p. 180.

[7] 'Luigi Dallapiccola: Fragments from Conversations', p. 299.

Marsia, dramatic ballet in one act (1942–43), after a scenario by Aurel M. Milloss; première: Venice, Teatro La Fenice, 9 September 1948, directed by Igor Markevitch. This work portrays the famous contest between the satyr Marsyas, discoverer of music, and the god Apollo, who reverses his lyre and continues to play without touching its strings. He then challenges Marsyas to reverse his flute and make music. The primitive being, raised to human dignity by the gift of art, is punished with death for his presumption.

[8] See Fedele d'Amico, '*Il Gusto di Dallapiccola*', in *Luigi Dallapiccola: Saggi, Testimonianze, Carteggio, Biografia e Bibliografia*, ed. Fiamma Nicolodi, Edizioni Suvini Zerboni, Milan, 1975, pp. 43–44 and 48.

Again, when he writes about Dante's account of Ulysses (*Inferno*, XXVI): 'Dante certainly did not fabricate his interpretation, for already in *The Odyssey* the poem of "the search" is grafted onto the poem of "the return"', Dallapiccola forgets – creatively! – that Ulysses is hardly free to shape his own destiny in the way of modern existential man. The hero's path is pre-ordained by the gods, and foretold by the oracles and seers, of Greek legend. Nor did Dante have direct knowledge of Homer's epos; his sources were Virgil, Cicero, Ovid, *et alii*.[9]

These are some suggestive misreadings of external signs, and they almost never invalidate the fascinating examples Dallapiccola adduces, or the conclusions he draws, in his writings on music. But how does he read 'the inner book of unknown symbols' that Proust mentions in the last volume of *The Search*?

As early as 1938, in response to an academic questionnaire, the composer discerned a *constant* factor in his creative process: 'the first idea that flashed into my mind, rather than being a germ cell, was the culminating point of the whole composition', he wrote concerning *Tre Laudi*, then one of his major works and one he subsequently described as a 'study' for *Volo di Notte*. In this, as in several later, dodecaphonic scores, including the mystery play *Job* (1950), the *punto culminante* does in fact coincide with the first passage written. Dallapiccola began the composition of *Job* with its penultimate episode (No. 6, for chorus) and immediately addressed the problem of weaving into the serial texture a quotation from the Gregorian '*Te Deum Laudamus*'. Many other works, however, were either composed straight through from beginning to end – all the purely instrumental pieces, and the instrumental movements of larger vocal works like *Requiescant* (1957–58) – or else in a more complicated order. *Il Prigioniero* originated from the central aria in three stanzas, *Ulisse* from a twelve-tone row conceived on 15 February 1960 during a brief train

---

[9] See Michelangelo Zurletti, '*Ulisse*', programme notes for the non-commercial, 'live' recording of the opera made by RAI Radiotelevisione Italiana, Rome, 15 January 1972.

ride from Asolo to Venice. But this row was later used in Act I, Scene 3 (the Circe episode), whereas Dallapiccola began the actual composition of the opera in July 1960 with the Prologue, Scene 1 (Calypso).[10]

A somewhat exceptional rule, then, this creative 'constant'! But a generalization typical of Dallapiccola, and one that serves 'neither as a mask for analytical laziness nor a pretext for mere rhetorical bombast. Rather, in this specific context,' concludes Fiamma Nicolodi, 'it only evinces his desire to translate "what is" into "what one would have it be"'.[11] In the widest possible context, of course, this 'translation' is the motivating force of all artistic endeavour. And transcendence, the goal.

The goal, if not the impetus, would be disavowed by those who aim to represent 'reality' in art. One of the manifold affinities between Luigi Dallapiccola and Ferruccio Busoni, whose ideas are the *données* of much of this book and its sequel, was their rejection of realism in opera, particularly the programme of so-called *verismo*. For Busoni the charm of the musical theatre lay in pretence, since the convention of the sung word would always be 'a hindrance to any semblance of truth'. In the future, he proposed,

> The opera should take possession of the supernatural or unnatural as its only proper sphere of representation and feeling and should create a pretence world in such a way that life is reflected in either a magic or a comic mirror, presenting consciously that which is not to be found in real life.[12]

---

[10] See Hans Nathan, 'On Dallapiccola's Working Methods', *Perspectives of New Music*, Vol. XV, No. 2, New York, Spring-Summer 1977, pp. 34–57.

'Frequently in constructing a poem the poet has to work backwards from his inspiration which provides the climax or finale of the work. This is how Dante would appear to have written the *Commedia*, working backwards from the vision of the Trinity of Easter, 1300. He had to nurse this vision within him for years before he could begin the poem, and his journey of return to that vision of perfection forced him to bring to the light of awareness all the horrors he had ever known of the imperfections of mankind'.   William Anderson, *Dante the Maker*, Routledge and Kegan Paul, London/Crossroad Publishing, New York, 1982, p. 11.

[11] Fiamma Nicolodi, '*Nota*' (Preface) to *Parole e Musica*, p. 14.

[12] Ferruccio Busoni, *The Essence of Music and Other Papers*, translated by Rosamond Ley, Constable, London/Dover, New York, 1965, pp. 39–40.

Busoni thought *The Magic Flute* came closest to his ideal of opera as 'a rare half-religious and elevating ceremony'. Goethe, he reminded us, wrote a continuation of it and had conceived his *Faust*, Part II, almost 'operatically'.[13]

Dallapiccola, too, saw the musical theatre essentially as a projection of moral and – ultimately – metaphysical issues. He was 'a man of faith and conviction', both as a Catholic and, in Sessions's broader sense of the phrase, as a creative personality. But also as an *artiste engagé*, though one who never sacrificed the universality of his message for narrow factionalism, Dallapiccola could not wholly retreat into an ivory tower. 'No matter how much we try to withdraw into ourselves,' he wrote in 1961, 'we are soon all too aware of the echo of the tragedies going on around us'.[14] Each of his stage works attempts a new synthesis of the concrete and the symbolic, of character rendered as individual psychology and as allegorical abstraction.

Rivière, the protagonist of *Volo di Notte*, for example, is both a realistically portrayed man of action and the personification of an idea – the ineluctable necessity for progress. But even in his first opera, Dallapiccola strives for something beyond dramatic integration of the two dimensions Massimo Mila defines as the 'naturalistic' and the 'sacral'.[15] At the climax of the opera (Scene 5), the wireless operator relays the pilot Fabien's last message as he flies momentarily above the stormclouds, just before plunging into the ocean: 'I see the stars! Even if I can't descend again, I want to reach them. Everything is shining – my hands, my clothes, the wings! Too beautiful . . . Beneath me all is hidden'. This desperate yet ecstatic recitative is counterpointed by a soprano voice (invisible, in the orchestra), intoning the melody of *Tre Laudi* No. 1, a setting of a mediaeval hymn to the Virgin:[16]

[13] *Ibid.*, p. 8.

[14] Luigi Dallapiccola, 'My Choral Music', transl. Madeleine M. Smith, in *The Composer's Point of View*, ed. Robert S. Hines, University of Oklahoma Press, Norman, 1963, p. 162. (*Cf. Parole e Musica*, p. 380.)

[15] Massimo Mila, '*L'"Ulisse" Opera a due Dimensioni*', in *LD: Saggi . . .* , pp. 31–41.

[16] *Tre Laudi* (1936–37) for soprano and thirteen instruments, texts from '*Laudario dei Battuti*' *di Modena* (1266).

Altissima luce con gran splendore,
In voi, dolze amore, aggia consolanza. . . .

O light consummate, splendid light,
Your sweet love gives us consolation. . . .

By means of such a simple juxtaposition, recalling Bach's
contrafacta – though here, conversely, it is a 'sacred' tune that
is fitted into a 'secular' context – Dallapiccola transfigures
the mundane, contemporary details of night flights and
radio-telegraphy, and imbues the musical fabric of the whole
opera with a mystical aura.

He also, not incidentally, sets spinning a wheel of self-
quotations (textual as well as musical) that will come to rest
only in the Epilogue of *Ulisse* or beyond. The stars Fabien
glimpses before his plane runs out of fuel are the same stars
glimpsed by the Prisoner, at the moment hope is about to be
revealed as the ultimate torture, and by Ulysses, alone at
last on the infinite ocean. This threefold allusion parallels
the threefold evocation of *le stelle* at the end of the *Inferno*,
Purgatorio, and *Paradiso*.[17] It is the insight of a composer – a

[17] 'Each of the three *cantiche* closes with the word "*stelle*"; this ending
serves to point eloquently to the upward way of the journey from now on
and seems to exhort the reader to look up also, on *his* journey in this life.'
                    Dante Alighieri, *The Divine Comedy*, translated, with a
                    commentary, by Charles S. Singleton, Princeton University
                                    Press, Princeton, 1970, Vol. I, Part 2, p. 644.
The final movement of *Sicut Umbra* (1970), for mezzo-soprano and four
groups of instruments, includes ideograms of nine different stellar
constellations. In his note for the recording (Argo ZRG 791), Dallapiccola
writes:
'I owe the inspiration for this work to a misprint in an anthology of
Spanish Lyrics (Edizione de Corrente, Milan, 1941) edited by Carlo Bo. On 5
April 1969 – exactly one year after finishing the score of my opera *Ulysses* – I
opened this book by chance at Juan Ramón Jiménez's poem "*Epitafio Ideal
de un Marinero*". My attention was caught by a word that I found marvellous: *firmamiento*. I am sure that had I known the correct spelling was
firmamento, exactly as in Italian, I would not have been so fascinated by that
word: but I only discovered that a long time after the publication of the
score.
'Even before choosing the other two Jiménez poems included in the
work, I started – with the idea of transcribing into music the shapes of
certain constellations – to calculate the distance and the position of the
stars, using a map of the night sky. . . . The title is drawn from the Book of

creator – who, in Busoni's words, 'brings to a single opera all that moves him, all that swims before his eyes, all that is within his powers to achieve: he is a musical Dante, [his opera] a musical Divine Comedy'.[18]

*　　*　　*

In 1969, as a respite from composition after the monumental labour of *Ulisse*, Dallapiccola made a selection of his critical and autobiographical writings that was published the following year in a volume entitled *Appunti Incontri Meditazioni* (Edizioni Suvini Zerboni, Milan; 193 pages). Most of the 24 pieces had appeared previously in various European and American periodicals, one of the earliest – 'Encounter with Anton Webern' – during his only stint as a regular music critic, for the Florentine review *Il Mondo*[19] in 1945–47. But Dallapiccola had begun publishing occasional essays a decade earlier, and by the time of his death in February 1975 these numbered 224 – not to mention over 80 unpublished texts[20] and the diaries which, according to the terms of his will, are not to be made public until 2015. Clearly, there was a need for an expanded edition.

This need was abundantly met with the publication in 1980 of *Parole e Musica* (Il Saggiatore, Milan; 603 pages). The editor, Fiamma Nicolodi, chose 65 texts written between 1930 and 1973 that reveal virtually every facet of Dallapiccola's critical and creative interests. They are arranged chronologically within each of five sections, subtitled Opera;

Job (Chapter VIII, Verse 9): *sicut umbra dies nostri sunt super terram* (our days on earth are but a shadow)'.

[18] *The Essence of Music*, p. 6.

[19] More precisely, Dallapiccola contributed reviews to *Il Mondo* (Florence) in 1945–46, and to its successor *Il Mondo Europeo* (Rome-Florence) in 1947 – both journals edited by his friend Alessandro Bonsanti. Between 1938 and 1947 he also published several articles in *Letteratura* (Florence), successor of the famous literary magazine *Solaria* (1926–36), whose programme Elio Vittorini described as 'anti-Fascist, European, universalist, anti-traditionalist'.

[20] Among them *Kohlennot* (1917), a one-act comedy in verse satirizing the privations of the War; and *Il Segreto* (1954), a libretto drawn from the story '*L'Enjeu*' by Villiers de l'Isle-Adam.

Reflections on Aesthetics, Teaching, and Culture; The [Second] Viennese School; Musicians;[21] and The Composer. The volume also comprises substantial introductions by Professor Nicolodi and Gianandrea Gavazzeni, together with exhaustive bibliographies of writings by and about Dallapiccola. Since the uncollected material consists largely of ephemerae (preliminary versions, programme notes, polemical articles, etc.), *Parole e Musica* is not likely to be superseded by another Italian edition for many years to come.

Dallapiccola's writings on music have been translated into English more often than into any other language except German.[22] It is perhaps appropriate, then, that the first non-Italian edition should be the joint enterprise of an American composer and a British publisher. Volume I of the Toccata Press Dallapiccola draws from *Parole e Musica* the eighteen essays and diary excerpts related to opera, from another source two letters of the composer to Wolfgang

[21] This section includes pieces about Vito Frazzi (1888–1975, Dallapiccola's composition teacher at the Florence Conservatory and composer of an opera based on Shakespeare's *King Lear*), Debussy, Ravel, Mahler, Busoni, Beethoven, Respighi, Shostakovich, Honegger, Messiaen, Casella, Wladimir Vogel, Hindemith, Varèse, Karl Amadeus Hartmann, and Gian Francesco Malipiero.

[22] Dallapiccola was fond of speaking German, and composed song cycles on poems by Goethe (*Goethe-Lieder*, 1953) and Heine (*An Mathilde*, 1955). He also published Italian translations of Busoni's letters (1955) and essays (1941; revised edition, *Lo Sguardo Lieto*, Il Saggiatore, Milan, 1977).

'Like Busoni, Dallapiccola nourishes himself, though not exclusively, from two disparate cultural traditions. On the one hand, imbued with Italian music (from the late sixteenth century to Casella and Malipiero, with comparatively little interest in the eighteenth century) and Italian and Latin literature, he is oriented to France: to Debussy, Ravel (but not Fauré), Mallarmé, Proust, etc. On the other hand, he is oriented to Germany and Austria: to Beethoven, Schumann (chiefly as a composer of Lieder), Wagner (but less to Brahms), the modern Viennese school, Heine, Thomas Mann, etc. He is thus capable of admiration for the "expressionism" (a favourite term of his) of such works as *Moses und Aron* and *Wozzeck* and equally fervent admiration for the "classicism" of *Valses Nobles et Sentimentales*. Outside these categories stands James Joyce, a writer who holds an unending fascination for the composer.'
                                                    Nathan, 'Luigi Dallapiccola: Fragments
                                                       from Conversations', p. 312, note 25.

Wagner and Léonide Massine,[23] and three scenes from *Ulisse* that are crucial for understanding not only the structure of that opera but also its continuity with *Il Prigioniero* and *Volo di Notte*.

'*Il libretto è già la musica*', Dallapiccola believed: the libretto is already the music. Pierluigi Petrobelli has shown that the libretto of *Ulisse* embodies the same principles of symmetry and mirror imitation which govern the structure of the basic musical material.[24] For example, the mirror principle determines the rhyme scheme of Ulysses's monologue in the closing scene:

No, non sono le Furie ad avventarsi		A
Su me per vendicare quei che uccisi,		B
Per rinfacciarmi i compagni perduti:		C
Sono i mostri (in me Circe li scoperse)		D
Che rodon questo cuore mai placato.	↓	E
Un uomo sono, un uomo che ha guardato	↑	E
Il mondo nelle foggie più diverse		D
E che intorno si vede sorger, muti,		C
Con occhi interroganti, mille visi,		B
Mentre nell'alma le memorie farsi		A
Sembran più dense e dolorose. . .		

My English version of this Epilogue, and of the corresponding solo scene at the beginning of the opera (pp. 276 and 267), preserves the rhyme scheme and, so far as possible, the feminine endings of the original verses.

The extremes of the opera are bridged by the transformation of Calypso's first line

Son soli, un'altra volta, il tuo cuore e il mare

---

[23] *LD: Saggi. . .*, pp. 90–91 and 104. This volume also contains letters from Berg, Boulanger, Casella, Copland, Hindemith, Kleiber, Maderna, Malipiero, Markevitch, Matisse, Messiaen, Milhaud, Nono, Poulenc, Scherchen, Schoenberg, Sessions, Toscanini, Varèse, and Webern, among others.

[24] 'Dallapiccola's Last Orchestral Piece', *Tempo*, No. 123, London, December 1977, pp. 2–6. The work to which the title of this article refers, *Three Questions with Two Answers* (1962), is based on the musical material more fully exploited in *Ulisse*.

–into Ulysses's last:

> *(Non più soli sono il mio cuore e il mare.*

Another unifying element is the refrain verse of Calypso's monologue–

> *Guardare, meravigliarsi, e tornar a guardare*

–'which recurs continuously throughout the opera as a sort of textual *leitmotiv*,' observes Petrobelli, 'and which presents, in its formulation, the very image of questioning'. The translation of *guardare* figuratively 'to search' (rather than literally 'to look') follows the English text of the essay 'Birth of a Libretto' prepared by Mario and Leaura Materassi for Dallapiccola's lecture at the University of Michigan, 4 October 1967, on the occasion of his being awarded the honorary degree of Doctor of Music. With considerable revision it is published in full for the first time in this book.[25] The Materassis quote several passages from Robert Fitzgerald's version of *The Odyssey*, and to his Book XI, 'A Gathering of Shades', I am also indebted for some bits of imagery in my translation of *Ulisse*, Act I, Scene 4, 'The Realm of the Cimmerians' (pp. 268–275).

But with the partial exception of 'Notes on the Statue Scene in *Don Giovanni*', all the remaining English translations presented here are by necessity completely fresh. The Mozart essay is typical of Dallapiccola's most important writings in its evolution through several preliminary versions, published in various languages, to the definitive text:

1. '*À Propos d'un Trait "Expressioniste" de Mozart*', in *Polyphonie*, No. 4, Paris, 1949, pp. 72–79; an issue devoted to the twelve-tone system.

2a. '*Appunti sulla Scena della Statua del "Don Giovanni"*', in *La Rassegna Musicale*, Vol. XX, No. 2, Turin, April 1950, pp. 107–115.

2b. 'Notes on the Statue Scene in *Don Giovanni*', transl.

[25] A very brief excerpt, entitled 'Birth of a Libretto', appeared in *The Listener*, Vol. II, No. 82, London, 23 October 1969, pp. 553–554. I am indebted to radio station WUOM, Ann Arbor, for a tape of the lecture.

Deryck Cooke, in *Music Survey*, Vol. III, No. 2, London, December 1950, pp. 89–97.

3. '*Consiterazioni in margine alla Scena della Statua nel "Don Giovanni" (1949–1969)*', in *Appunti Incontri Meditazioni* (1970), pp. 39–59; reprinted, with notes by Fiamma Nicolodi, in *Parole e Musica* (1980), pp. 39–65.

In this case the final form of the essay was achieved mainly by adding material in versions 2a and – especially – 3. A translation of the new sections could therefore be grafted, without undue difficulty, onto Deryck Cooke's English version, 2b.

Dallapiccola's revision of 'The Genesis of the *Canti di Prigionia* and *Il Prigioniero*' was a somewhat more complex process. Shortly after it appeared in the July 1953 issue of *The Musical Quarterly*,[26] Colin Mason noted the 'defensive tone' of recurring references to the dodecaphonic system. For example:

> One day, in a mood of *Galgenhumor*, I wrote the *Sonatina Canonica su 'Capricci' di Niccolò Paganini* in a way as proof that, while in the *Sex Carmina Alcaei* I had dealt with problems associated with twelve-tone music, I was able to write in regular tonality, using a stated theme.

By the time the definitive Italian text was published (1970), however, Dallapiccola no longer felt a need either to justify himself or 'to refute the widely held belief that the twelve-note method of composing is . . . an entirely mechanical and cerebral activity, incompatible with spontaneous feeling or inspiration'.[27] And while he retained the subtitle 'An Autobiographical Fragment', Dallapiccola expunged many other references of a personal nature – some as brief as a phrase, others the length of a paragraph. The opening paragraph, for instance, recalls the distinction Sessions made between the composer and the critic:

---

[26] Vol. XXXIX, No. 3, pp. 355–372, translated by Jonathan Schiller. Dallapiccola never published the Italian text of this version, but a preliminary version entitled '*Qualche Cenno sulla Genesi de "Il Prigioniero"*' appeared in *Paragone*, Vol. I, No. 6, Florence, June 1950, pp. 44–54.

[27] Colin Mason, 'Dallapiccola and the Twelve-note Method', *The Listener*, LI, London, 29 April 1954, p. 757.

> . . .For a writer to talk about himself, interpret himself, and analyse himself is part of his profession; but this is not so for a musician who, in place of writing about events, can suggest at the most states of mind, since he is used to devoting his attention to the abstract matter of sound rather than to the exactness of the written word.

Considering the nature and extent of the composer's revisions, I have not attempted to salvage Jonathan Schiller's rather attractive translation.

Finally, for different reasons I have chosen not to reprint the first English translation of an essay about opera to be based on Dallapiccola's definitive text. The essay in question is the one that lends part of its title to the 1980 edition of his writings: '*Parole e Musica nel Melodramma (1961–1969)*'. Despite a claim of completeness, the version offered as 'Words and Music in Italian Nineteenth-Century Opera' in *The Verdi Companion*[28] leaves out eight of the thirteen musical examples and omits or misplaces a number of phrases and sentences; what is more, it consistently mistranslates the specialized Italian term *melodramma* as the English 'melodrama' (see p. 133, note 1). Nor has the analysis of the terzetto from Act II of *Un Ballo in Maschera* been rendered with nearly the requisite clarity and accuracy.

'Words and Music . . .' may well be Dallapiccola's most important and enduring critical essay. Certainly, it now seems the one least subject to 'the limitations of personality' of which Sessions wrote in 1939. Granting such limitations, 'The fact remains' – continued Sessions, in 1947 – 'that some of the greatest critics of the past have been creative artists whose generosity or whose vital curiosity have enabled them to bring their best powers to the task of criticism, and who could see their individual predilections or personal destinies at times in the perspective of their love for music as such'.[29]

---

[28] Transl. Alvary E. Grazebrook, ed. William Weaver and Martin Chusid, W.W. Norton, New York, 1979, pp. 193–215.

[29] 'The Scope of Music Criticism', *Roger Sessions on Music*, p. 151. In a memorial tribute (1975), Sessions wrote:

'Luigi Dallapiccola was, in the only valid sense of the word, a truly great composer. . . .

'Dallapiccola was not only a profoundly cultivated human being; he was also a rarely generous, compassionate, and humane one. He was vividly

All the writings in this book are instinct with that generosity and vital curiosity. But if Luigi Dallapiccola is counted among the greatest critics, as already he is numbered among the great composers of this century, it will surely be for the acuity of insight and intensity of love that illuminate his pages on Giuseppe Verdi.

Acknowledgements

If one could properly 'dedicate' a translation, I should first like to pay my mother, Louise Shackelford, that much-merited, long-overdue homage. Without her loyal, patient, unfailingly tactful support, this book might never have been completed or even essayed.

Equally discreet, unstintingly generous, were the advice and assistance offered by Laura Dallapiccola. At an early stage of the planning for a single miscellaneous volume of her husband's writings, she encouraged, without ever seeking to impose, the present scope and direction of my two-part anthology. At a later juncture she read the typescript and made numerous invaluable suggestions for improving its clarity and fidelity. With Professor Fiamma Nicolodi, Signora Dallapiccola was always available to elucidate doubtful points and identify obscure references (obscure not by intention, of course, but through cultural and – already – temporal distance). And with Professor Irma Brandeis, she illuminated the 'impervious' poetry of Tommaso Campanella: tangential here, but altogether typical of both Luigi and Laura Dallapiccola's meticulous, passionate philology.

---

aware of the world in which we live, and was devoted to the cause of human liberty, both on the individual and on the political level. He was always ready to take the initiative in cases where he felt that injustice had been done, and to commit himself without reserve, as he always did to his personal beliefs. His nature was in essence a deeply religious one, which means, quite simply, that he was constantly aware of the human condition, in its profoundest as well as its most immediate aspects, and that he remained unfettered by limitations of a sectarian, narrowly partisan, or doctrinaire kind. This too is reflected, richly and eloquently, in the music he has left us' (pp. 387–388).

Fernando Farulli was unhesitatingly generous in allowing the reproduction of his designs for the 1968 premiere, in Berlin, of *Ulisse*.

I am deeply indebted to the Rockefeller Foundation, for the invitation to spend two months in the Spring of 1977 at its magnificent Villa Serbelloni in Bellagio, on Lake Como. Edizioni Suvini Zerboni and Il Saggiatore, the Milanese publishers respectively of Dallapiccola's music and prose, have been extraordinarily helpful and mindful of the pecuniary constraints upon a nascent enterprise. And Arthur Hammond deserves my gratitude for checking the accuracy of the music examples.

The excerpts from *Il Prigioniero, Job* and *Ulisse* are reproduced by courtesy of Edizioni Suvini Zerboni, and that from *Volo di Notte* courtesy of Universal Edition; our thanks to both houses.

The essay on *Falstaff*, and excerpts from the essays on *Rigoletto* and *Simon Boccanegra*, first appeared in English as 'Reflections on Three Verdi Operas' in *19th Century Music* (Vol. VII, No. 1, Davis, California, Summer 1983); 'Two Encounters with Antoine de Saint-Exupéry', in *MadAminA!* (Vol. V, No. 1, Englewood, New Jersey, Spring 1984). I am grateful to the editors of these journals for allowing me to reprint this material.

Finally, I should like to thank the following authors, publishers, and copyright holders for kindly permitting me to quote from their works and editions: Felix Aprahamian, for the lines from his translation (1981) of *L'Enfant et les Sortilèges* by Ravel and Colette, libretto with the recording on HMV ASD 4167/Angel DS–37869; Edward Arnold Ltd. and Da Capo Press, Inc., for the passages from Ferruccio Busoni's *Letters to His Wife*, tr. Rosamond Ley, 1938 and 1975; Bantam Books, Inc., for the excerpt from 'Don Juan' by E.T.A. Hoffmann, in *German Stories*, ed. Harry Steinhauer, 1961; Basil Blackwell Ltd., for the material from *The Ulysses Theme* by W.B. Stanford, 1968; Boosey & Hawkes Music Publishers Ltd., for the quotation from 'Dallapiccola's Last Orchestral Piece' by Pierluigi Petrobelli, in *Tempo*, No. 123, December 1977; The British Broadcasting Corporation, for the extracts from 'Dallapiccola and the Twelve-note Method' by Colin Mason, in *The Listener*, 29 April 1954, and from 'Dallapiccola's Odyssey' by David Drew, in *The Listener*, 17 October 1968; Cambridge University Press, for the passages from *The Cambridge Italian Dictionary*, ed. Barbara Reynolds, Vol. I, 1962, and from *Verdi in the Age of Italian Romanticism* by David R.B. Kimbell, 1981; Cassell Ltd. and Oxford University Press, New York, for the excerpts from *The Operas of Verdi* by Julian Budden, Vols. II (1978) and III (1981); Chatto & Windus Ltd. and Princeton University Press, for the lines from *C.P. Cavafy: Collected Poems*, tr. Edmund Keeley and Philip Sherrard, ed. George Savidis, 1975;

Chatto & Windus and Random House, Inc., for the quotation from *Time Regained* by Marcel Proust, tr. Andreas Mayor, in *Remembrance of Things Past*, Vol. III, 1981; Chatto & Windus and Viking Penguin Inc., for the extract from *The World of Odysseus* by M.I. Finley, 1978; Constable & Company, Ltd. and Dover Publications, Inc., for the material from *The Essence of Music and Other Papers* by Ferruccio Busoni, tr. Rosamond Ley, 1965, and from Busoni's 'Sketch of a New Esthetic of Music', tr. Theodore Baker, in *Three Classics in the Aesthetic of Music* 1962; The Crossroad Publishing Company and Routledge and Kegan Paul, Ltd, for the passage from *Dante the Maker* by William Anderson, 1982; Decca Record Company Ltd., for Dallapiccola's programme note on *Sicut Umbra* (c. 1975), with the recording on Argo ZRG–791; J.M. Dent & Sons Ltd., for the quotations from *The Man Verdi* by Frank Walker, 1962; J.M. Dent & Sons and Farrar, Straus Giroux, Inc., for the excerpt from *Mozart* by Wolfgang Hildesheimer, tr. Marion Faber, 1982; Doubleday & Company, Inc., for the lines from *The Odyssey* of Homer, tr. Robert Fitzgerald, 1963; Dover Publications, Inc., for the line from *Salome* by Oscar Wilde, tr. Lord Alfred Douglas, 1967; Faber & Faber Ltd., for the passage from *Style and Idea: Selected Writings of Arnold Schoenberg*, ed. Leonard Stein, 1975; Faber Music Ltd. and Mrs. Deryck Cooke, for 'Notes on the Statue Scene in *Don Giovanni*' by Luigi Dallapiccola, tr. Deryck Cooke, in *Music Survey*, December 1950, and for the quotation from Cooke's translation of 'On the Twelve-Note Road' by Dallapiccola, in *Music Survey*, October 1951; Victor Gollancz Ltd. and Random House, Inc., for the material from *The Memoirs of Hector Berlioz*, tr. and ed. David Cairns, 1977; Harcourt Brace Jovanovich, Inc., for the excerpts from *Night Flight* by Antoine de Saint-Exupéry, tr. Stuart Gilbert, preface by André Gide, 1932; Harvard University Press, for the extract from *Homer's Odyssey* by John H. Finley, Jr., 1978; W. Heffer & Sons Ltd. and Hans Nathan, for the quotations from 'Luigi Dallapiccola: Fragments from Conversations', presented by Hans Nathan, in *The Music Review*, November 1966; David Higham Associates Ltd., for the passage from *The Divine Comedy* of Dante, tr. Dorothy L. Sayers, Vol. I (*Hell*), 1949; Indiana University Press, for the material from *Essays on the Odyssey: Selected Modern Criticism*, ed. Charles H. Taylor, Jr., 1969; W.W. Norton & Company, Inc., for the lines from Goethe's *Faust*, tr. Walter Arndt, ed. Cyrus Hamlin, 1976, and from *Seven Verdi Librettos*, tr. William Weaver, 1977; Oxford University Press and Eulenburg Books, London, for the excerpts from *Ferruccio Busoni: A Biography* by Edward J. Dent, 1933 and 1974, and from Dent's article 'The Nomenclature of Opera', in *Music and Letters*, XXV, 1944; Oxford University Press, New York, for the quotation from *Opera in the Twentieth Century* by Ethan Mordden, 1978; Penguin Books Ltd., for the extracts from *The Consolation of Philosophy* by Boethius, tr. V.E. Watts, 1969, from *Pinocchio* by Carlo Collodi, tr. E. Harden, 1974, and from Dante's *La Vita Nuova*, tr. Barbara Reynolds, 1969; *Perspectives of New Music* and Hans Nathan, for the material from 'On Dallapiccola's Working Methods' by Hans Nathan, Spring-Summer 1977; Princeton University Press, for the passages from *The Divine Comedy* of Dante, tr. with commentary by Charles Singleton, Vol. I (*Inferno*), 1970, from *Either/Or* by Søren Kierkegaard, tr. David F. and Lillian M. Swenson, Vol. I, 1971, and from *Roger Sessions on Music: Collected Essays*, ed. Edward T. Cone, 1979; Random House, Inc., for the excerpts from *Opera as Drama* by Joseph Kerman, 1956, and from Nietzsche's *Beyond Good and Evil*, tr. Walter Kaufmann, 1966; Routledge & Kegan Paul Ltd. and Princeton University Press, for the quotations from *The Tragic Sense of Life* by Miguel de Unamuno, tr. Anthony Kerrigan, 1972; G. Schirmer, Inc., for the extracts from articles in *The Musical Quarterly* by Heinrich Jalowetz ('On the Spontaneity of Schoenberg's Music', October 1944), Richard F. Goldman ('Current Chronicle: New York', July 1951), and Luigi Dallapiccola ('The Genesis of the *Canti di Prigionia* and *Il Prigioniero*', tr. Jonathan Schiller, July 1953); B. Schott's Söhne, Mainz, for the lines from the libretto of *Moses und Aron* by Arnold Schoenberg, tr. Allen Forte, with the recording on Philips 6700 084; Secker & Warburg Ltd. and Alfred A. Knopf, Inc., for the material from *The Magic Mountain* (1927 and 1969) and *The Tales of Jacob* (1934 and 1976, in *Joseph and His Brothers*) by Thomas Mann, tr. H.T. Lowe-Porter; Simon & Schuster, Inc., for the extracts from *The Odyssey: A Modern Sequel* by Nikos Kazantzakis, tr. Kimon Friar, 1958, and from *Oedipus the King* of Sophocles, tr. Bernard Knox, Washington Square Press, 1959; Thames & Hudson Ltd., for the passages from *Homer and the Heroic Age* by J.V. Luce, 1975, and from *Verdi: A Documentary Study*, ed. William Weaver, 1977; University of California Press, for the excerpt from *Theory of Harmony* by Arnold Schoenberg, tr. Roy Carter, 1978; University of Chicago Press, for the quotation from *The Wisdom of the Sands* by Antoine de Saint-Exupéry, tr. Stuart Gilbert, 1979; University of Michigan Press, for the material from *Italy: A Modern History* by Denis Mack Smith, 1969; University of Oklahoma Press, for the extracts from 'My Choral Music' by Luigi Dallapiccola, tr. Madeleine M. Smith, in *The Composer's Point of View*, ed. Robert S. Hines, 1963; Weidenfeld & Nicolson Ltd. and Alfred A. Knopf, Inc., for the passage from *Mussolini* by Denis Mack Smith, 1982.

RUDY SHACKELFORD

Publisher's Note

This book would be incomplete without one further acknowledgement. When Rudy Shackelford and I were at the early stages of planning *Dallapiccola on Opera* and its sequel, I suggested that we ought to discuss a fee for the sizable amount of work that translating, editing and annotating both volumes would entail. This was his reply: 'Like Busoni, I "bleed internally" when it comes to doing something for a profit which is really a labor of love, particularly in connexion with Dallapiccola whose life and work remain my highest example of personal and aesthetic conduct'.

MARTIN ANDERSON
Toccata Press

I

Songs of Imprisonment
Songs of Liberation
Pieces of a Life

The Genesis of
Canti di Prigionia
and
Il Prigioniero
(1950-1953)
An Autobiographical Fragment

To Massimo Mila (for 14 August 1970)[1]

A few days after the world première of *Il Prigioniero*,[2] I happened to dine with Igor Markevitch, for whom I had already played my opera on the piano. He had listened to the broadcast and seemed very favourably impressed by it.[3] At a

---

[1] On the occasion of the Turinese music critic's sixtieth birthday.

[2] Italian Radio (RAI), Turin, 1 December 1949; Hermann Scherchen, conductor.   –LD (Author's notes are initialed LD throughout the book; all others are editorial.)

'At Zurich again, late one afternoon in the Autumn of 1948, I was playing the recently completed *Il Prigioniero* for Scherchen on the piano in one of the Radio studios. As the last notes were fading into the air, I heard the Maestro's voice: "I want to hear the entire opera again". "When?" I asked, "After dinner?" "No, right away." He wouldn't be put off, so without demur, without even rising from the piano, I began once more at the opening bar. After the second run-through he explained: "I wanted to hear everything. One passage – the only spot that has, in a certain sense, the character of a *reprise* – seemed too brief. Now I understand. It's right, and I am satisfied".

'And so he had made me play the whole opera again in order to comprehend it better: all things considered, a further proof of his love for the music'.   *'Ricordo di Hermann Scherchen', Parole e Musica*, pp. 172–173.

[3] Igor Markevitch (1912–83) re-organized the orchestra of the Florentine Maggio Musicale in the post-War period. Dallapiccola was much

certain moment Markevitch sprung such a direct and unexpected question that I was embarrassed – as embarrassed as one would feel if suddenly denuded. He asked precisely what were the secret reasons that had made me dwell for such a long period of my life on prisons and prisoners, and whether I had named my daughter Annalibera to contrast something lovely and tender with a motif that so strangely dominated my artistic output.

Only then did I realize in a flash that *Canti di Prigionia* had occupied me from 1938 until 1941, and that *Il Prigioniero* had required four years of work, from 1944 to 1948. Even though I had written other compositions of quite different character during that decade (suffice it to mention *Liriche Greche*[4]), I had lived spiritually among prisons and prisoners for ten years, counting the extended period of preparation for the libretto of *Il Prigioniero*. This occurred to me only as a result of the question Markevitch chanced to ask.

Not all moments are equally suitable for surveying an

-----

impressed by the Italian première of *Psaume* for soprano and orchestra, which Markevitch conducted during the twelfth ISCM festival at Florence (4 April 1934). On 2 December 1949 Markevitch wrote to Dallapiccola:

'Yesterday we listened to *Il Prigioniero* with great excitement. The performance seemed excellent, and I thought very highly of the singer [Magda László] you discovered. (Scherchen in top form.)

'What magnificent work you do! And how proud you can be of having completed such an important opera! It's incredible how the dramatic tension is maintained throughout, and your performance at the cottage [on Bernard Berenson's estate at Settignano, near Florence] was so fresh in our memory that we could follow along very easily. A first-rate broadcast: the score was clearly interpreted. . .'.   *LD: Saggi . . .*, p. 80.

[4] A triptych of song cycles for voice and chamber ensemble, on texts by Sappho, Anacreon, and Alcaeus, translated by Salvatore Quasimodo:

I. *Cinque Frammenti di Saffo* (1942);

II. *Due Liriche di Anacreonte* (1944–45), dedicated to Domenico de' Paoli;

III. *Sex Carmina Alcaei* (1943), dedicated to Anton Webern on his sixtieth birthday and, in 1945, to his memory.

'Those were the years when Europe, long surrounded by barbed wire, was being ever more quickly reduced to a heap of ruins. I sometimes found relief from that continuous lack of balance to which we had become conditioned in the supreme equilibrium of the Greek lyrics. They helped me endure the tragic events and, perhaps, provided the necessary contrast to the atmosphere of *Il Prigioniero*, the opera I was composing'.

LD: Saggi . . ., pp. 122–123.

entire life at a glance, nor does every moment seem equally propitious for making confessions. I don't recall how I answered the question, but I probably dodged it with a witticism.

To review the past is not easy – on the contrary, it is sometimes difficult and painful. Even an artist, by nature intensely introspective, often finds it hard to specify exactly what gave his imagination its first creative impetus.

Psychology maintains that the experiences of childhood and adolescence exercise a preponderant, almost unique influence on the formation of the personality, particularly the personality of the artist. Shortly before the first stage performance of *Il Prigioniero*,[5] an American journalist inquired whether by chance I had ever been in prison. I answered no. Yet if I now wished to take a journey into my *temps perdu*, I would see that there was one supremely important event in my life: the twenty months of internment at Graz, from 27 March 1917 to 18 November 1918. And this exile, however important it may be in its own right, becomes even more significant when one considers that it coincided with the onset of my adolescence.

Before delving into the heart of this matter, I must try to describe a remote era and a milieu obviously unfamiliar to the youth of today. It is the period just preceding World War I, 'in the beginning of which so much began that has scarcely yet left off beginning'.[6] The background is the family of a teacher of classical languages at the only Italian secondary school permitted by the Austro-Hungarian government in the middle of that tiny peninsula called Istria.[7] The small town of Pisino, with a population of little more than 3,000, was located along the railroad from Trieste to Pola. Is it accurate to speak of a 'bourgeois' environment in a 'bour-

---

[5] Maggio Musicale, Florence (Teatro Comunale), 20 May 1950; Bronislaw Horowicz, producer, Enzo Rossi, scene designer, Hermann Scherchen, conductor.   –LD

[6] Thomas Mann, *The Magic Mountain* (1924) [translated by H.T. Lowe-Porter, Secker & Warburg, London/Vintage Books, New York, 1969, p. ix].   –LD

[7] The Italian schools were under the jurisdiction of the local authorities; there were other schools at Capodistria and Pola.   –LD

geois' state – the Austro-Hungarian Empire – disregarding
the pejorative connotation this word later acquired? Only up
to a certain point. One should not forget that the little
Istrian peninsula where I was born lies at the crossing of
three borders. When the train stopped at the station in my
hometown, the conductor called out: 'Mitterburg, Pisino,
Pazin'. It is well known how hospitable frontier countries are
to mixtures of race and culture; moreover, the mentality one
encounters in border regions is very different from that
generally found in the interior. How can this mentality be
defined? Perhaps as 'restless'.

In the era before the First World War, only thieves and
murderers were usually imprisoned. The fact that the
Dreyfus case had roused the conscience of all Europeans at
the end of the 19th century is proof of the importance
attached to justice and individual liberty. How many bourgeois families jealously preserved for years and years, as if it
were a relic, the issue of *L'Aurore* in which Émile Zola
published his famous '*J'accuse!*'

I was ten years old and just beginning high school when,
in 1914, the first phase of World War I convulsed Europe.
For several years I had devoted my spare time to the study of
piano (a cultural pursuit not uncommon among bourgeois
families in Central Europe), without even suspecting that
music would one day become my only *raison d'être*. Our home
life continued to be calm and uneventful. Sometimes I would
hear about the Irredentist movements of Italian-speaking
subjects of the Austro-Hungarian Empire;[8] I was also aware
of the rivalry between Italians and Slavs. But in a region like
mine, one of mixed population, all of this seemed quite
unexceptional.

And so my childhood passed calmly. One afternoon,
following a piano lesson, the teacher asked to speak with my

---

[8] The Irredentists (from *Italia irredenta*, 'unredeemed Italy') wished to
emancipate all Italian lands under foreign rule, among them Southern
Tyrol (Trentino) and Istria, then controlled by Austria. 'To the countrymen
of Goethe and Wagner, the *lago di Garda* was the *Gardasee*'.
        Denis Mack Smith, *Italy: A Modern History*,
    University of Michigan Press, Ann Arbor, 1969, p. 142.

mother. He told her that, in his opinion, I had a special talent for music and should be encouraged to become a musician. It was my distinct impression that the teacher's advice, far from reassuring my mother, profoundly upset her. Believing the life of an artist to be full of disappointments and bristling with difficulties, like any mother she felt that her first duty was to remove her child as far as possible from every source of pain. Certainly, she never again mentioned the advice my first music teacher gave, at least not in my presence.

When I was six years old, a crime created a great sensation in our province: a woman had killed her husband. My parents never spoke about such disturbing events in front of us children, yet who can say, after all, just what may trouble the mind of a child? And then, aren't children mysteriously aware of everything that's going on?

One evening my father returned home with a newspaper tucked under his arm. I was standing at the window, gazing out at the dark, almost deserted street, dimly lit by scattered gas-lamps. My father whispered into my mother's ear: 'Mrs Volpis has been sentenced to six years in prison'. I pressed my forehead against the windowpane as if to gain a better view of the street and the passers-by and for the first time I realized how cold the glass could be in winter. A moment later I was curled up in the window-niche, counting to six on my fingertips, horrified that a human being could be shut in a cell for a period of time which to me seemed endless. Six years: my whole life until that day. I often caught myself thinking about the woman prisoner whose face and appearance and first name I shall never know.

On 29 June every year, in the main square of my home town, the popular feast of St Peter and St Paul was celebrated with a band and a game of lotto. We boys keenly anticipated this holiday for, among other things, the chance to sit at a table in the café and enjoy a big dish of ice cream. Back in 1914, before the advent of radio, news of even the most momentous happenings arrived only the following day. Suddenly the air seemed charged with whispered confidences, vague and fragmentary rumours whose gravity a boy of ten could scarcely assess:

'A telegram has arrived at the post office. . .'
'The celebration must be discontinued at once. . .'
'It appears something has happened at Sarajevo. . .'
'His name is Gavrilo Princip. . . '
'That's right, a twenty-year-old Serbian student. . .'.
And finally, the official bulletin: 'Archduke Franz Ferdinand, heir-apparent to the Austro-Hungarian throne, and his wife, Countess Sophie Chotek, have been assassinated at Sarajevo'. One month later war broke out.

Such cataclysms, needless to say, have special repercussions in border regions. But when Italy entered the War,[9] the reverberations became deafening: for the first time there was talk, even in my small town, of concentration camps. Emperor Franz Joseph had firmly resolved to 'discipline' the Italian residents of the Trentino and Trieste and Istria, to put a bridle on those freedom-loving rebels who had so often disturbed his already ill-starred reign. It was necessary to teach the Irredentists – those last heirs of the Risorgimento – a decisive lesson. Law-abiding citizens were arrested and deported. Spies lurked everywhere. Leibnitz, Mittergraben, Oberhollabrun . . . the names of certain cities took on a sinister ring, if not nearly so tragic as those of Auschwitz, Dachau or Buchenwald a quarter of a century later.

Life was changing rapidly, just how rapidly we who were caught up in it failed to realize at that moment. Only today, many years later, can I express the swiftness of the change when I recall meeting a friend of my own age in 1916, on the morning the newspapers reported that the Austrian prime minister Count Karl von Stürgkh had been assassinated by the Socialist Friedrich Adler. Winking at me, my friend whispered: 'Another one gone'. Thus even twelve-year-olds had been infected with the new mentality: human life had lost much of its value.

On 21 November 1916, Franz Joseph died. Charles I, his successor, a man doubtlessly aware of many urgent problems – among them the necessity for a united Europe – was crowned too late at least to attempt a solution. One of his first steps was to abolish the concentration camps which had

---

[9] Italy declared war against Austria-Hungary on 23 May 1915.

aroused such profound indignation throughout civilized Europe at the time. The Irredentists, the political suspects – or rather the '*P.U.*', *politisch unverlässlich* ('politically unreliable') – were to be expelled from the border zones and sent to the interior of Austria. The school my father had directed with such love, where he had taught for so many years, was closed overnight on the grounds that it was a 'protest school' (*ein Trotz-Gymnasium*), in the jargon of the higher authorities. And so my family, escorted by a policeman, was obliged to arrive at Graz on 27 March 1917.

There, in the capital of Styria, we had to begin our life anew. But how? With the minuscule pension my father had been allotted after the suppression of his school? We were never treated harshly. My father was under no particular obligation, except to report periodically to the police. However, the sudden change from the tranquil rhythm of the first ten years of my life to what later happened was a little too abrupt. I had the impression that an injustice had been done and felt deeply humiliated.

The food situation, already very serious when we arrived at Graz, deteriorated from one day to the next. We heard that by taking the train to Feldbach or Fehring and walking several kilometres, one could get comestibles from the farmers, who had begun to doubt the value of money and preferred payment in bedsheets or blankets. And this we would do when school wasn't in session.

For a teenager 125 grammes of bread per day is not sufficient. Fortunately, at Graz there was an opera house which, despite the war and the privations everyone suffered, managed to give respectable performances. Standing in the gallery, a boy of thirteen could listen effortlessly to such operas as *Die Meistersinger* or those of *The Ring*. And what is really surprising, during the performance he scarcely noticed hunger pangs.

Did my mother still remember what my piano teacher had told her one afternoon not many years ago? Did she recall how it upset her then? Was she troubled by my constantly growing love for music? Did it strike her that by sending me to the opera every evening she was pushing me in the very direction she would most want to avoid? I don't know. Certainly, she was in no position to choose. Eighty cents wasn't enough to purchase black-market bread, but it could be used to buy a ticket for the gallery at the opera. Unable to give me bread, my mother sent me to the theatre.

One could spend a sleepless night, to be sure, after being terrified by the final scene of *Don Giovanni*.[10] It might remind one of the Inferno or the 'weeping and gnashing of teeth'. But insomnia is an altogether private matter, not something to be discussed with others. By age fourteen, in any case, I had acquired a sufficiently profound knowledge of Wagner.

In my heart I had already decided to become a musician the evening I first saw *The Flying Dutchman*,[11] and yet I was afraid that if I spoke about it my family might be opposed. Finally, a few years later, after dropping some rather vague hints about my plans for the future, I realized that my father wouldn't stand in the way provided I finished my high school education. 'The day of ignorant musicians is past,' he admonished me whenever I complained that it seemed a waste of time to memorize the derivation of molecular formulas or the elements of crystallography.

The War ended, and I returned to my home town.[12] The mood there was festive. From every side came assurances that war was a thing of the past – assurances which may at least partially account for the hedonistic psychosis of the post-War period. Woodrow Wilson had visited the major European capitals and was everywhere accorded a hero's

---

[10] At that time, following a tradition established by Gustav Mahler, the Epilogue was omitted and performances of *Don Giovanni* ended with the Statue scene.   –LD

The practice of ending the opera with Don Giovanni's descent to hell had actually been observed, with rare exceptions, throughout the 19th century and into the early years of the 20th. It has recently been criticized: see Wolfgang Hildesheimer, *Mozart*, translated by Marion Faber, J.M. Dent, London/Farrar Straus Giroux, New York, 1982, pp. 231–233.

[11] 'On 18 May 1917 my father took me to a performance of *The Flying Dutchman*. This was the first time I heard an opera of Wagner. Previously I had heard operas by Rossini, Verdi, Puccini, etc. It is certain that even before Wagner's overture came to an end, I had decided to become a musician and also, if I must be frank, to become a great musician. For a thirteen-year-old boy it is easy to make big decisions.'

'Luigi Dallapiccola: Fragments from Conversations', p. 310.

[12] He returned to Pisino on 21 November 1918: '. . . three days of travel in a cattle car; there were no other possibilities'.   *Ibid.*, note 24.

welcome. In such a psychological climate, in the atmosphere of freedom regained, it was almost pleasant to recall the 'tyrants' of the House of Habsburg, especially the petty scion of Charlemagne and Charles V and Maria Theresa whose reign lasted sixty-eight years.

But it's time to introduce a new character: a childhood friend, indeed the only friend I have kept from childhood until today.[13] Just one year older than I, he was very sensitive, extremely intelligent and curious about all things cultural, an 'artist' to his fingertips.

One day while we were strolling in the public park of our small town, my friend told me with deep emotion that his French teacher had read in class and commented on '*La Rose de l'Infante*' from *La Légende des Siècles* [1859] by Victor Hugo:

> *Elle est toute petite, une duègne la garde.*
> *Elle tient à la main une rose, et regarde.*

How much Hugo's poem retained of the historical or the real was of no importance to us. And with verses like these, what did it matter that the Infanta's name was not in fact Marie?

> *Quel doux regard, l'azur! et quel doux nom, Marie!*
> *Tout est rayon; son oeil éclaire et son nom prie.*

The Infanta, attended by her duenna, is holding a rose in her hand and contemplating a pool of water in the garden. Behind a window of the palace in the background appears Philip II:

> *Dans le vaste palais catholique romain*
> *Dont chaque ogive semble au soleil une mitre,*
> *Quelqu'un de formidable est derrière la vitre;*

Evidently not the Escorial, the palace is more likely Aranjuez. But why should the poet prefer 'architectural' reality to the beauty of his imagination? Now anyone who could have gazed into the depths of Philip's eyes would have seen reflected in them neither the sky nor the garden nor his daughter, but a fleet of ships sailing northwards: the Invincible Armada.

The sun has set. A sudden puff of wind stirs the water, the

---

[13] Ezio Pattay (Pisino 1903–Florence 1958).

trees, even the rose held by the Infanta, and rudely deflowers it. The petals fall into the pool, which seems to foam up again, and they are scattered. The destruction of the rose is perhaps the first disappointment the little creature has suffered. Since she cannot understand why it has happened, she looks up at the sky as if searching for the wind. To the Infanta's silent question the duenna responds with the very words Philip II is said to have uttered on learning that the Invincible Armada had run into a storm and been sunk:

> *Tout sur terre appartient aux princes, hors le vent.*

I believe that the idea of Philip II as a threat hovering over mankind ('*Sa rêverie était un poids sur l'univers*') has been fixed in my mind ever since that day. But if it seemed possible in 1919 to establish a parallel between the son of Charles V and the tyrants of the House of Habsburg, I felt not many years later that Philip II could be identified with other, much more terrible figures.

*   *   *

I was working on *Volo di Notte* when strange rumours began to circulate, discreetly at first and *sotto voce*, later quite overtly. Would the Fascists launch an anti-Semitic campaign, slavishly aping Hitler's vile example? These rumours were hastily scotched by the *Corrispondenza Politico-Diplomatica* in mid-February 1938, but knowing from experience the meaning of official denials I gathered that Mussolini had yielded once again.[14]

---

[14] 'Possibly it was during his four days in Germany in 1937 that he saw the political usefulness of anti-semitism, and his views developed rapidly in 1938 as he moved closer to a German alliance. Subsequently he tried to excuse himself by accusing the Germans of exerting pressure to push him into a racialist policy, but it is hard to discover evidence of any such pressure; the motive was rather his own spontaneous decision to show solidarity with nazism and provide a convenient scapegoat for the years of austerity that he meant to impose on Italy'.

> Denis Mack Smith, *Mussolini*, Weidenfeld & Nicolson, London/ Alfred A. Knopf, New York, 1982, p. 221; see also H. Stuart Hughes, *Prisoners of Hope: The Silver Age of the Italian Jews 1924–1974*, Harvard University Press, Cambridge (Mass.), 1983, p. 58.

Five months later, on 15 July 1938, the newspapers published the 'Charter of Race' drafted by a group of 'Fascist scholars' (!) – an obscenity made all the more loathsome by the admixture of pseudo-scientific concepts.[15] On 1 September the race campaign became a reality.

As precious as the truth is to me, I should quite willingly have omitted the last few paragraphs. Having written them, I am happy to be able to say that the Italian people not only refused to support the race campaign – they overwhelmingly opposed it.[16]

If I had suffered so much as an adolescent from what seemed to me the unjust internment at Graz, how could I describe my state of mind at five o'clock on that fateful afternoon of 1 September 1938, as I heard the voice of Mussolini broadcasting the edicts of the Fascist government? I should have wished to protest, yet I wasn't so naïve as to suppose that the individual is not powerless in a totalitarian regime.

Only through music could I vent my indignation. Little did I imagine that works of the kind I felt welling up inside me – works like *La Mort d'un Tyran* (1932) by Darius Milhaud and *Thyl Claes* (1938–45) by Wladimir Vogel, Schoenberg's

[15] 'In July the newspapers had to print an impertinent declaration signed by a number of well-known university professors who had the audacity to state that Italians were Nordic Aryans of unmixed stock since the Lombard invasions and should be alive to the "peril" from this less than one-tenth of 1 per cent of the population'.

Mack Smith, *Italy: A Modern History*, p. 462.

The anti-Semitic campaign thwarted publication of Dallapiccola's Italian translation of *Die Neue Instrumentation* (Berlin, 1928–29) by Egon Wellesz. The manuscript, entitled *La Strumentazione Moderna* (1935–36, 796pp.), remains unpublished. See *Parole e Musica*, p. 562.

[16] Among the many notes taken in preparation for the libretto of *Il Prigioniero*, I find the following:

'One would have to despair of human nature if this brutality had been universal. Fortunately, a great many Catholics abhorred the massacre of St Bartholomew [23–24 August 1572]. One group, the executioners, was admirable. They refused to act, saying that they killed only after sentence had been passed. At Lyons and elsewhere the soldiers refused to shoot, saying they could not fire except in war'.

Jules Michelet, '*Guerres de Réligion*', *Histoire de France*, A. Lemerre, Paris, 1887, p. 451.   –LD

Ode to Napoleon Buonaparte (1942) or *A Survivor from Warsaw* (1947), to mention only a few — would soon be defined precisely as 'protest music'.

I had just read the biography of Mary Stuart by Stefan Zweig [1935], and I am indebted to this book for the knowledge of a brief prayer which the Queen of Scots wrote during the last years of her imprisonment:

> *O Domine Deus! speravi in Te.*
> *O care mi Jesu! nunc libera me.*
> *In dura catena, in misera poena, desidero Te.*
> *Languendo, gemendo et genu flectendo,*
> *Adoro, imploro, ut liberes me.*

> O Lord Almighty! I trusted in Thee.
> O Jesus, dear Saviour! now liberate me.
> In harsh chains, in grievous pain, I long for Thee.
> Languishing, sighing, and bending my knee,
> I entreat, I beseech Thee to liberate me.

These verses, centuries old, seemed to mirror a perennial human condition — hence our present-day condition. (I have never believed that the 'contemporary reality' is only what we read in the newspapers, and besides I am convinced that a wide gulf separates history from reportage.) For this reason, I intended to transform the Queen's personal prayer into a collective song; I wanted everyone to shout the divine word *libera*. Who could say whether, in the depths of my unconscious, there might still dwell the memory of that woman prisoner whose penalty had traumatized my childhood?

All of a sudden the music began to impel me, so forcefully that I had to interrupt work on *Volo di Notte*. I made a first sketch of the '*Preghiera di Maria Stuarda*' in short score, awaiting the chance to give it definitive form when I should have completed my opera. During the four-day hiatus devoted to the 'Prayer', I could not possibly think of anything else: that is, I still didn't know whether it was destined to remain an isolated piece or to become part of a larger composition. Only several months later did I clearly realize the necessity of a major development. Consequently, I had to search for other texts and investigate the writings of other illustrious prisoners — those who had struggled and believed.

The twelve-tone system intrigued me, but I knew so little about it![17] Nevertheless, I based the entire composition on a twelve-tone series and, as a symbolic gesture, counterpointed a fragment of the ancient liturgical sequence '*Dies irae, dies illa*'. Given the world political situation a few weeks after the Munich Conference, it did not seem inappropriate to think about the Last Judgement. Furthermore, I was convinced that the use of the '*Dies irae*' in the manner of a *cantus firmus* would facilitate the comprehension of my ideas. 'Comprehension,' let me repeat: not success nor the possibility of frequent performances. Never in my life – not even for an instant – have such motives influenced my actions or my thoughts. In *Canti di Prigionia* I called for the vibraphone because it was necessary, although I knew that in all of Italy, in 1938, not one could be found.[18] (Who would have imagined that only a few years later, this instrument was to be hailed as the solution of every problem – not excluding the problem of Good and Evil?)

In two phrases from *De Consolatione Philosophiae* by Severinus Boethius,[19] I found the text I needed for the

---

[17] See Dallapiccola's essay, 'On the Twelve-Note Road', translated by Deryck Cooke, *Music Survey*, Vol. IV, No. 1, London, October 1951, pp. 318–332. It will appear in Volume Two of the Toccata Press anthology of his writings.

[18] 'It is the timbre of Dallapiccola's *Canti* that makes them unique; this is the product of an imagination in sound that has had few equals. The songs use an "orchestra" of two pianos, two harps, xylophone, vibraphone, six timpani, ten large chimes, three tam-tams (large, medium, and small), cymbals (free and suspended), triangle, and various drums. It is useless to attempt a description of the sounds that Dallapiccola makes these instruments produce. In a sense they are evidence . . . of the genius of Varèse, who may first have suggested them. The indebtedness of Dallapiccola, if indebtedness there is, should surely be credited to *Ionisation* rather than to *Les Noces*'.

Richard F. Goldman, in *The Musical Quarterly*, July 1951, p. 407.

[19] *Felix qui potuit boni*   Happy the man whose eyes once could
Fontem visere lucidum,   Perceive the shining fount of good;
Felix qui potuit gravis   Happy he whose unchecked mind
Terrae solvere vincula.   Could leave the chains of earth behind.
– Book III, Chapter 12

– *The Consolation of Philosophy*, transl.
V.E. Watts, Penguin Books,
Harmondsworth, 1969, p. 113.

second movement, which occupied me during the Spring and Summer of 1940: a kind of scherzo, with an instrumental introduction to which the *pianissimo* dynamic lends an 'apocalyptic' quality. For the finale, I devoted much time to the setting of a madrigal by Tommaso Campanella [1568–1639], only to realize the incongruity of following two Latin texts with one in Italian. What is more, I felt that two verses of this madrigal – those preceded by the amazing line '*Se nulla in nulla si disfà giammai*' ('If nothing ever dissolves into nothingness') – would not be amenable to musical interpretation, since they are pure thought.[20]

So the search for a text resumed. I found the last words of Socrates extraordinarily attractive, to be sure, but how cold and unapproachable they sounded in the two learned Latin translations I was able to consult! A letter of Sébastien Castellion[21] looked promising, but after a few days I again realized my mistake.

On 19 August my wife and I happened to be at Covigliaio, a small mountain retreat in the Apennines. That evening Hitler gave an extremely bellicose speech in the Reichstag,

---

[20] '*Non può altronde, chi a sé pria non è morto, /Morte patir o torto*' ('It is further true that he who is not already dead to himself cannot suffer either death or wrong'), from *Quattro Canzoni: Dispregio della Morte* ('*Madrigale*' I of *Canzone* I, transl. Prof. Irma Brandeis).

[21] Part of a letter written by Calvin's great opponent, dated Basel, 1 July 1555. Dallapiccola would set this text to music in the Summer of 1952, as the first movement of *Canti di Liberazione* (1955) for chorus and large orchestra.

'I can now say, in retrospect, that *Canti di Prigionia* was not to be my last choral work on a Latin text. Even in 1941 I wished to compose another, analogous in structure, designed as the continuation, contrast to, and conclusion of the preceding work. . . .

'The war was over. We now had a little daughter, whom we decided to call Annalibera. For her I had written, during a long trip from Canada to Mexico, a set of piano pieces entitled *Quaderno Musicale di Annalibera*. It was based on a rather special twelve-tone series, which I used also in the first movement of *Canti di Liberazione*, sketched during my second visit to the United States, in 1952. "*Libera*" – "*liberazione*": the root is identical. Those who know the *Quaderno Musicale* will possibly discover something of it in *Canti di Liberazione*, despite the thousands of changes. And I hold the title in special regard just for this analogy: "*libera*" – "*liberazione*"'.

    LD: Saggi . . ., pp. 128–129; see 'My Choral Music', pp. 166–170.

announcing the imminent bombardment of Great Britain. It reminded me of the horrors Girolamo Savonarola had prophesied, which later came to pass. Sir Samuel Hoare, then Foreign Secretary, in answering Hitler exhorted the people to pray.

Finally I hit upon it! Hadn't the tragic monk of the Convent of St Mark written something similar in the *Meditatio in Psalmum 'In Te Domine Speravi'*, left unfinished at his death?

> *Premat mundus, insurgant hostes, nihil timeo*
> *Quoniam in Te Domine speravi,*
> *Quoniam Tu es spes mea,*
> *Quoniam Tu altissimum posuisti refugium Tuum.*

Let the world oppress, let the foe rise up, I fear nothing:
For in Thee, O Lord, have I trusted,
For Thou art my hope,
For Thou hast placed Thy refuge on the summit.

I owe the first performance of '*Preghiera di Maria Stuarda*' to the Belgian Radio (NIR) of Brussels and its director Paul Collaer, to whom the score is dedicated. It took place on 10 April 1940, the last broadcast from that courageous radio station I was to hear before its five-year silence. For in May, Nazi troops occupied Belgium.

The première of the complete triptych[22] was given in sinister circumstances at Rome. It was unusually cold, and the streets were swarming with police and Fascist militia: I am speaking of 11 December 1941, the day Mussolini decided to declare war on the United States. After this performance, *Canti di Prigionia* was easily forgotten in the surge of events and personalities. Apart from the prattle in the daily papers, no one took further notice of it until after the War. I am grateful to Fedele d'Amico for writing the first

[22] *Canti di Prigionia* consists of:
I. '*Preghiera di Maria Stuarda*' (Florence, 22 July 1939), dedicated to Paul Collaer;
II. '*Invocazione di Boezio*' (Covigliaio, 14 July 1940), to Ernest Ansermet;
III. '*Congedo di Girolamo Savonarola*' (Florence, 13 October 1941), to Sandro and Luisa Materassi.
First complete performance: Rome, Teatro delle Arti, 11 December 1941; Fernando Previtali, conductor.

important article about the *Canti*[23] and to the International Society for Contemporary Music, which 'rediscovered' my work during its first post-War festival (July 1946), in London.

In June 1939 my wife and I decided to visit Paris, to see once again at such an unsettled time a city we especially cherished. Events were coming to a head. Everyone now *knew* that another provocation on Hitler's part would mean war. Everyone knew it, as I said, except the man who more than anyone else should have known: Joachim von Ribbentrop.

And yet, life continued at its normal pace. Neither before nor after 1939 have I seen Paris more joyous or hospitable. Used books were being sold, as always, on the banks of the Seine, and it was there we obtained the works of Count Villiers de l'Isle-Adam. On our return journey, my wife suggested the story '*La Torture par l'Espérance*'[24] as a potential dramatic subject – perhaps, she added, the theme for a pantomime.

Thus, by sheer coincidence, the reading of this extremely cruel tale at once brought back the vision of a menacing tyrant. Philip II, the 'Official' at Saragossa, and the fanatical, blood-tinged pomposity of certain 16th-century Spanish choral music began to haunt my spirit. The route from reading a story to drafting a libretto is hardly direct.

[23] '*Canti di Prigionia*', in *Società*, Vol. I, No. 1, Florence, January–June 1945, pp. 95–100. Dallapiccola wrote to d'Amico on 3 August 1946:

'I was very warmly received in London and, later, in Paris and Brussels, and did some useful work for my colleagues. . . . Six sections of the ISCM voluntarily asked me to restore their relations with the Italian section. Very stormy sessions: for thirty-five minutes I had to try to defend Alfredo [Casella] . . . finally, an agreement was reached "in the English manner" *between Dent* and me*. For the English are alarmingly well-informed about every Italian intellectual current of the War years'.

LD: Saggi . . ., p. 73.

* Edward J. Dent (1876–1957), English musicologist, critic, and organizer, founded the ISCM in 1923 and directed it until 1938.

[24] In *Contes Cruels, Nouveaux Contes Cruels*, Éditions Garnier Frères, Paris, 1968. Translated by Anthony Bonner as 'Torture Through Hope', in *Great French Short Stories*, edited by Germaine Brée, Dell Publishing, New York, 1960, pp. 175–181.

But I recall that on the evening of the première of *Volo di Notte*, 18 May 1940, I had already decided that sooner or later, if I survived the War, I would adapt '*La Torture par l'Espérance*' for the stage.

Meanwhile, I felt that I should become thoroughly acquainted with the character of Philip II as reflected in history and poetry. Here is the unique case of a great king – great, certainly, if Miguel de Unamuno so passionately affirms it![25] – exonerated by historians and condemned by poets: by all the poets known to me, with the partial exception of Paul Verlaine. (Verlaine is no more than a partial exception, of course, since his initial inspiration was clearly the last verse of the poem, stupendous in its solemn immobility – '*Philippe II était à la droite du Père*' – the cornerstone of an entire poem quite untypical of Verlaine's personality and full of very apparent sutures.[26]) Taking note of the historians' judgement, I sided with the poets.

At that time I also reread *La Légende d'Ulenspiegel et de Lamme Goedzak*, the Flemish epic by Charles de Coster. In this book, which a few years earlier had filled Wladimir Vogel with its spirit of liberty,[27] several elements immediately struck me as advantageous for the opera I was avidly planning. Between 1942 and 1943 I kept jotting down hundreds of facts and anecdotes and trivia. By then I had almost become an expert in the history of that obscure period usually called the Wars of Religion.

Months passed and events progressed. More compellingly than ever I saw the necessity of writing an opera that could

[25] 'Would the world have been the same without our Charles I, without our Philip II, our great Philip?'
  Miguel de Unamuno, *The Tragic Sense of Life in Men and Nations*, translated by Anthony Kerrigan, Princeton University Press, Princeton/Routledge and Kegan Paul, London, 1972, p. 333.

[26] Paul Verlaine, '*La Mort de Philippe II*' in *Poèmes Saturniens* (1866).

[27] 'In this work [the epic oratorio *Thyl Claes*], Vogel demonstrates very lucidly that the twelve-tone system lends itself not merely to creating vague atmospheres but can also permit harsh, strongly rhythmic episodes – in the past, others have expressed serious doubts about this. Most interesting of all is that the system need not be so tyrannical as to exclude, *a priori* (as many would like to believe), expression and humanity'.
  '*Wladimir Vogel*' (1947), *Parole e Musica*, p. 344.

be at once moving and contemporary despite its historical setting, an opera that would depict the tragedy of our time – the tragedy of the persecution felt and suffered by the millions and tens of millions. Entitled simply *Il Prigioniero* ('The Prisoner'), the opera would not adopt as its protagonist Rabbi Aser Abarbanel, whom we meet in the story by Villiers de l'Isle-Adam and whose presence would only limit the scope of the now universal problem.

Events progressed, and I became increasingly receptive to certain details that would some day find their place in the libretto. During the war years we usually went to bed very late, for in the evenings between eleven and midnight there was always a chance of catching the bulletins broadcast in German by the London radio.[28] (German not being widely understood in Italy, these broadcasts were much less censored than those in French or English.) After listening to the 'late news', I usually took a walk along the Viale Margherita[29] where I was living at the time.

One of the many solitary walks of those years remains especially memorable. Above the motionless tableau of the blacked-out city, a clear winter sky and the full moon: 'a night for the RAF' we used to joke a bit cynically, quite indifferent to the danger of a raid by the Royal Air Force. Strolling slowly beneath the leafless trees, I had the eerie sensation of being choked by two moonlit branches casting their shadows over me. It lasted only an instant, but just long enough for me to see and feel the embrace of the Grand Inquisitor, hidden by the tree trunk, awaiting his beloved victim.

Nazi troops occupied Florence on 11 September 1943. As

[28] 'Everyone was listening to the London radio, even the generals and the fascist leaders who wanted to know what was really happening'.

Mack Smith, *Italy: A Modern History*, p. 480.

Massimo Mila detects a parody of the London radio bulletin in Scene 2 of *Il Prigioniero*, 'the exalting (but lying) narrative by the Jailer of the Flemish revolt and the victory of the Beggars. . . . "Camp Veere has now been taken by the Beggars; they're at the gates of Vlissing; at Gorcum they are fighting . . .".

Notes for the recording (CBS 61344), directed by Carl Melles.

[29] Now Viale Spartaco Lavagnini.   –LD

if that weren't enough, London radio announced the following evening that Mussolini had been 'liberated'. Although Mussolini was everywhere discussed freely and without inhibitions,[30] it was clear that the recrudescence of Fascism and the advent of the 'republic' of Salò backed by the S.S. made it very imprudent to continue living at our house in town. A friend generously offered us asylum in his villa at Borgunto, north of Fiesole.[31] Here I finished *Sex Carmina Alcaei* and then fell silent.

In that period I was too beleaguered to find even the modicum of tranquillity necessary for my work, but the forced idleness was still more annoying. How to pass the time? Certainly not by reading the newspapers, the contents of which were more disgusting than ever. If a friend turned up to our door without having telephoned in advance, I invariably asked: 'What's the bad news now?' Igor Markevitch, who bicycled out to see us on 6 November, answered: 'They've started rounding up the Jews'. A few days later we left for Como, where we could prepare to escape to Switzerland. But this plan was foiled by all kinds of obstacles,

[30] In my diary I find this entry, dated 14 November 1943:

'Long, intolerable trip. We have only left Milan about three-quarters of an hour when the train stops. Ten, fifteen, twenty minutes of waiting. In our third-class compartment, jam-packed with people of all sorts, there are two chorus girls probably from a small-time variety show. "What station is this?" one of them asks. She saunters down the aisle, looks out of the window, and says to herself, "Oh, we're only at Lodi", then starts humming:

Io non vengo da Lodi per lodare,
Né vengo da Piacenza per piacere,
Ma vengo da Predappio per predare . . .

("I don't come from Lodi to praise, nor from Piacenza to please, but I come from Predappio [Mussolini's birthplace] to prey . . .".) This was evidently part of one version of a popular song that made a hit during the forty-five-day administration of Marshal Badoglio. The other girl pokes her with her elbow and says, "Are you crazy?" "Who cares?" answers the first. "We're out of danger now." She shrugs her shoulders with indifference. Not a sign of reaction from the other passengers'.   –LD

[31] Leone Massimo's villa 'Le Pozzarelle', where Dallapiccola and his wife stayed from September 1943 until February 1944.

and we had no other choice than to return to Borgunto with only the hope that we might survive.

In 1942, at the request of the unforgettable Paolo Giordani,[32] who was planning to publish an anthology of piano pieces, I had written a 'Study' on Caprice No. 14 by Paganini. One year later in the solitude of Borgunto, as a way of killing time (*Galgenhumor!*), I had the idea of borrowing more material from the works of the supreme violinist, and in a week I sketched three pieces which, together with the one already completed, would form the *Sonatina Canonica*.

Seeking information about the term 'torture', I consulted the *Encyclopaedia Britannica* in Vittorio Gui's villa at Regresso di Maiano and, in Giacomo Devoto's home at San Domenico, the *Enciclopedia Italiana*.

On 9 December 1943, after receiving a warning, I felt strongly that my wife had better take shelter for a while in Florence, in an unoccupied apartment placed at her disposal by a trusted friend. At dusk I would go down to visit her, carefully selecting a different street each evening. Alessandro Bonsanti said to me: 'After all, they're our wives and they've been forced to flee. I'd like to wring somebody's neck!'

A rather long corridor led to my room in Borgunto. Returning there one evening, I actually *saw* the corridor of the 'Official' at Saragossa. And thus another detail valuable

---

[32] Paolo Giordani, friend and advocate of contemporary composers, directed the Milanese publishing firm Edizioni Suvini Zerboni from 1932 until his death in 1948. Dallapiccola dedicated *Il Prigioniero* to the memory of Giordani, 'who believed in this opera after simply reading the libretto, who spurred and encouraged me and helped me so generously to complete it' (*LD: Saggi . . .*, p. 75).

About the *Sonatina Canonica*, the composer wrote to Fedele d'Amico (see note 23 on p. 50):

'It's a little set of "pranks" (*sguerguenze*, in the dialect of Pistoia) on several Paganini Caprices. Just as Liszt created a pianistic equivalent of the Paganini technique, so – all differences granted – I decided to employ a contrapuntal equivalent of the same technique. There's even a *canon cancrizans* where the trills and turns are in retrograde, all with very few changes in the original harmony. Luckily, the piece is very difficult (it's dedicated to Scarpini), so there's no danger of its being played by the girls at the Conservatory'.

for the staging of the cruel story by Villiers de l'Isle-Adam was added to my store.

Once her position had been clarified and a police officer assured me that I would be warned of renewed danger, my wife returned to Borgunto. Between Christmas Eve and New Year's Eve of 1943, I made a first draft of the libretto of *Il Prigioniero* and read it for a small circle of friends at the Bonsantis, in San Domenico, on 4 January 1944. After the protagonist's last words – after he mutters almost unconsciously, though in a distinctly questioning tone, '*La libertà?*' – there was a moment of silence. Then Bonsanti interrupted: 'For my part, I dare hope those others will end at the stake'.

Finally, on 10 January, I had the first sufficiently clear musical idea, the one that generated the aria in three stanzas '*Sull' Oceano, sulla Schelda*' at the centre of the opera. In this idea I immediately perceived many possibilities for transformation. That same evening we learned from London radio the outcome of the Verona trial.[33] I completed the draft of the central aria in a couple of weeks, but for many months thereafter work on *Il Prigioniero* would fail to progress.

At the beginning of February, the villa in Borgunto was requisitioned by a German command. We had no choice but to return to our apartment in the Viale Margherita and remain there until we received the next warning. Then some fraternal friends would cordially welcome us to wait long days and interminable evenings with them for the hour of liberation. The sirens sounded their alarms seven or eight times a day.

Personally, I was not worried about the air raids: I didn't expect to be killed by an Anglo-American bomb. What totally unnerved me were the insidious persecution and the constant threat of anonymous denunciations – always carried out, in fact – the vulgar journalistic prose and the petty Fascist functionaries sporting the Roman eagle on their caps, who stared meaningfully when they met you in the street. (Everything seemed to be finished, yet the

---

[33] Mussolini had his son-in-law, Count Galeazzo Ciano (Fascist foreign minister), and four other party leaders executed as traitors because of their vote which toppled his regime on 25 July 1943. See Mack Smith, *Mussolini*, pp. 302–305.

masquerades continued.) Like so many others, I was paying a bitter price for the tremendous outburst of joy on 25 July, the happiest day of my life.

The summer days of 1944 were long: the houses had neither water nor lights. We waited, absolutely incommunicado, for those who had devised some ingenious means of operating their radios to bring us news. No longer was there talk about music. When friends gathered, we tried to make sense of the current situation – never succeeding, of course.

On 20 July Pietro Scarpini[34] knocked four times as usual at our door. Months earlier we'd have spoken of Liszt or Busoni or Schoenberg; that evening, when asked if there was any news, Scarpini only replied: 'Yes, Hitler is *not* dead'. So even in Germany, somebody was taking the initiative? We felt relieved, but we would still have to wait almost ten terrible months for something decisive to happen.

Florence suffered all but her last indignity. The Nazis had some lorries equipped with large hooks and used them to rip out the tram-car cables, stripping the plaster from the houses. These specialized teams were called 'rescue squads'. And finally, the ultimate outrage. The bridges of Florence had been mined. At daybreak on 4 August, several flashes followed by frightful explosions seemed to announce that our waiting was nearly over. The Allied troops crossed the Arno on 11 August, and the next day Sandro Materassi[35] and I went under a scorching sun to survey the centre of an almost unrecognizable city, stepping precariously over shards of glass and masonry debris, skirting as best we could the piles of rubble. We didn't even attempt to console one another, for our eyes were full of tears.

[34] Pietro Scarpini (b. 1911), pianist, colleague of Dallapiccola's at the Luigi Cherubini Conservatory in Florence; gave the world premières of *Sonatina Canonica* (1946) and *Tre Episodi dal Balletto 'Marsia'* (1950), participated in the first Italian performance of *Musica per Tre Pianoforti (Inni)* (1936).

[35] Sandro Materassi (b. 1904), violinist and partner in the Materassi-Dallapiccola Duo from 1930 to 1970; dedicatee of '*Congedo di Girolamo Savonarola*' and the two versions of *Tartiniana Seconda* (1956).

Opposite, from Il Prigioniero, *Scene 4: The Prisoner, who has just escaped from the dungeon of the 'Official' at Saragossa but who will soon fall into the embrace of the Grand Inquisitor, exclaims – 'I have not hoped in vain. . . . The stars! The sky!'*

Returning home after a war does not really guarantee an immediate resumption of work. What is more, we could only return twenty-eight days after the liberation, and too many repairs were needed, first of all in the badly leaking roof. To think I had hoped to be able to take up, bright and early on the morning after the liberation so as not to lose more time, exactly where I had left off!

Suddenly, from the depths of the unconscious, emerged the memory of the trip my family and I had taken to Graz twenty-seven years earlier. And with this memory surfaced the thousand details I believed were forgotten and buried forever in my innermost self.

As a parting gift, a friend had presented me with a brass medal that depicted St George slaying the dragon. The inscription read: *In tempestate securitas.* 'A good omen', remarked my father after examining the medal.

A gentleman boarded our coach at the Styrian frontier and immediately buried his eyes in the Graz *Tagespost*. He was reading the political section on page one, and seated opposite him I could see the last page with its conspicuous announcement of the opera to be performed that evening: '*OTELLO*' (how can I forget the beauty of those bold gothic letters?), 'Opera in Four Acts, by Giuseppe Verdi'. Leo Slezak played the title role. 'Performance beginning at 7:30'. How many times I asked my father if the train would be very late!

For in my unbridled adolescent egoism, heedless of the fatigue and anxiety of a day-long journey, I naturally expected my family to take me to the theatre – my family driven from its home, faced with a very dim prospect and endless uncertainties. As luck would have it, the train arrived at eleven, so the problem that had vexed me for several hours during the trip was solved by force of circumstances.

Twenty-seven years later, I must have been quite deluded still if I imagined that I could resume work on the morning after the cessation of combat. Had I then learned so little from life? And yet, adolescence was far behind me! But perhaps it was again only my love for music and the awareness that, apart from music, life would have very little to offer me.

Certainly, *Il Prigioniero* could not make notable progress before January 1945. I sketched two scenes and, in the meantime, composed a couple of chamber pieces.[36] In 1946 I suddenly became blocked. Weariness, exhaustion. Only then did I realize that the hardships and anxieties of the War years, the worries of the immediate pre-War period – the *Anschluss* of Austria and the question of the Sudetenland, the fraud of Munich and that fateful 14 March 1939 when Hitler entered Prague (reading the announcement on the kiosk of the afternoon newspaper, I felt faint and had to lean against the wall, and I remember looking high above me towards the deep blue sky and murmuring *'Sed libera nos a malo'*) – all this together with the privations and the feverish work of the post-War period had demanded a superhuman effort of everyone.

Fortunately, in July I was able to set out on a journey. After years of isolation, that first contact with people of many nations was unforgettable.[37]

After London and Paris, I went to Brussels. But one morning, without bidding my friends adieu, I boarded the train for Antwerp – not only to see its many artistic treasures, but still more to contemplate the vast estuary of the Scheldt (no longer a river and not yet the sea), that mirror of water where the Revolt of the Beggars against Philip II took place. From the Scheldt one views an infinite horizon. 'Swans of liberty,' I sang in my heart.[38]

---

[36] As mentioned above, Dallapiccola conceived the first musical idea of the opera, the idea embodied in the central Aria in Three Stanzas *'Sull' Oceano, sulla Schelda'*, on 10 January 1944, shortly after he finished the first draft of the libretto. The second scene as a whole, containing this Aria, is dated 3 February 1945, and the other parts of *Il Prigioniero* were completed in the following sequence: Scene IV, 4 August 1945; Scene III, 25 August 1946; Prologue, 6 April 1947; Scene I, 25 April 1947.

[37] 'The sessions were always intensely cordial. To the joy of renewing old friendships and repairing those lines of communication so abruptly severed on 1 September 1939 was added our unconfessed delight in having survived. Because of this very special atmosphere, the twentieth ISCM festival, organized in association with the London *News Chronicle*, may be remembered much longer for its human importance than for the considerable artistic achievement'.   *LD: Saggi . . .*, p. 123.

[38] 'On the ocean, on the Scheldt, in sunshine, in rain, in snow, in hail, winter and summer, glided the ships of the Beggars to and fro.

Then on to see Ghent, something of a fortress. There I climbed the bell tower where 'Roelandt' had resounded, the proud bell that figures so prominently in *Il Prigioniero*.[39] And thus I regained the strength to resume work, and finished a first draft of my opera on 25 April 1947.

The orchestral score was completed on 3 May 1948.

'All sails out like mantling swans, swans of white freedom. . . .'
      Charles de Coster, *The Legend of Ulenspiegel and Lamme Goedzak*,
      translated by F.M. Atkinson, Heinemann, London, 1928, p. 600.
[39] 'Then he [Emperor Charles V] looked upon Roelandt, the great bell, and hanged from the clapper the fellow who had sounded the alarm to call the city to defend her right. He had no mercy for Roelandt, his mother's tongue, the tongue with which she spoke to Flanders: Roelandt, the proud bell, which saith of himself:

Als men my slaet dan is 't brandt.
Als men my luyt dan is 't storm in Vlaenderlandt.

When they ring me there is fire.
When they toll me there is storm in Flanders.

'Finding that his mother spoke too loud and free, he took away the bell. And the folk of the flat country say that Ghent died because her son had torn out her tongue with his iron pincers'.   *Ibid.*, pp. 59–60.

Job

A Mystery Play

(1967)

Harald Kreutzberg[1] danced that evening, 13 June 1949, at the Teatro della Pergola in Florence. He danced, and every moment seemed to offer the audience a fresh revelation. Then the penultimate work on the programme: *Job Struggles with God*. So completely did it absorb my attention and receptivity that I cannot remember the final piece of the evening.

On leaving the theatre, my wife and I talked about Job. Neither of us could have guessed that Carl Jung was just then contemplating one of his major works, *Antwort auf Hiob*,[2] written in the Summer of 1950. We resolved to reread the Book of Job the next day, but our conversation was interrupted by meeting the artistic director of the Teatro Comunale of Florence.[3] Without beating around the bush, he said that he regretted my allowing the world première of *Il Prigioniero* to be given as a radio broadcast. And he added: 'We could have worked together in secret, without telling anyone . . .'. I replied that, while I wasn't conversant with the operations of subsidized institutions, I was astonished all the same that we should have had to work surreptitiously, as if the performance of one of my works were at least something to be ashamed of. And there the conversation abruptly ended.

Evidently the artistic director knew more about it than I.

---

[1] Harald Kreutzberg (1902–68), celebrated German dancer and choreographer.
[2] *Answer to Job*, translated by R.F.C. Hull, Princeton University Press, Princeton, 1973 (originally published in Zurich in 1952).
[3] Francesco Siciliani (b. 1911).

Perhaps he already knew that by programming *Il Prigioniero*, he would unleash the fury of many of his colleagues. But could he have suspected even then what would happen between January 1950 and the date of the performance? Letters to the government, one of which said: 'It is a disgrace that an opera which casts a dim light on the Holy Spanish Inquisition should be performed in Italy during the Holy Year'. In other words, *Il Prigioniero* was essentially an attack on the Catholic Church. Of all the insults hurled at me during the first half of 1950, this was the only one that deeply wounded me – and the only one I haven't forgotten – on account of its absolute bad faith.[4]

And so went that period of my life I once described in a letter as 'Inquisition without cowl, auto-da-fé without flames'.

To make life impossible for him: this was the watchword for a couple of years. And no doubt they succeeded in making my life impossible, even in a *material* sense. All the same, the

---

[4] 'On the other hand the Communist Party, whose attentions had been lavished on me in the past, took issue with my article "Planned Music" (published in *Il Ponte*, Florence, January 1950). They didn't know that I had written the libretto of *Il Prigioniero* in 1942–43, when I was combatting only one kind of dictator, but pretended to believe my barbs were aimed at the Soviet dictator of 1950. So in the Spring of 1950, I had the honour of being "*a Dio spiacenti e a' nemici sui*" ("displeasing to God and to his enemies" [Dante, *Inferno*, III: 63]) – displeasing, that is, to the Catholics and the Communists alike.'

'The Birth-Pangs of *Job*', *Musical Events*, Vol. XV, No. 5, London, May 1960, p. 26 (translation revised).

On 4 July 1957 Dallapiccola wrote to his publisher, Edizioni Suvini Zerboni:

'I was very interested to read about the possibility of *Il Prigioniero* being performed at Moscow. . . . Speaking as the composer, I can have no objection to this performance, on condition that the sponsor promises to insert a note in the programme exactly as follows:

'"Experience has taught me, unfortunately, that the subject of my opera *Il Prigioniero* lends itself to an interpretation contrary to my intention. When I began making notes for the libretto in the Summer of 1942, tyranny and the horrors of war were widespread in most of Europe, and there was no possibility of misunderstanding that the Spanish Inquisition should be considered a symbol, not be taken literally.

'"As a believer I want to emphasize that there is nothing against the Catholic Church in *Il Prigioniero*, but only a protest against tyranny and oppression"'.   *LD: Saggi . . .*, pp. 91–92.

première took place at Florence and wasn't quite the flop they had hoped for, despite a less than mediocre performance (though the conductor was none other than Hermann Scherchen), despite the atmosphere of open hostility that infected everyone, even the stage-hands, who were encouraged by it to act badly. Only two persons were friendly towards me then: the artistic director, who committed himself wholeheartedly to the difficult score – difficult, certainly, for him; and an obscure prompter, whom the producer Bronislaw Horowicz overheard roaring from the stage: 'It makes no difference to me whether it concerns Verdi or Dallapiccola! My duty is to do right, and I want to do right!'

Immediately after the two performances of *Il Prigioniero*, I left for Brussels and London.[5] On returning I asked the artistic director of the Teatro Comunale in Florence how Rome had reacted to the opera. (Naturally, I meant the reaction of the authorities, since the opinion of the critics was of no importance to me.) And here is exactly what he said: 'They've *cashed in* on the success'.

*   *   *

However, in mid-March, two months, that is, before the première, my faithful old friend Guido M. Gatti had paid me a visit.[6] He wanted to talk about the newly formed Amfiparnaso

[5] In London I happened to meet the sculptor Jacob Epstein, whose studio was dominated by an eleven-foot-tall marble colossus 'Behold the Man'. This *Ecce Homo* was sorrowful in a different way from all the others I had seen before. Veiled by a nameless suffering, the eyes seemed about to lose their last ray of light. The lips, which at first appeared to express indignation, on closer examination revealed deep compassion – compassion for the fate of mankind. Just at that moment I felt the statue had a special meaning for me, and I asked Epstein for a photograph of it.   –LD

[6] 'After a catastrophe, it takes much time and effort to get back on one's feet. And so three years after the end of the War in Europe, on 3 May 1948, the day I finished the score of *Il Prigioniero*, my wife – who evidently not to disturb me had said nothing for several weeks about everyday problems – alerted me that our bank account was down to 500 lire. I wrote to you for help the same day, and you telephoned the next morning, inviting me to Rome and commissioning the music for a documentary.* At the time it was our salvation.'   '*Lettera a Guido M. Gatti*' (1965), *Parole e Musica*, p. 167.

* *Accademie Straniere in Roma*, directed by Vittorio Carpignano for Lux Film.

Society of Rome, whose aim was to present short operas written especially for the occasion together with operas of the past that weren't part of the regular repertory. Gatti told me that Vincenzo Tommasini, Goffredo Petrassi and Alberto Savinio had already promised new works,[7] and that the Society had considered asking me for a mystery play (*sacra rappresentazione*), inasmuch as I had composed *Tre Laudi* more than a decade earlier. 'That was fourteen years ago,' I replied, 'and in the meantime we have been through World War II. I don't believe I am capable any longer of painting a picture on a gold background.' Nor was this the first time I had been compelled to note how political events had influenced me. The brutality of the Ethiopian campaign, the disasters of the Spanish Civil War had changed me. I couldn't imagine now a return to the brightly coloured anecdotage that inspired *Sei Cori di Michelangelo Buonarroti il Giovane*, which must remain a unique work in my catalogue.[8] Granted: in the *Laudi* I had taken a step forward, at least insofar as I was thinking for the first time of melodic lines comprising all twelve tones possible in our tempered system.[9] I neither accepted nor declined

[7] Respectively, *Il Tenore Sconfitto ovvero La Presunzione Punita*, *Morte dell' Aria*, and *Orfeo Vedovo*; performed at the Teatro Eliseo, Rome, 24 October 1950.

One of the revivals was Rossini's *Il Turco in Italia*, which had not been performed in Italy since 1855; Maria Callas played the role of Donna Fiorilla. Although the Associazione Amfiparnaso* failed for financial reasons, the tradition of chamber opera in Italy was given a new lease on life with the inauguration of the Piccola Scala at Milan and the Teatrino di Corte at Naples.

* *L'Amfiparnaso* (*The Slopes of Parnassus*, 1597) is a madrigal comedy by the Modenese composer Orazio Vecchi.

[8] In three sets: I. (1933) for mixed chorus a cappella; II. (1934–35) for small chamber choir, women or boys, and seventeen instruments; III. (1935–36) for mixed chorus and large orchestra; texts by Michelangelo the Younger, nephew of the sculptor. See 'My Choral Music', pp. 154–160.

[9] '*Job* was the first work of mine of any considerable scope in which I had used a single twelve-tone row. The *cantus firmus* (the *Te Deum Laudamus*), which I used here and there, was also arranged, with appropriate transpositions, in such a manner as to achieve the "full chromatic". I had made use of only one "transformation" of the row: namely, that which is obtained by the omission of six notes among the individual tones – the one, that is, which

Gatti's offer. I merely said I would think it over and let him know.

That evening, when my wife returned home, I told her about Gatti's visit and the proposal he had made. Her reaction was instantaneous: 'If the authorities were so scandalized by *Il Prigioniero*, why not answer them with a *Job*?' Needless to say, we were under no illusion that the question Job asks God could even be noticed by the boors who, after too many years of 'Minculpop', had been called back to occupy the positions they once held during the *ventennio*.[10]

The next day in my studio I assembled thirty-four different editions of the Book of Job in several languages, with various commentaries. Then it was a matter of reading and absorbing them all, before selecting the words and establishing the overall *form* of the composition. It is a delicate operation, of course, to choose words for the musical theatre from pre-existing literary works: delicate, because the words, immobile on the printed page, must assume another quality and another dimension in order to help create the character on stage. With regard to form, I realized at once that in a mystery play, a structure composed of separate pieces – or 'numbers', as they used to be called – would be more than acceptable, even in the 20th century. A series of tableaux, one after another, following the development of the story. The Bible itself gave such

---

adopts tones 1, 8, 15, 22, etc. (Note that this transformation appears only in the passage "*Beato l'uomo cui corregge Iddio: Non c'è morte senza peccato, né sofferenza senza colpa*" ["Behold, happy is the man whom God correcteth: there is no death without sin, nor any suffering without guilt"] – and, of course, in the other parallel passages. Now, this is the only passage that I did not draw directly from the Book of Job but rather from one of the writings of a Father of the Church.)'   'My Choral Music', pp. 167–168.

[10] One of the functions of the Ministry of Popular Culture ('Minculpop', formerly the Ministry of Propaganda) was to regulate all theatrical activities according to the directives of the Fascist regime. The *ventennio* – or *il ventennio nero* – were the twenty 'black' years of Fascism, from October 1922 (the March on Rome) to July 1943.

'The vagaries of the censorship were notorious. Fisher's *History of Europe* was confiscated from bookstores in 1939 by order of a new dignitary called the Minister of Popular Culture. An index of prohibited books was also drawn up for libraries, in which, along with Robert Graves and Axel Munthe, Machiavelli and Boccaccio were in 1939 declared "unsuitable to the fascist spirit". By this time the lunatic elements of fascism were clearly in full control'.   Mack Smith, *Italy: A Modern History*, pp. 419–420.

61

© *Edizioni Suvini Zerboni, 1950*

precise indications for the musical form of one of the pieces (No. 2, the scene of the messengers) that it would have been absurd to disregard them. Let us read verses 14–19 from Chapter I of the Book of Job:

> And there came a messenger unto Job, and said, The oxen were plowing, and the asses feeding beside them:
>
> And the Sabeans fell upon them, and took them away; yea, they have slain the servants with the edge of the sword; and I only am escaped alone to tell thee.
>
> While he was yet speaking, there came also another, and said, The fire of God is fallen from heaven, and hath burned up the sheep, and the servants, and consumed them; and I only am escaped alone to tell thee.
>
> While he was yet speaking, there came also another, and said, The Chaldeans made out three bands, and fell upon the camels, and have carried them away, yea, and slain the servants with the edge of the sword; and I only am escaped alone to tell thee.
>
> While he was yet speaking, there came also another, and said, Thy sons and thy daughters were eating and drinking wine in their eldest brother's house:
>
> And, behold, there came a great wind from the wilderness, and smote the four corners of the house, and it fell upon the young men, and they are dead; and I only am escaped alone to tell thee.[11]

As we see, the Bible gives us an exact indication: 'While he was yet speaking . . .' – a quartet. And it would be useless for me to try to convey how enthusiastically I accepted this suggestion, since I had not had an opportunity before then to come to grips with a quartet on the stage. Another ensemble piece would have been possible, at least in certain respects, in the scene of Job's 'friends'.[12] The culminating point of the

[11] King James version.

[12] '. . . the Book of Job has been called a "poem of pessimism", but perhaps it could be more aptly described as a "poem of revolt". This makes it clear that while Job is prepared to endure the tribulations visited on him by God, he rebels when he realizes that his fellow-men have no compassion for him. The attitude of Job's friends, who can only censure him, who will not admit that he has been punished without having sinned, is as far as one

Opposite, from Job, *No. 5: Job – having asked God 'Wherefore do the wicked live, become old, yea, are mighty in power? . . .' – demands an answer.*

whole work is the penultimate scene (No. 6), obviously based on chapters 38–41 of the Book of Job, where God amidst the whirlwind answers the famous question – the boldest question any man ever dared address to the Deity. And this climax would be reserved for the chorus.

It also seemed clear that the presence of a narrator (*storico*) – a reciting voice – was not out of place in a mystery play, although I should have been very careful not to resort to such a contrivance in an opera, for example. The narrator's task would be to introduce the dramatic action, bring it to a close, and link several episodes with very brief interpolations.[13] It remained only to decide how to resolve the strife between God and Satan. Considering how extremely important it was dramatically, I felt that with two speaking choirs stationed at different points on the stage I could convey the significance of this conflict to the audience more clearly than by the use of the singing chorus.

*   *   *

I am unable to comment on the première of *Job*, in Rome, because I didn't hear it. On that evening, 30 October 1950,

---

can imagine from a Christian mentality'.

    '*Dichiarazioni sul mio "Job"*' (1950, first published in the programme notes of the Teatro Comunale, Bologna, 13 October 1984), p. 3.

[13] 'The first movement corresponds to the seventh, in that the work begins and ends with the *storico*; likewise, in terms of tension and volume of sound, the second movement (the quartet of the messengers) corresponds to the sixth (the singing chorus interpreting the voice of God). There is also a parallel between the third movement, where God consigns the body of Job to Satan's power, and the fifth, which portrays the protagonist's final solitude. In the centre stands the fourth movement, the scene of Job with his friends.

    'It may be very helpful for the listener to know at the outset that the entire work, which lasts about thirty-five minutes, has the form of an *arch*'.

                        ibid., pp. 1–2.

    The *storico* ('historian') in *Job*, who narrates the events in the third person, should be distinguished from the Radio-telegraphist in *Volo di Notte*, Dallapiccola's first opera. The latter identifies himself with Fabien almost to the point of becoming the pilot's alter ego, and relates his messages in the first person. *Cf.* pp. 74 and 83 *et seq.*

the stage of the Teatro Eliseo was 'invaded' by singers who hadn't been paid for previous performances. Endless arguments, bills being signed, promises made – I couldn't understand very much in that hullabaloo. But I still remember the outrage of one very fat singer who then received 300,000 lire per engagement and whose weight, I am told, has since decreased in inverse proportion to the fee she now commands.

The première of *Job*, slated for nine o'clock, began exactly at ten-thirty, in an atmosphere one can easily imagine. As I said, I didn't hear it. I was back stage, trying my best to keep a door closed to prevent the uproar and the quarrels from disturbing the performance too much.

Ten years later one remembers these things without bitterness.[14]

---

[14] 'The Birth-Pangs of *Job*', p. 27 (translation revised). *Cf.* Gatti's letter of 16 November 1950 and Dallapiccola's reply, in *L.D.: Saggi* . . ., pp. 83–84.

Pages from a Diary
Alexander Moissi

Milan, 27 March 1951

I left Florence this morning. Tomorrow I shall deliver the score of *Job*, ready for printing, to my publisher. In the railway compartment opposite me are three gentlemen, one of middle age sitting between two youths. On my left, a beautiful woman, distinctly an American type.

The train has just departed. The middle-aged man addresses me, we introduce ourselves, and since my travelling companion has scant Italian I suggest that we converse in German. (The 'American' removes a notepad and pen from her purse.)

The man facing me is a producer, born in Czechoslovakia, educated at the School of Dramatic Art in Berlin. I don't inquire, but the two youths probably belong to the class of 'assistant producer'. Loquacious, my travelling companion. On trains, of course, one often runs into people with the gift of gab. Jeremiads ad infinitum on the general state of the theatre, which he considers beneath all criticism, on the absolute lack of genuinely talented producers the world over (hardly an astonishing statement coming from a producer). And finally, devastating critiques of actors and actresses, living and dead, with quotations from the tragedies and comedies they would have slaughtered. Difficult to get a word in edgewise, so fluent and incessant is the producer's monologue – obviously part of his repertoire.

A question prompted me, but I hesitated. Had the passage of time aggrandized a memory of early adolescence? No, I wasn't mistaken: I had never witnessed such a bold assertion of personality before that Sunday afternoon I heard Alexander

Moissi[1] in *Oedipus Rex*. I have never forgotten his declamation of certain lines:

> . . . *selber komm'*ich *hieher, ich,*
> *Mit Ruhm von allen Oe-di-pus genannt.*

Here I am, myself, world-famous Oedipus.[2]

In the score I shall deliver to my publisher tomorrow, isn't there perhaps still a trace of the lesson I received then, thirty-four years ago?

> *Questo, tutto questo dico* i–o, i–o, *Job*.

And wasn't there something akin to it earlier, in *Volo di Notte*?

> I–o, i–o *solo, Rivière* . . .

I finally manage to interrupt the producer and ask his opinion of Moissi. Nonplussed for a moment by having his monologue turned into a dialogue, the producer replies in a blasé tone:
    'I remember Alexander Moissi only as a great *poseur* . . .'
    'Having admired him so much in *Oedipus Rex* many years ago . . .'
    'Yes,' admits the producer with an air of condescension, 'in *Oedipus Rex* he was remarkable. . . .'
    'So you heard it, too?'
    'More than heard.' And he continues: 'When I was a student at the Berlin Academy, our teacher said one morning on entering the classroom: "What a nuisance! Tomorrow that *poseur* Moissi begins rehearsals for *Oedipus Rex* and he has written to me requesting forty extras. So at ten sharp tomorrow morning, twenty girls and twenty boys will be at the theatre". One of us asked: "But what will we have to do?" The teacher answered: "How should I know? The stage will probably be dark. As the curtain rises you rush pell-mell onto the steps of the Palace of Thebes – girls on the left, boys on the right, mind you! – and stretch out face downwards. . . . Your entrance will probably be accompanied by a roll on the bass

---

[1] Renowned Austrian actor (1879–1935), particularly associated with Max Reinhardt's theatre in Berlin and Vienna.
[2] Sophocles, *Oedipus the King*, translated by Bernard Knox, Washington Square Press, New York, 1959, p. 2; subsequent quotations from pp. 11 and 1.

drum or tremolo on timpani. At the end of the dialogue between Oedipus and Creon, the Priest will say: 'My sons, stand up', and nod when you should exit. Nothing complicated, you see".

'Next morning we arrive at the rehearsal on time. As instructed, we come onstage in a riot and hurl ourselves onto the steps of the palace. Moissi appears under the spotlight clad in a white tunic, with outstretched arms, his voice tuned to the note A, and begins:

O ihr des alten Kadmos Kinder, neu Geschlecht . . .

My sons! Newest generation of this ancient city of Thebes!

He makes no gesture, nor can he, being already crucified.[3] Well, we forty arose and climbed the stairs of the palace to form a circle around him, so affecting was the tenderness in that word "*Kinder*". . . .'

I thanked the producer for his story, not failing to add that in my opinion what Moissi had achieved at the first rehearsal was the result of a great actor's magic – something no mere *poseur* can possess.

The beautiful American sitting on my left evidently knew German. Nor did she suffer from inhibitions, for while aware that I was keeping an eye on her, with admirable impudence she jotted down on her notepad verbatim, in English, the conversation in the railway coach.

Will it be published?

*   *   *

P.S.: One can always learn something – even on a train, even

---

[3] Moissi's extended arms gave him the appearance of a man bound to the cross. In *Cinque Canti* (1956) for baritone and eight instruments, Dallapiccola causes the notation at several points in the third song to produce the symbol of the crucifix (*cf.* p. 253, n. 27).

'Ideograms of all sorts abound in the composer's music,' observes Hans Nathan. 'Another non-auditory one can be found in the *Concerto per la Notte di Natale dell' Anno 1956*, movement IV, where the lines, of course consisting of the tones of the row, are curved in such a way as to form circles. This occurs at Jacopone da Todi's mystical words "*Amor, amor, tu se' cerchio rotondo*" and again later near the word "*amore*".'

'Luigi Dallapiccola: Fragments from Conversations', p. 305, n. 19.

at my age. The professor at the Academy had defined Alexander Moissi as a *poseur*, and for decades the producer has continued to regard him as such and calls him a *poseur* today, despite the marvellous experience he took part in.

We who teach bear serious responsibilities. I must always exercise the strictest control over what I say during my classes at the Conservatory.

Two Encounters with
Antoine
de Saint-Exupéry
(1951)

I had scarcely begun the first musical draft of *Volo di Notte* when it struck me that sooner or later I should have to approach Antoine de Saint-Exupéry, if only to get his permission to extract a libretto from *Vol de Nuit*, the short novel which had made him internationally famous overnight. I didn't know how accessible the writer would be, and so I asked Domenico de' Paoli,[1] who was living in Paris at the time, to do his best to arrange an interview during my first visit there. De' Paoli found a way of approaching him, and we went to the aviator-novelist's apartment, Place Vauban 7, one morning in the last week of June 1937. But de' Paoli had already spoken with Saint-Exupéry – or 'Saint-Ex' as he was called in French artistic and social circles, after the venerable custom of abbreviating long names, making them sound friendlier and more familiar. He had told him that an Italian composer was so captivated by the story of his renowned novel, he wished to base a work on it. Apparently the writer didn't immediately understand: would it be a symphonic poem, he asked? When he learned that it was intended for the theatre (even if not to be designated an 'opera'), he expressed no appreciation for an idea that probably seemed unrealizable on the stage. Anyhow, he sent me in care of de' Paoli a card with very friendly

---

[1] Domenico de' Paoli (b. 1894), Italian music critic, dedicatee of *Due Liriche di Anacreonte*.

greetings and a copy of *Vol de Nuit*, inscribed with thanks for liking his little book.

I was rather tense that morning in June, as I went up to the apartment in Place Vauban 7. The wait of several minutes seemed all too brief, busy as I was examining the bookcases, the books, and the work-table. A door stood ajar, and I still recall how my curiosity was piqued by the four fingerbones and red-enamelled nails of a woman's hand that appeared just above the handle of the door at a certain moment and softly closed it. I had neglected to inquire about Saint-Ex's appearance. The sight of his gigantic figure and deeply scarred face, the grip of his enormous, strong hand made me reproach myself a moment for this oversight, as I could hardly contain my astonishment. I resolved never to go to another important interview unprepared. But that was only for an instant, because his scarred face broke into the most friendly smile. Then it was time to begin.

'The stage is divided by a partition into two rooms. Much the smaller, on the viewer's left, is Rivière's study, containing a desk and several chairs. In the left-hand wall, a door and a window; almost the entire remaining space covered by a big map. The rear wall is made of glass, and through it a large door opens from the office (on the viewer's right) onto the airfield. In the distance, beyond the airport, the city of Buenos Aires should also be visible, gradually illuminated at nightfall'.

Here the writer's lively voice interrupted me: 'And everything takes place on this one set?' A second smile appeared on the face that attentively scrutinized me – an enigmatic smile this time though not, I think, even tinged with irony. I begged Saint-Ex to hear me out. When I had finished telling him about the Radio-telegraphist, a kind of narrator (*storico*) from Greek tragedy who acts as intermediary between what happens on earth and the drama that unfolds beyond the clouds, the writer, whose interest in my exposition was steadily growing, smiled once more. His third smile was one of satisfaction with my solution to the problem of staging. 'Now I'm relieved,' he said.

The brief conversation that followed revealed his human qualities above all – qualities which would be fully illuminated in *Terre des Hommes* [*Wind, Sand and Stars*, 1939]. He was a man who loved his fellow-men, and far from searching out and emphasizing their faults, he seemed bent on accentuating their virtues.[2] The education in hatred, which Maurice Sachs[3] would later have to list among the characteristics of the next generation, was foreign to him and he would certainly deplore it today. I am sure that his desire to highlight the good qualities of men at all costs greatly encouraged me that day in my work. He was a man who had faith in the future and considered the present extremely ephemeral. When I returned to Paris a year later, in June 1938, I hoped to revisit the writer and play him the music I had meanwhile composed. But at that time he was in the South of France, and so I had to be content with sending him the libretto. He telephoned a few days later, to say he was very pleased with it.

I happened to see Saint-Ex for the second time in June 1939. He was no longer living at Place Vauban but had moved to an apartment on rue Michel-Ange, in the sixteenth arrondissement. He invited me to spend the evening before his departure there with his guests: the publisher Gaston Gallimard, whom I had already approached; the Minister of Aviation, Pierre Cot, then one of the chief targets of the Fascist press; and several young men and women, all passionate mountaineers. How serene Saint-Ex was that night, too! The adventures that inspired *Terre des Hommes*, perhaps his most nearly complete literary success, had neither aged him nor affected his nerves. He was always the same, reasonable and benevolent by nature, full of plans for the future.

Did friends and technicians discourage him from embarking on a bold new journey because his liver was enlarged? No matter, he would proceed undaunted. In *Pilote de Guerre* [*Flight to Arras*, 1942] he speaks not of this but other voyages: he

---

[2] 'Too well we know man's failings, his cowardice and lapses, and our writers of today are only too proficient in exposing these; but we stood in need of one to tell us how a man may be lifted far above himself by his sheer force of will'.   André Gide, preface to *Night Flight* by Antoine de Saint-Exupéry, transl. Stuart Gilbert, Harcourt Brace Jovanovich, New York, 1932, pp. 3–4.

[3] Maurice Sachs (1906–45), French writer, secretary and friend of Jean Cocteau, who wrote about Sachs in *Journal d'un Inconnu* (1952).

evokes dazzling visions of childhood and talks about the 'watchmaker' – Voltaire's watchmaker, of course. I informed the writer, without regret, that negotiations initiated by a German theatre to give the world première of *Volo di Notte* had failed, due to Goebbels' veto,[4] but that a performance at the 1940 Florentine Maggio Musicale was likely. I had heard that in the Spring of 1939, at a time of particularly serious political tension, the French were openly hostile towards Italians who visited their country, yet no such animosity came to my attention. My last sojourn in France before the outbreak of the War I remember as one of the happiest periods in my life. We drank champagne that evening and, late at night, the young people sang mountain songs. Three, four, five songs – the last one (I don't know if it was intentional) in Italian. The singers addressed me, as though in homage, and I was moved. We parted. Saint-Ex squeezed my hand tightly and declared his friendship.

---

[4] Dallapiccola elaborated on this episode in the programme of the Brunswick State Theatre, 31 March 1965 ('*Sehen, was anderen verborgen bleibt*'), p. 296:

'[After hearing the opera at Venice, 7 September 1938, Alfred Schlee of Universal Edition had said:] "I know a German city that could give the world première of your *Volo di Notte*". "Which city?" I asked, very surprised and pleased. "Brunswick."

'Several weeks later I began corresponding with the Intendant, Karlheinz Gutheim, who was obliged to write to me on 11 March 1939: "We have left no stone unturned, we've done our utmost to sponsor the première of *Volo di Notte*. But it has proved impossible to get permission from the Reich's Ministry of Propaganda, on which we depend. We greatly regret, therefore, having to put aside this project and so many others . . .".

'[Subsequently, a letter from the Reichstheaterkammer to the publisher Ricordi, dated 8 March 1941:] "We are returning the score and the stage design. As you know, this opera was submitted to the Reich's drama critic two years ago, and you were advised at the time against publicizing it in Germany. Our position is the same today, notwithstanding the performance at the 1940 Maggio Musicale. Past experience has shown that German theatre-goers reject the sort of music which is too atonal. Therefore, it would not be profitable for the publisher to assume the expense of translation and adaptation. Our best advice, consequently, is to give up the idea of publicizing this opera.

"Heil Hitler.   Association of Theatrical Publishers,
                                                    [signed] Stadeler"'.
                                                    LD: Saggi . . ., pp. 133–134.

How many times I thought of him during the War years! How I missed him the evening of the première in Florence. How intensely I remembered him that fateful 10 June 1940! I didn't know then about the flight he had just made over Arras, described in *Pilote de Guerre*. And I thought of him once more when I learned of the death of his fraternal friend Henri Guillaumet, to whom he dedicated *Terre des Hommes*.

I never again saw the brave man who, with his book, had influenced me so greatly during several years of my youth. The War years changed everything, and the youthful self-assurance that carried me through the composition of my first dramatic work gave way to the darkness and despair of *Il Prigioniero*. Much later, at the end of *Job*, a glimmer of hope finally appeared. Would those years also have changed the man whom, though I met him only twice, I venture to call 'friend'?

It was the duty of Domenico de' Paoli, who had introduced me to Saint-Ex, to communicate in 1945 the news of his death. His few disconsolate words were accompanied by a newspaper clipping, which said that the aviator-writer had failed to return from a war-time flight.[5]

---

[5] 'He took off at 8:30 on July 31, 1944; the weather reports were good, the engines running smoothly, and the plane soared lightly into the shimmering morning air, northwards towards France. At one-thirty Saint-Exupéry had not returned and his friends were growing more and more anxious, as by now only an hour's fuel remained in his tanks. And at two-thirty he still had not returned. . . .'

Stuart Gilbert, translator's introduction to *The Wisdom of the Sands* by Antoine de Saint-Exupéry, University of Chicago Press, Chicago, 1979, p. xii.

For the Première of
Volo di Notte
(1940)

Like every musician, and especially every Italian musician, I have longed since my difficult formative years for a chance to try my mettle one day in the theatre. While it has given me great peace of mind to destroy several inchoate attempts of that period, which now seems so remote, I retain some of my early ideas about the fundamental concepts of 'drama', 'tragedy', and 'theatre'. The frequently inappropriate use of this terminology has contributed more than is commonly supposed to the confusion about the theatre that still reigns today, both among the public and among many musicians.

It appears that I distinguished clearly between a theatre based on action and one based on words. In Goethe – the Goethe of *Iphigenie in Tauris* and *Torquato Tasso*, for example – words are much more important than action, and the same may be said about the plays of Ibsen and Pirandello. Even then I noticed that the word 'theatrical', used too often by people of scant culture and taste, cannot help sounding synonymous with 'vulgar'.

In the concept of drama I saw particularly the artistic solution to a problem of *crescendo*: a crescendo of emotion, which usually subsides in a resolutive catharsis. And this catharsis can be brought about in opera, needless to say, only by the music. It matters little whether the crescendo is manifest or latent. The essential thing is that it be present.

While studying several major modern operas, I observed how individual composers had solved, time after time, the problem that for me represented the core of the drama. Debussy achieves a vast crescendo during Acts I to IV of *Pelléas et Mélisande* and resolves it in the concluding Act V. In the turbid *Wozzeck*, Alban Berg keeps tightening the screws throughout fourteen scenes, and only in the final scene does he admit a pale shaft of sunlight.[1] Darius Milhaud, in the first part of *Christophe Colomb*,[2] arrays five large and extremely diverse musical frescoes: Queen Isabella praying to St James of Compostela; the boisterous southern port of Cadiz; the mysterious council of the Mexican gods; the sailors' mutiny; and, as final resolution, the '*Te Deum*' for the discovery of America.

The first impressionist opera, the first big expressionist opera, and the first modern opera of 'the masses' all have in common that the composer's utmost effort is a drive towards the final scene, a convergence on the conclusion. Otherwise, for the listener, Debussy's opera would end *musically* in Act IV with the death of Pelléas – that is, with its *dramatic* close – and Berg's opera with the drowning of Wozzeck, and the first part of *Christophe Colomb* with the appearance of the dove, the messenger of peace.

Milhaud, Berg, and Debussy obviously did not want to fall into the 'error' (if I may be permitted this almost irreverent word) made by the Ritter von Gluck. One of the greatest composers the history of opera can claim, Gluck seems, for example in *Alceste*, to exhaust his musical possibilities at the very moment the dramatic tension ceases. The final pages of *Alceste*, from the appearance of the *deus ex machina*, are undeniably cold and conventional; yet, in spite of this weakness, the opera remains a masterpiece.

If I have dwelt up to this point on several common traits of modern opera, I must remind you that the musical situation is different in the so-called *verismo* opera. Here the pace is swift, the brevity of the episodes can indicate a very high degree of

---

[1] Joseph Kerman also perceives 'a large recurring musical rhythm from tension to relaxation. This is felt between many scenes and the orchestral interludes following them, but comes forward in all force only on the largest scale: between the opera as a whole and its final interlude, following Wozzeck's death and preceding the twenty-one-bar epilogue with the children. The first level on which *Wozzeck* is experienced is as a series of horrors mounting to a great release of tension in this last and longest interlude'.   *Opera as Drama*, Vintage Books, New York, 1956, p. 230.

[2] Grand opera with film (1928), in two parts and twenty-seven scenes, text by Paul Claudel. Première: Berlin, 5 May 1930.

effectiveness; no place is reserved for the conclusive catharsis. Consider the ending of *Il Tabarro*, my favourite opera by Puccini: a model of concision and brutality. And who does not recall the close of *Cavalleria Rusticana*?

I was told that Mascagni's famous score, in the early version submitted to the Sonzogno Competition,[3] included a fugal finale – later eliminated for dramatic reasons – on the words '*Hanno ammazzato Compare Turiddu!*' ('They've murdered comrade Turiddu!'). I don't know how much truth there is in this story since, on the occasion of the opera's fiftieth anniversary, legends are so rife. Personally, I am inclined to believe there *was* a fugue, for then we could finally understand the question one of the judges asked the twenty-six-year-old composer (as reported by a great newspaper): 'How on earth was a youngster like you able to display such a mastery of counterpoint?' Having removed the fugue and revised the ending to the one everybody knows, Mascagni ensured the *dramatic* effectiveness of his opera.

Although I thought I had gleaned from my studies the solution to the problem of drama in that of the crescendo, I naturally did not delude myself that others hadn't reached the same conclusions long before me. On the contrary, I was overjoyed to find a confirmation – and such an authoritative confirmation! – of what I was trying to clarify for myself in *Weltgeschichte des Theaters* by Joseph Gregor.[4] With great lucidity Gregor examines the elementary, primordial concept of 'drama' and demonstrates that a subject almost ideally suited to the stage may be found, for example, in the meagre telegrams received by the editorial office of *Neue Freie Presse*, Vienna, between 9 and 16 May 1902, on the day following the terrible eruption of Mt Pelée in Martinique. We may summarize the salient points of these dispatches:

---

[3] A competition for one-act operas, established by the publisher Edoardo Sonzogno in 1884; *Cavalleria Rusticana* won the prize in 1888. The conductor L. Mugnone advised Mascagni to eliminate the four-voice choral fugato that originally ended the opera.

[4] Joseph Gregor (1888–1960), renowned Austrian theatre historian and playwright, associated with the Viennese artistic-dramatic circle of Hugo von Hofmannsthal, Max Reinhardt, and Richard Strauss. His fundamental book *Weltgeschichte des Theaters* was published in 1933 by Phaidon of Zurich.

Paris, 9 May. A plantation owner residing in Paris is informed by an employee that it is impossible to put ashore at Saint-Pierre, because the coast is covered with ashes.

Paris, 9 May. The Ministry of the Navy receives the message of a cruiser from Fort-de-France: 'I arrive from Saint-Pierre. Entire city destroyed by an eruption. All inhabitants seem to have perished. I have brought on board thirty survivors. Eruptions continue'.

Paris, 9 May. Communications with Martinique are interrupted due to breakage of cables. Flag at half-mast on the Ministry.

London, 9 May. Two steamers approaching the region lost all or part of their crews.

New York, 9 May. Not only are there 25,000 dead at Saint-Pierre, but in the environs thousands face starvation. Provisions on the way from all quarters.

London, 9 May. Latest eruption also at St Vincent.

London, 11 May. Details. On 8 May, around eight o'clock, eruption of white-hot lava from Mt Pelée volcano. Sea of fire covering the whole coast. Losses upwards of 30,000.

Paris, 12 May. Shipwrecks floating at sea; subterranean rumblings; more chasms and deep ravines cleave the countryside.

London, 12 May. Danger of epidemic at Saint-Pierre.

London, 12 May. Number of victims estimated at 50,000; another 50,000 without food or shelter.

St Thomas, 12 May. Lava still flowing towards the north of Martinique.

London, 13 May. Crater dormant. Provisions and water arrive from various directions.

London, 13 May. Island still overcast. Ruins of city continue burning.

Paris, 13 May. Great calm and unspeakable grief.

London, 14 May. Threat of plague despite mass cremation.

Paris, 14 May. Changes in soil in the northern part of the island. Changes in geographic conformation: new hills and valleys.

New York, 14 May. Hundreds of corpses looted. Arrest of six robbers laden with jewelry.

While it is sometimes difficult to ascertain the remote, obscure origins of works long hoped-for and loved and endured, I believe I can say that the fundamental idea of *Volo di Notte* is implicit in this series of telegrams.

In 1934 I happened to read *Vol de Nuit*, the short novel that made the writer-aviator Antoine de Saint-Exupéry famous overnight. It impressed me strongly, but I didn't immediately perceive the possibility of extracting a dramatic work from it. What is more, when this possibility was suggested to me, I became apprehensive and dismayed. The subject was undoubtedly fascinating, but the *mise en scène* presented a host of serious difficulties. I gave it much thought. *Volo di Notte* would have to be condensed into one act – an act of rather large proportions, perhaps, but a single act nonetheless. Any interruption would deprive the drama of that continuous inner drive which seems to me its fundamental *raison d'être*.

Saint-Exupéry observes in his novel a strict unity of time (the entire story unfolds between dusk and three a.m.), and this unity would naturally have to be preserved in the libretto. Maintaining the unity of action might not be particularly difficult; several secondary episodes would have to be sacrificed and nothing more. But how to solve the problem of unity of place in a drama that progresses on two levels: in the troubled mind of Rivière, director of the airline, a reflective man condemned to solitude by his own greatness; and simultaneously, very far from the airline office, in the space of the skies?

Chance came to my rescue. In a remark to which others might not have attached particular significance, I glimpsed the solution to the most serious problem, that of the 'third unity'. At the end of November 1934, the BBC broadcast the British première of the very recent *Perséphone* by Igor Stravinsky.[5] Hearing this work deeply moved me and my fellow listeners. How could we resist the temptation to talk about it a little? In the course of the discussion, someone asked me whether a figure like Eumolpus, the narrator (*storico*), transported to the stage of a modern opera, could not take the form of a radio-telegraph operator. Here, in embryo, was the solution to the problem of unity of place: the Radiotelegraphist, the modern Magus, who knows more and learns

---

[5] Melodrama in three scenes for tenor, mixed chorus, children's choir, and orchestra, on a text by André Gide; composed between May 1933 and January 1934. Première: Ballets Ida Rubinstein, Paris Opéra, 30 April 1934, conducted by the composer.

it sooner than anyone else. He reminds us both of the messenger in Greek tragedy and of Lynceus in *Faust*,[6] who observes from the watch-tower the cruel destruction of the cottage of Philemon and Baucis.

We are all quite familiar with *Vol de Nuit*, but a synopsis will not be out of place if only to show *how* I read the novel. It is a drama of the will. "'It's a matter of life and death," said Rivière, "for the lead we gain by day on ships and railways is lost each night". . . . Rivière had no notion when or how commercial aviation would tackle the problem of night flying but its inevitable solution must be prepared for'.[7] (In 1931, when Saint-Exupéry wrote the novel, technicians still considered night flights extremely hazardous.)

It is precisely these early experimental night flights that my 'one-act' depicts. Three aeroplanes are en route: one from Chile, one from Patagonia, one from Paraguay. Rivière, who initiated the night service and is solely responsible for the enterprise, awaits their arrival at Buenos Aires, after which he will signal the departure of the mail to Europe. The Chile flight arrives, having passed through a storm; the plane from Paraguay lands without incident; but the Patagonia courier fails to reach its destination. Rivière, faced with the partial success of his undertaking, aware of the outspoken opposition of his co-workers and the shabby, covert hostility of his subordinates, gives the starting signal to the flight for Europe. Rivière, a man of faith, pays no heed to small defeats or to the mediocrity of those around him. With his faith he saves his pure, courageous idea.

The stage is divided by a partition into two rooms.[8] Much the smaller, on the viewer's left, is Rivière's study, containing a desk and several chairs. A large map covers almost the entire left-hand wall, in which there are also a door and a window; another door, with curtain, in the partition. On the viewer's right, an office containing desks, chairs, a typewriter. A door in the right-hand wall, and next to it a big wireless transmitter and a stand for Rivière's coat and hat. The whole

---

[6] Goethe, *Faust*, Part II, Act V.

[7] Saint-Exupéry, *Night Flight*, p. 52.

[8] Some of the details of staging are drawn from the preface to the full score of *Volo di Notte*, Universal Edition (No. 13882), Vienna.

rear wall is made of glass, and through it a large door opens from the office onto the airfield. In the distance, beyond the airport, the city of Buenos Aires should be visible, gradually illuminated at nightfall.

Scene 1. We are introduced immediately to Rivière, a man both tough and compassionate ('Love the men under your orders – but do not let them know it,' he advises Inspector Robineau[9]), a man who understands the reason for his solitude. Rivière has not renounced life willingly, but by force of circumstances. And yet, from time to time his words are tinged with a certain melancholy: the brief exchange with an old foreman, the echo of a dance orchestra that reaches him from the distant city – everything reminds him of what he has missed in life, of what people generally enjoy.

Scene 2. Meanwhile, the plane from Chile arrives and the pilot Pellerin tells how he was surprised by a cyclone while flying at high altitude over the Andes.

Scene 3. We learn shortly from the Radio-telegraphist that the mail flight from Patagonia, piloted by Fabien, is in serious trouble. Rivière orders weather reports from several radio stations: from Trelew, from Comodoro Rivadavia, San Antonio, and Bahia Blanca the bulletins grow more ominous by the minute. Fabien is doomed. His plane has just enough fuel to last for half an hour.

Scene 4. The pilot's wife, alarmed by his delay, goes for news. Here we have the meeting of the man, Rivière, and the woman, Simone Fabien. She lives only for her love, he only for his idea. Between the two there is no point of contact. While Rivière glimpses in this woman the sadness of the human condition, Simone Fabien sees in him only the enemy who crushes her, the enemy she cannot possibly combat. But she alone guesses Rivière's secret: that although he dominates and is feared by everyone, he is an unhappy man.

Scene 5. While Rivière is convinced that nothing more can be done to save the pilot Fabien, he orders the Radio-telegraphist to make contact with him. At first the wireless operator relates the messages received. Then all at once he hears Fabien's

[9] *Night Flight*, p. 33.

voice: from this moment until the end of the scene, his personality is split. The operator begins to speak in the first person, and gradually, with increasing emotion, we see him transformed as it were into the pilot himself. We 'hear' Fabien speak to us out of the storm. His eyes no longer distinguish the masses of sky and of land. He asks the men to advise what course to take and implores them not to abandon him. We 'hear' Fabien in the vertiginous descent of the plane he can no longer control. We 'hear' him launch the only landing flare he has on board and realize, with horror, that the storm has carried him so far off course he is flying over the ocean. At this moment Fabien falls into a trap. Through a rift in the clouds he sees a star, then two stars. If he ascends he can never get down again. He knows full well he is doomed, yet his lust for light is such that he cannot but climb. Now we 'hear' Fabien enraptured. The light! How luminous are his hands, his clothes, the wings! An ecstasy of brief duration. His last communication surprises us: 'We're out of fuel'.

Scene 6. Meanwhile, the plane from Paraguay approaches. At the airport, news of Fabien's death spreads rapidly, and the workers and mechanics revolt. The shouting throng invades the office. But the uproar is calmed, as if by magic, when Rivière firmly orders the departure of the Europe mail. In the face of such confidence, the mob is subdued: those very men who not long ago had uttered the name of Rivière with savage ferocity were now repeating it almost in a tone of religious fervour. Rivière's will has conquered; the post departs for Europe. Once more Rivière is alone in his study. The shifts have changed and Inspector Robineau, too, has gone. Rivière can meditate in the silence of night. He thinks about what Simone Fabien had told him, and indeed he is conscious of 'bearing his heavy load of victory'.[10] Even he, in the final analysis, is a wretched creature: he believes that he holds sway, but there is someone above him. . . . He shuffles the papers on his desk and resumes work.

Although theatrical tradition still seems to favour costume operas or stories set in vaguely defined epochs, I felt that

[10] *Ibid.*, p. 87.

in my first encounter with the theatre I should choose a subject drawn from contemporary life. Not to say a 'modern subject', for 'modern' is meaningless, and I wouldn't like anyone to think I am so deluded as to assume that writing about aeroplanes is all that's required to be 'at the height of fashion'.

In setting to music the libretto of *Le Nozze di Figaro*, Mozart chose a subject of his own time, as Verdi did in *La Traviata*. Characters like the Count and Countess Almaviva, Figaro, and Cherubino, immortalized in literature even before they entered music, are really characters of that period which just preceded the French Revolution. The 'comedy of intrigue', as it was happily called, has for its milieu the elegant ambiance of that era; and by the same token, Violetta and Germont, who are anything but rare specimens of the mid-19th century, move in the world of the salon. (Verdi had quite different reasons for not wishing the characters of *La Traviata* to be dressed in contemporary costume.[11])

I chose as the protagonist of my 'one-act' the director of an airline, locked in his prison of glass. Should this choice seem somewhat bizarre today? Yes, but only to that cadre of critics so emboldened by the ephemeral power of writing for a newspaper that they try to secure performances of their own operas – the manuscripts of which have turned yellow after thirty years of obscurity in a drawer – and sometimes succeed. For my part, I don't believe that an accusation of 'originality at all costs' can stand an inquiry conducted with a minimum of good faith. Because in this instance Antoine de Saint-Exupéry has found a lyrical expression of our time, an expression that, as art, attains universal significance. Rivière's feelings are those of all men who work and struggle to reach an ideal.

It has been said that technical conquests have killed poetry.

---

[11] 'Verdi meant *La Traviata* to be given in contemporary dress. When the Venetian authorities rejected this revolutionary idea, he suggested the period of Louis XIII. Eventually the work was set in the time of Louis XIV and was not seen in Italy in 1850s costumes until the end of the century, when such costumes were already historical'.
    William Weaver, ed., *Verdi: A Documentary Study*, Thames and Hudson, London and New York, 1977, caption for plates 129–133.

U. E. 11902

Volo di Notte, *Scene 5: The Radio-telegraphist relates the last message from the doomed pilot Fabien – 'I see the stars! . . .' – while a soprano voice (invisible, in the orchestra) intones the melody of* Tre Laudi *No. 1 –*

'Altissima luce con gran splendore . . .'. *(Reproduced by kind permission of Universal Edition, Vienna.)*

In my opinion they have killed absolutely nothing, but if it were true we could no longer understand the poetry of the past. And since even the machine is a product of man, it takes part in the whole of life – poetry not excluded.

Poetry as a spiritual essence is eternal: only the circumstances change, and the forms in which it is manifested. If we are compelled to create poetry today, I think it right to choose the forms most relevant to our time. In every age, bravery has been a source of poetic inspiration. But why continue indefinitely to extol the Argonauts, for example, who have only moved us vicariously through the work of art, when a Lindbergh can thrill us with direct and pristine emotion? Let us then make art out of our personal experiences, those which are likely to be the most authentic.

I have designated *Volo di Notte* neither 'opera' nor '*melodramma*'.[12] 'One act' I have written, not wishing to be more specific. 'Opera' is too vague, '*melodramma*' too definite in meaning – so definite, indeed, that Verdi himself abandoned it after *Un Ballo in Maschera*. Obviously, it seemed inadequate for his final and boldest conquests. It is unimportant that the definition '*melodramma*' has been revived by Ottorino Respighi, for example in *La Fiamma*, where it is used with plainly polemical intent. For polemic has nothing to do with art.

In any case, between the two kinds of polemics – between the usually apparent *parti pris* of those who wish to advance a step or two and are fully vindicated (sometimes a few years later) by events and achievements, and the plea of those who would like to retreat several kilometres – I naturally side with the former. For the same reasons I prefer adventure to quietism, I admire the person who prepared to fly into the stratosphere and loathe the one who cut the cords of the gondola at night with a penknife.

I was instinctively suspicious of a certain 'return to Bach' proclaimed some years ago from highly authoritative professorial chairs. I am not connected with the 'neo-classicists', and anyone who so labels me must have a very faulty grasp of the meaning of this term. That 'Musical Manifesto' of 17 December 1932 seemed absurd, both in its general outlook and its

---

[12] See p. 133, n.1.

apocalyptic tone.[13] It reminded me of the Talking Cricket and my early childhood: 'Good night, Pinocchio. May Heaven preserve you from dangers and assassins!'[14] And the various 'returns to normality' recommended in recent years struck me as the most abnormal and sick that one could imagine, since for people today nothing should be more true or more normal than the life of today.

'In the idea of creation the idea of the new is implicit,' wrote Ferruccio Busoni. The advent of the new, like the birth of a child or the growth of a plant through the earth towards the light, contains something violent and not altogether 'comfortable'. If the creator is well acquainted with the reality of this 'discomfort', in a certain sense it is understandably reflected onto the listener as well, who can react in many ways to the intrinsic, necessary aggressiveness of the new. (I say 'intrinsic' because I am not interested in extrinsic aggressiveness, tainted with the polemical element.)

Each new work inevitably provokes discussions, for among every audience, alongside a minority attracted by the new – sometimes sincerely attracted, sometimes only out of snobbishness – there exists a strong conservative majority. One example of a minority for which we should all be grateful was the group of Paris Conservatoire students whose demand for repeat performances saved *Pelléas et Mélisande* in 1902 from the din of whistling. This was a case of a 'plebeian' minority. A unique instance of 'aristocratic' minority is that of Queen Marie Antoinette who, with her authority and diplomacy, saved one of the *Iphigénie* operas by her old teacher Christoph Gluck.[15] I believe that the minority was on the right side, as much in the first case as in the second. And is it necessary to recount the vicissitudes of *Lohengrin*, of *Tristan* and Ludwig II of Bavaria?

The majority, on the other hand, has always been conserva-

[13] The notorious manifesto was signed by Ottorino Respighi, Giuseppe Mulè, Ildebrando Pizzetti, Riccardo Zandonai, Alberto Gasco, Alceo Toni, Riccardo Pick-Mangiagalli, Guido Guerrini, Gennaro Napoli and Guido Zuffellato. See pp. 111–112.

[14] Carlo Collodi, *Pinocchio*, translated by E. Harden, Penguin Books, Harmondsworth, 1974, p. 67.

[15] *Iphigénie en Aulide*, Paris, 1774.

tive – an attitude as old as mankind and one that will persist until man's end. In this connexion, I never tire of quoting the colloquy between Faust and Mephistopheles which precedes the descent to the 'Mothers':

> Faust: *Den Müttern! Trifft's mich immer wie ein Schlag!*
>   *Was ist das Wort, das ich nicht hören mag?*
> Meph.: *Bist so beschränkt, dass neues Wort dich stört?*
>   *Willst du nur hören was du schon gehört?*
>
> *Faust*: The Mothers! Still it strikes a shock of fear.
>   What is this word that I am loath to hear?
> *Meph.*: Are you in blinkers, rear at a new word?
>   Would only hear what you already heard?[16]

A gentleman I met at the theatre a few evenings ago showed a friendly interest in the progress of the rehearsals of *Volo di Notte*. When he asked the reason for my tranquillity, I replied: 'I am always calm when my mind is at peace'. I might have added that a negative reception can disturb a composer only when an opera is not published. My opera has been printed, and so there is always the chance for what I like to call an 'appeal'. As for the reception by the press – see here! we shan't even touch on this subject. Because it is beneath my dignity to believe that a critic, even the most intelligent and impartial critic, can express an opinion about the result of years of work after a cursory audition at the dress rehearsal.

In an interview some years ago, Charlie Chaplin spoke about his difficult adolescence and not too easy early manhood. When asked about his present wealth, Charlie replied: 'Oh, nothing's easier to get used to than money!' While I have never been in a position to attest the truth of Charlot's words, from an artist's point of view I *can* say that nothing is easier to get used to than disapproval and scathing reviews. I will go further: given the well-known distance between the majority and the minority which I mentioned earlier, and granted that savage reviews are often inspired by extra-artistic factors (and can therefore harm no one), I am convinced that in many cases the bad notices themselves contributed significantly to the spread of contemporary artists' names.

---

[16] Goethe, *Faust*, Part II, Act I, translated by Walter Arndt, W.W. Norton, New York, 1976, p. 158.

Volo di Notte is divided, dramatically and musically, into six
well-differentiated scenes. From both a musical and a dramatic standpoint, the six scenes have one feature in common:
each is preceded by an Introduction.

If in the *melodramma* the action developed during the
recitatives and was interrupted by occasional moments of
lyrical stasis, expressed musically in arias, duets, ensembles,
etc., in the music drama as conceived by modern composers
the crescendo is implemented by concise and continuous
action. The feelings of the characters are therefore expressed
throughout the plot as a whole, and there is no need for a full
stop to allow them individual expression. Yet we would not
wish to deny lyrical elements their place, even in modern
opera; it is only that they are no longer the basis of our
dramatic material.

In order to clarify the architecture of the work and to
express my thought and feeling as coherently as possible, I
have occasionally used closed forms – not as they were used in
melodramma, but rather in the instrumental sense of the term.
Thus the nucleus of Scene 3, where the wireless operator
begins relating the ominous news about the Patagonia flight,
is a 'Rhythmic Study'; Scene 5, between Rivière and the
Radio-telegraphist, a 'Chorale with Variations and Finale';
and that part of the final scene which follows the revolt, a
'Hymn'.

This kind of structural process is not new: it is easy enough
to find examples of instrumental closed forms (chaconne and
passacaglia) in 17th-century opera. And, at the end of his
career, having abandoned the form of the *melodramma*, Verdi
seemed occasionally to turn towards a reconsideration of
instrumental forms. How else can we explain Act III, Scene 5
of *Otello*, where Iago sings –

*Essa t'avvince
Coi vaghi rai.*

She ensnares you
With her lovely glances.[17]

---

[17] Translated by William Weaver, in *Seven Verdi Librettos*, W.W. Norton,
New York, 1977; also the source of the subsequent English versions of Verdi
operas quoted in this book, except that of *Simon Boccanegra*.

– if not as a backward glance, a new interpretation of the
Scarlatti sonata?[18] Likewise the first scene of *Falstaff*, from the
initial C major to the dominant pedal: doesn't it closely
resemble a sonata exposition?

I have deliberately mentioned some great examples from
the past, for when modern composers adopt this structural
plan instead of much easier plans – especially those composers
who detest dilettantism and carelessness, who wish to be very
scrupulous in their own work – they are accused of being
'cerebral'. (The unbridled acrimony against 'the moderns'
sometimes backfires, of course. A few years ago, an over-
zealous, too hasty critic even passed Georg Büchner off as a
contemporary. . . .)

As for the vocal part, I have often kept it in the foreground.
The words, at least the crucial words, are always audible.
Experience has taught us that very little of the text of an opera
is understood at first hearing; a second hearing often suffices
for much better comprehension. To say that the words in
19th-century *melodramma* are audible is no refutation. We hear
the words in *Rigoletto* and *Il Trovatore* because we know them
by heart; but the text of a *Simon Boccanegra* or *Luisa Miller*,
precisely because it isn't so familiar, seemed very mysterious
to the audience of the Maggio Musicale in 1937 and 1938.

I have used *parlato* (speech) in various ways, particularly
when a sharp contrast of sonority was needed to articulate the
simultaneously progressing action in Rivière's study and in
the Radio-telegraphist's office. I have not employed true
'leading themes'. The unity of the opera is secured rather by
two principal rhythms, and by some melodic and harmonic
motifs always recognizable in their transformations. The most
typical example of this mutability is found in the chorus: the
countenance of the Mass, whatever feelings it expresses,
remains the same.[19] Among the many criticisms levelled at

[18] Verdi expressed his admiration for the sonatas of Scarlatti in a letter to
Giulio Ricordi, dated 2 November 1864 (*Carteggi Verdiani*, IV, p. 241).

[19] 'This anonymous mass has no words to sing; it participates in the
events *from the outside*; it sings offstage.

'Only at one point, right in the middle of Scene 6, does the chorus
suddenly assume a most important function. It will now have a text and will
appear on the stage.

me since the beginning of my career, I believe I have been spared the charge of incoherence. That is worth noting.

The music of *Volo di Notte* should not seem inordinately difficult to anyone who is prepared to listen attentively and, if possible, without too many preconceptions. (For there's hardly a failure of preparatory harmony among us who does not have *his* concept of 'theatre', who doesn't know how opera should be made. By the same token, the dullest concert-goer, when he hears a performance of Beethoven, invariably finds that the executant has not yet loved enough or suffered enough to undertake the music of the 'divine deaf man'. . . .)

The human ear has made considerable progress in recent decades. The idea of 'dissonance' is no longer so restricted today as it was at the turn of the century, and I am convinced the moment will come when dissonance – that is to say 'movement' – will be universally recognized and justified in the art of music, which is the art of movement par excellence. When the dissonance is acknowledged, it will be time to study pure sound – sound in its primordial essence.

The music of *Volo di Notte* develops those characteristics of 'sound' which have already been observed in my compositions after *Divertimento in Quattro Esercizi*,[20] particularly in *Sei Cori di Michelangelo Buonarroti il Giovane* and the more recent *Tre Laudi*: a 'study' for the opera, just as the *Sarabande und Cortège* by Busoni are studies for his *Doktor Faust*. I think I have succeeded in advancing my earlier investigations of timbre, form and melody. The clarification of expression, the purifica-

---

'From the airport (bar 880) comes a confused murmur. The mixed chorus, divided into two (placed at some distance from each other), begins, humming. The news that the mailplane from Patagonia, piloted by Fabien, has crashed in the sea, has come through to the mechanics, skeptical as they are about the bold ideas of Rivière, and they have decided to rebel. This time distinct and articulate words are heard: "*E Fabien? Perduto*" ("What about Fabien? – Lost"). The two choruses, now close together, alternate on the question and answer. . . . The chorus bursts onto the stage. Now at last it participates from the *inside* in an event, not a visible event, but one none the less direct and plain. The chorus becomes the conscience of Rivière and in the same moment acquires a consciousness of itself.'

'My Choral Music', pp. 174–175.

[20] For soprano, flute, oboe, clarinet, viola, and cello (1934), on anonymous 13th-century poems; dedicated to Alfredo Casella.

tion of material, progress, and improvement are in the final analysis the things that interest me the most – indeed, I would say the only things. This much I feel I have in common with Rivière.

And let no one maliciously misinterpret me when I add that, like Rivière, I have unlimited faith in the future.

*　　*　　*

My *Volo di Notte* was first staged at the Teatro della Pergola in Florence, on 18 May 1940. It was a 'sensation', almost a success despite protests and raging arguments. People at that time, however, were pre-occupied with much more serious and pressing problems than the première of an opera. . . . We were on the brink of war. I recall a critic from Bologna, who had come to the dress rehearsal, proudly exhibiting his invitation from the Reichsmusik-Kammer to the 'Victory Concert' at Bayreuth, 15 August 1940. This concert, as the whole world knows, never took place.

The next day I was the subject of a long piece in *Il Popolo d'Italia*, the Fascist daily. Full of cheap shots, all of no consequence needless to say. But let me extract a few gems: 'What a narrow definition of heroism, what a limited perspective, from the human point of view! Should we send our aviators to see this opera in order to tone up their nerves and revive their enthusiasm?' And later: 'We Italians also expect to participate in the impending European upheaval . . .'. So the music critic predicted the declaration of war twenty-three days before that fateful 10 June. . . . And at the end: 'The applause drowned out the protests – very feeble protests, it's true. But everybody knows Florence is the bastion of certain intellectual factions that like to be called Europeans. . . . They are Europeans only in their ties to the international ideal. . . '. The word 'international' at that time signified Communist or, at least, anti-Fascist.[21]

---

[21] *LD: Saggi* . . ., pp. 121–122; in French.

II

From Malipiero to Mozart
Comments and Communications

Comments on
Contemporary Opera
(1960)

Conspicuous by their absence from the following remarks are those 20th-century operas that form the so-called repertory. Precisely because they are endowed with sufficient musical and dramatic merits to be counted 'successes' in the traditional mould, operas of this sort have gained ready admittance to theatres around the world. They are accepted unconditionally by the public, almost without reservation by the critics, and by the 'authorities' with enthusiasm. The times can still change radically. What has been consecrated by tradition will not, therefore, be re-examined.

When *Tosca* was first performed, it is safe to assume that the 'authorities' came for the most part from that class which had drunk at the Carduccian spring, perhaps a bit ingenuously but with undeniable fervour:

A te, de l'essere
Principio immenso, . . .

Sixty years later, many things have changed. Today, the 'authorities' sing with doubtful intonation *'T'adoriam, Ostia divina'*.[1] And yet, if we tried to inform our authorities, the very ones who so zealously and peevishly inspect Brigitte Bardot's décolletage, that the first act of *Tosca* presents a real *love scene*

---

[1] A sardonic allusion to the anti-clericalism of Giosue Carducci's famous 'Hymn to Satan' (1863) and to the latter-day clericalism of the Christian Democratic Party, as exemplified by a popular religious song beginning *'T'adoriam, Ostia divina'* – both of them antipathetic to Dallapiccola's feeling of religion.

set in church, we would run the risk of not being understood. We might as well speak to them in a foreign language, since the 'repertory' is beyond discussion.

Rather, let me try briefly to underline a few of the changes I consider most significant in 20th-century opera. These changes are responsible in no small part for the public's frequent incomprehension and for the difficulty so many modern operas face in being accepted by our subsidized theatres.

One could say, on the whole, that love was the vital impulse of 19th-century opera (and of its *verismo* offspring). Love, and hence jealousy – often complicated by political vicissitudes or family rivalry. But love was always in the foreground, the medium through which the characters communicated with one another.

Pelléas et Mélisande is, in this sense, an opera securely anchored to tradition. It also owes a great deal to tradition from the standpoint of 'structure'. Debussy has planned a dramatic *crescendo* from the beginning up to the death of Pelléas (Act V functions as a conclusion), a crescendo which sometimes enlarges the meaning – that is, the *weight* – of even an individual word. I shall limit myself to one example.

Pelléas and Mélisande meet six times during the fifteen scenes of the opera. Notice how, in the course of the even-numbered encounters, the verb *tomber* assumes increasing significance. Second meeting [Act II, Scene 1]: Mélisande's ring falls into the well; fourth meeting [Act III, Scene 1]: her hair falls from the tower; sixth meeting [Act IV, Scene 4]: the stars fall. At this point, the fall of Pelléas under Golaud's sword is inevitable.[2]

But what happened later? Composers who felt the need to renew opera seem almost unanimous in discarding first of all the love element, which had charmed audiences the world

[2] 'Maeterlinck's play is fairly loaded with such recurring images, which gather force as the piece proceeds. To mention only one: the half-peaceful, half-sinister image of the blind man, *l'aveugle*. . . . At the first mention of the word, its effect may be slight, but at each successive repetition the listener half-consciously recalls all the others, so that rich associations and inter-associations are set up in the imagination.'
Kerman, *Opera as Drama*, p. 186.

over for a good century. The traditional 'love duet' vanished.[3] Man without love has become terribly alone, and when man is alone Care easily invades his heart.[4] Of course there are still duets, even between Wozzeck and Marie. But their colloquies seem to move along parallel paths: an encounter, a communication, is out of the question. To describe Act II, Scene 3 of *Wozzeck*, one is tempted to coin the term 'hate duet'.

The searing solitude of man without love, this inmost drama, lurks where one least expects it. Instructive in this regard is the deceptively light '*fantaisie lyrique*' by Ravel, *L'Enfant et les Sortilèges*. As the story unfolds, the Child feels lonely – desperately lonely. He sees that the animals of the forest love each other, and the cats sing nothing less than a real love duet (one that unfortunately strikes the large majority of the audience as amusing, if not positively droll!). Yet the Child is able to save himself at the eleventh hour. By uttering the word '*Maman!*' he casts his own spell, the last and greatest sorcery of the opera. The eternal word liberates him from solitude. Thanks to this magic word, the opera attains its catharsis: far from the *Verklärung* of romantic opera it may be, but a true catharsis nevertheless.

Altogether different is the situation in Busoni's *Doktor Faust*. Solitude is here again at the root of everything. (Faust's servant Wagner, later elevated to Rector Magnificus, may not even be equal to a conversation with him!) The very act of conjuring the powers of Hell is nothing other than an attempt to *communicate* with someone, seeing that Faust has lost contact with human beings.

The game is up. Faust has not achieved what he set out to do. Nothing remains, therefore, but death. After the final

---

[3] 'A love-duet on the public stage is not only shameless but absolutely untrue, not untrue in the beautiful and right feeling of artistic transmission, but altogether wrong and fictitious besides being ridiculous. . . . Anyone who has made a third in the company of lovers will have felt this to be painful. It is to a whole audience that this happens during a love duet.'
Busoni, *The Essence of Music*, pp. 10–11.

[4] '*Die Sorge, sie schleicht sich durchs Schlüsselloch ein*' ('But Care – she will creep through the keyhole unseen'): Goethe, *Faust*, Part II, Act V, Arndt translation, p. 289.

appearance of the Students from Cracow, at the end of the penultimate scene, the protagonist is happy to die.

Vorbei, endlich vorbei!
Frei liegt der Weg, willkommen
Du, meines Abends letzter Gang,
Wilkommen bist Du!

All is over at last; the way is free; the evening's end
   is welcome.[5]

Faust will leave a spiritual legacy; others will carry on his work. Everything must continue. *Doktor Faust* does not conclude, as Mephistopheles, in the guise of Night Watchman, proves with his final question: '*Sollte dieser Mann etwa verunglückt sein?*' ('Has this man met with an accident?'). If attributed to the Night Watchman, this question could refer simply to a mishap suffered by the man lying in the street. If, on the other hand, we imagine Mephistopheles speaking, his '*verunglückt*' takes on the connotation of perdition: the devil asks whether that man is damned.[6]

There is no more certainty. *Doubt* has entered the opera house.

---

[5] Edward J. Dent, *Ferruccio Busoni: A Biography*, Oxford University Press, London, 1933, p. 303; republished in 1974 by Eulenburg Books, London.

[6] In a letter dated Chicago, 31 March 1915, Busoni writes:

'And if I obey the inner logic, this ending is inevitable. This man [Faust] is wise enough to be able to make his own laws, but he has not used his wisdom well, for he is guilty of several murders and really no good deed can be put down to his credit.

'Then, as a nightwatchman, the devil, no longer connected with evil, is brought into everyday human affairs, so that the situation is hardly symbolic any longer.

'Finally, Faust himself says,
    "If life is only an illusion,
    What else can death be?"

'So that a doubt is raised as to the reality of the idea of the devil, which therefore lessens its importance.

'What has the last Act got to do with the devil? A man, ill, disappointed, tormented by his conscience, dies of heart failure and is found by the nightwatchman. The last word, too, is "a victim" (and not "condemned", or anything like it).'

Ferruccio Busoni, *Letters to His Wife*, translated by
Rosamond Ley, Edward Arnold, London, 1938/
Da Capo Press, New York, 1975, pp. 252–253.

A monologue is the obvious vehicle for the artistic expression of solitude, this contemporary condition. Nevertheless, I wouldn't venture to say that Moses, in Schoenberg's opera *Moses und Aron*, is less alone than the Woman in his monodrama *Erwartung*. Moses sees all too clearly that the enormous problem he had addressed (but what am I saying? – the problem God had assigned him!) has not been solved. And here, at the end of Act II, is one of the most desperate invocations recorded in the history of opera:

> *So habe ich mir ein Bild gemacht, falsch, wie ein Bild nur*
> *sein kann!*
> *So bin ich geschlagen! . . .*
> *O Wort, du Wort, das mir fehlt!*

> Then I have fashioned an image too, false, as an image
> must be.
> Thus am I defeated! . . .
> O word, thou word, that I lack![7]

Need it be emphasized that Busoni was destined not to finish *Doktor Faust*, nor Schoenberg *Moses und Aron*? Today everyone knows the text Schoenberg had prepared for Act III, and we can read some interesting remarks at the end of the score which may explain why the music for this last act was never composed. But the opera as such really ends with the protagonist's desperate entreaty.

It appears that the image against which Moses was struggling gained the advantage over Schoenberg himself at a particular moment. Because from the standpoint of the theatre – of images, therefore, and not only ideas – the opera finds its conclusion in the personal drama of Moses. The text of Act III is pure thought, pure religious meditation – even, one might add, a warning: and incapable of being translated this time into images, into drama.[8]

---

[7] Libretto translated by Allen Forte, copyrighted by B. Schott's Söhne, Mainz (no date); included in the recording of *Moses und Aron* conducted by Michael Gielen (Philips 6700 084), p. 18.

[8] 'If one observes certain minute details . . ., it becomes clear that the composer writes a work for himself above all and tries therein to make his dream come true, without caring in the least about contingencies.

'An excerpt from *Moses und Aron*, "The Dance around the Golden Calf", was published in 1951 by Hermann Scherchen's Ars Viva Verlag; on page

Nor does Gian Francesco Malipiero's opera *Torneo Nottur-no* actually conclude. '*Il Disperato*' can indeed slay '*Lo Spensiera-to*', whose death, however, settles nothing.[9] And by the same token, the question at the end of my own opera *Il Prigioniero* ('*La libertà?*') implies that the action is not yet finished.

Why do I especially love opera? Because it seems the most suitable medium for the exposition of my thought (not that I consider opera a philosophical treatise, of course . . .). I should like some day, after all the question marks – mine and others', to succeed in expressing a 'certainty'. The difficulty of this personal problem is what fascinates me.

I am also intrigued by opera as a general problem, whether for the composer or the performer. The composer's task is to attain at least relative purity in a production which is essentially impure, given the many diverse factors involved in its realization. (Today, fortunately, we no longer resort to 'sure-fire' formulas, such as the ridicule of stock characters – the stammerer, the deaf man, the cuckold – in *opera buffa*. Every contemporary opera is *sui generis*, and its problems must be faced and solved without formulas.) The performer's task is also very exacting. A symphonic concert, if carefully rehearsed, has an excellent chance of success. But in the opera house a mistaken lighting effect can be as disastrous as a wrong tempo, an inappropriate gesture can plunge the most tragic moment into absurdity. All this, each evening, amounts to a game of chance. The almost unattainable prize is perfection.

139, we find the indication "four naked virgins". Well then, in the complete score of the opera published by Schott there is a note: "Nude insofar as the law permits and the *mise en scène* requires". There seems to be a striking parallel between this "writing for oneself above all" and that sense of solitude endemic to the works and personalities of our century'.

From an unpublished radio talk Dallapiccola gave in response to the inquiry '*Hat die Oper eine Zukunft?*' ('Does Opera Have a Future?'), Bremen, Spring 1960.

[9] In Malipiero's *Nocturnal Tournament* (1929), '. . . the seven "nocturnes" follow the paths of two principals, the Desperate Man and the Carefree Man, who enjoin the nightly contest from forest to tavern to prison, until at last the Desperate kills the Carefree and escapes from his dungeon to . . . liberty? No, no liberty for the Desperate, for he sees life too clearly to enjoy it'.   Ethan Mordden, *Opera in the Twentieth Century: Sacred, Profane, Godot*, Oxford University Press, New York, 1978, p. 225.

Actually, nowadays, the performance of an opera is troublesome. If we were dealing with an audience of 'the people' – genuine people, I mean – the difficulties might be somewhat less serious.[10] Instead, we have to contend with a certain wealthy middle class (the season-ticket holders!) who regard the tenor's high C as just recompense for a trying day – several committee meetings in the morning, tea at five, cocktails at six-thirty – and the soprano's C as equivalent to the price of the ticket. The 'subscribers', as a rule, have no problems and don't wish to be bothered with problems. All they ask is that the evening be as carefree as possible. The administrators of our subsidized theatres know their audience and are wary of new productions that require many rehearsals and promise uncertain receipts at the box office. In many cases the acceptance of new operas (operas by living composers) seems to be dictated more by opportunism than by artistic considerations.

Schoenberg writes in a fundamental essay on Gustav Mahler: 'For the great artist must somehow be punished in his lifetime for the honour which he will enjoy later. And the esteemed music critic must somehow be compensated in his lifetime for the contempt with which later times will treat him'.[11]

What a pity Schoenberg never contemplated the interesting figure of the critic-composer! Today, it is easy for an influential critic to get his operas performed: much easier than for a

---

[10] '"Go towards the people", it has been said. How many are the interpretations of this famous phrase! And so I, too, arrogate the right to interpret it.

'To go towards the people is all very well. We modern musicians have never feared the masses, but we wish they were truly the people and not that curious agglomeration of persons who even today constitute nearly the entire audience at theatres and concerts. The people, especially in our country, have demonstrated their lack of prejudice and their willingness to accept many things in due course. And the people, in their profound humility, know how to regard the creative artist.'

'*Di un Aspetto della Musica Contemporanea*' (1936), *Parole e Musica*, p. 218.

[11] 'Gustav Mahler' (1912, 1948), transl. Dika Newlin, in *Style and Idea: Selected Writings of Arnold Schoenberg*, ed. Leonard Stein, Faber & Faber, London/University of California Press, Berkeley, 1984, p. 462.

composer without the power of a newspaper behind him.

But these are problems that have nothing to do with art. Nor should a composer be asked to take up the cudgels in order to change a situation designed only to humiliate him.

Further Comments on
Opera
(1969)

For at least the past fifty years we have heard that opera is finished, dead, buried. If this were really so, I don't think new theatres would continually be built, nor could I account for the fact that even in a country like the United States, with no operatic tradition, young people are still so eager to try their luck in the musical theatre.

At a time when we have reached a decisive turning-point in history, when religious, cultural, social, and political issues are sifted for answers to the thousand burning questions of the day, it would be patently abnormal if opera, too, were not a focus of controversy. Fortunately, it is. Radical pronouncements and even insults are therefore welcome! They can only serve to scotch the rumour of opera's untimely demise. Nobody speaks of the dead.

Today there are many who ask whether it can be justified that the government (and hence the taxpayers) should subsidize a kind of theatre accessible to only a small minority of citizens. Do we need, then, to close the opera houses? Or is opera, as others claim, a 'cultural amenity' which the state must make every effort to maintain?

I believe that opera houses should be supported, but for different purposes. No longer should they partake of mundane pageantry often bordering on the vulgar, nor offer opportunity for 'amusement'. Instead, they ought to become finishing schools for singers (in music and acting) and orchestra conductors, and without undue extravagance in production prepare musical performances so as not to lose touch com-

pletely with the tradition of this great art form, the opera.[1]
Let's not forget that an 'active tradition' does exist! Opera
houses should be considered living museums – I don't blush at
the word 'museum' – since music, if it isn't performed, ceases
to exist for most people.

As no one proposes to shut the picture galleries and
museums of ancient art that every state maintains, so then
should opera theatres continue to function as curators of an
immense cultural heritage.

And modern opera? There are operas which absolutely
cannot be mounted in 18th- and 19th-century theatres. Others
can still be produced in theatres of more or less traditional
design with some expedients – and what composer has never
had to make a few practical concessions?

It is no longer uncommon to see certain dramatic presenta-
tions staged, for example, in a stadium or a hangar. Why
couldn't something similar work for new forms of musical
theatre? If opera remains vital and viable, as I hope, it will
finally be forced by circumstances, probably within a few
years, to create its own more suitable environments. Historically, it has always done so.

I cannot end these notes without acknowledging the televi-
sion companies – impossible to overpraise them! – that
encourage avant-garde theatre and bring it to an extremely
vast and variegated audience, that support it generously,
affording composers the possibility and pleasure of experimentation.

All things considered, I don't absolutely see the need for
destruction. Time, the supreme judge, has already managed
to do away with a great deal and will continue to eliminate
much more. As Verdi wrote, '. . . the *music of the future* does not
frighten me'.[2] Nor is it likely that the sons of our space age will
be frightened by the music of the past.

---

[1] In 1871 Verdi had proposed 'In each theatre a singing school for the
public, free of charge, the pupils being obliged to work in the theatre for a
given time'. See Julian Budden, *The Operas of Verdi*, Vol. III, Cassell,
London/Oxford University Press, New York, 1981, p. 266.

[2] In a letter to Francesco Florimo, dated 4 (5?) January 1871, which also
contains the famous aphorism 'Return to the past; and it will be a step
forward'.   *Ibid.* (*Cf.* Weaver, *Verdi: A Documentary Study*, pp. 225–226.)

In Memoriam
Gian Francesco Malipiero
(18 March 1882–1 August 1973)

I still remember, more than forty years later, how moved I was to shake his hand when we were introduced in the hall of a Venetian hotel, in September 1932. Malipiero was for me, at that time, the greatly beloved composer of *Sette Canzoni*, of *Poemi Asolani*, and *Le Stagioni Italiche*.

Will you say I knew little of the Maestro's music? True. But don't forget that in Italy, forty years ago, concert programmes were characterized by the most parochial conservatory taste. Much the same policy prevailed at the Ente Radiofonico Italiano (with its notorious monogram *EIAR*), which selected the music for broadcast I wouldn't say according to the culture and taste of its directors – granted that they were totally destitute of culture and taste – but rather in conformity with the composer's political connexions. (We know the monogram was interpreted 'È *Indispensabile Avere Raccomandazioni*'.) And the politics was solely and supremely the line of the National Fascist Party.

One of the rare exceptions to the rule of radio programming – one that has remained strongly stamped on my memory – occurred in Autumn 1932, when Alfredo Casella presented *Torneo Notturno*, an opera by Gian Francesco Malipiero. This is not an opera in the traditional sense of the term. The composer had already given us evidence, in *Sette Canzoni*,[1] of his ambition to create a new form of musical

---

[1] Part II of the triptych *L'Orfeide* (1918–22), which also includes *La Morte delle Maschere* and *Orfeo, ovvero l'Ottava Canzone*. Première of the complete triptych: Düsseldorf, 5 November 1925; première of *Sette Canzoni*: Paris Opéra, 10 July 1920 (see p. 168, n.7).

theatre ('my theatre', he called it), a thousand miles equidistant from Verdi and from Wagner. Malipiero himself designated *Torneo Notturno* not an 'opera', but 'seven Nocturnes'.

I believe I wrote the Maestro a letter after hearing the work: probably just a few lines of congratulation, timid and reserved. For in our brief encounter in the hall of the Venetian hotel, he had seemed extremely sensitive, and I knew that sensitive persons, finding it hard to bear the admiration of others, take refuge in irony or coldness to mask their true feelings. I don't recall what I wrote on that occasion. But I can now say that for me it was a memorable evening, not unlike the evening I first saw *The Flying Dutchman* at the age of thirteen; or when, at sixteen, I heard Debussy's *Ibéria*[2] or, at twenty, *Pierrot Lunaire*;[3] or finally, in 1935, when the *Klang* of

---

[2] 'Put yourself in the place of a boy who, at the age of fifteen, goes to Bologna for Easter – his first trip to Italy after the War. This was in 1919. I was in the company of my old uncle, who was very fond of me. We of course stopped, enchanted, in front of the window of the music store of Pizzi. I saw: Claude Debussy, *Pelléas et Mélisande*. And I asked my uncle, who was an ardent music lover: "Do you know this work, *Pelléas et Mélisande*?" "It's Debussy's masterpiece," he replied. I was ashamed that he, though not a musician, knew the name of a composer I had never heard of before. After I returned home, I resumed my piano lessons. And then by way of "*La Cathédrale Engloutie*" I began to discover what there was in Debussy. . . . It had such an effect on me that for three years I did not write another note because I understood that I would have merely imitated Debussy. A few years later, precisely at the age of twenty, I needed *Pierrot Lunaire* to regain my balance. . . .

'[In 1926] I heard, for the first time, *Le Martyre de Saint-Sébastien* under Toscanini at La Scala (in a box, Gabriele d'Annunzio – with two ladies; on the stage, Ida Rubinstein). This was the most important lesson in orchestration I ever had'.

'Luigi Dallapiccola: Fragments from Conversations', pp. 310–311.

[3] 'My orientation was decided on the night of April 1st, 1924, when I saw Arnold Schoenberg conduct a performance of his *Pierrot Lunaire*, in the Sala Bianca of the Palazzo Pitti [at Florence]. That night the students, with typical Latin gaiety, were indulging in the usual whistling before the performance began; the public for their part caused an uproar, stamping their feet and laughing. But Giacomo Puccini did not laugh on that occasion. He listened to the performance with the utmost attention, following it with the score, and at the end of the concert asked to be introduced to Schoenberg'.

'On the Twelve-Note Road', *Music Survey*, October 1951, p. 318.

Anton Webern's music first struck my ears.[4] Certainly, for
weeks thereafter, when I awoke I caught myself humming the
theme of the '*Canzone del Tempo*':

Chi ha tempo e tempo aspetta, il tempo perde,
Il tempo fugge come d'arco strale . . .

Seize the day or lose your chance forever,
The hours fly like arrows from a bow . . .

Those were the years when I was searching for myself.

How not to recall the poisonous, nauseating nationalistic
rhetoric of that time? How not to preserve the memory of
endless polemics, so very bitter and for the most part basely
appealing, about *italianità* and 'internationalism' in music? (In
Fascist jargon, this word had become a synonym for 'anti-
Fascist' and even 'Communist'!) How to forget that on 17
December 1932, a few weeks after the tenth anniversary of the
'March on Rome', all the daily newspapers of the peninsula
published that scurrilous 'Musical Manifesto' – a none too
subtle attack on Malipiero and Casella, then the only vital
forces in Italian music – signed by ten personages including
composers, pseudo-composers, and critics who had tried to
compose in their youth.[5]

Naturally, Malipiero's music was branded 'international'.
Was it perhaps because the world première of *Sette
Canzoni* had been given at Paris, *Orfeo, ovvero l'Ottava Canzone*
at Düsseldorf, *Tre Commedie Goldoniane* [1920–22] at Darmstadt, *Filomela e l'Infatuato* [1925] at Prague, the trilogy *Il*

---

[4] Concerto for Nine Instruments, Op. 24, world première: thirteenth
ISCM festival, Prague, 5 September 1935, directed by Heinrich Jalowetz.
See 'Meeting with Anton Webern (Pages from a Diary)', *Tempo*, No. 99,
London, 1972, pp. 2–7.

[5] See p. 91, n. 13. Without naming Casella and Malipiero, the authors of
the *Manifesto di Musicisti Italiani per la Tradizione dell'Arte Romantica dell'Ot-
tocento* attacked their anti-Romantic stance and their 'so-called objective
music' – music 'without human content', merely 'mechanical games and
mental gymnastics'. Pizzetti, the spokesman of the group, had earlier
debated with Casella (1913–14) on the young composers' attitude towards
Verdi, and with Malipiero (1921–22) on the place of 19th-century music in
conservatory instruction.

Mistero di Venezia[6] at Mainz, *I Corvi di San Marco* at Coburg, *Torneo Notturno* at Munich [15 May 1931], and *La Favola del Figlio Cambiato* [1932–33] at Brunswick? Malipiero has very wisely chosen the locations of his first performances. We must remember that when the Italian première of *La Favola del Figlio Cambiato* was given at Rome, the Head of the Government, Cavaliere Benito Mussolini, appeared there in person to forbid further performances – indignant, probably, at finding in the opera none of the optimism and bogus patriotism so prized by dictators.[7] (My music would be judged by the same standards, and for a very long time, beginning a few years later.)

Well, in *Torneo Notturno* it seemed to me that Malipiero had discovered the old, authentic spirit of Italian music, the spirit which – to tell the truth – I had never found in *verismo* operas nor in the operas of those who signed the 'Manifesto'. It was my impression in 1932, as it remains today, that Malipiero had resumed the line of the grand Italian tradition, the tradition which made our music great and universal. But many others, too many, were unaware or preferred not to notice – another sign of the provincialism that totally dominated Italy for years on end.

The whole of *Torneo Notturno* seems to be centred musically in the '*Canzone del Tempo*', a setting of three octaves by Poliziano. I think the poet probably wished above all to display his literary virtuosity, by treating the word *tempo* in the manner of an ostinato: it occurs eight times in the first stanza, twice in the second, and fifteen times in the third. For the composer, this word takes on the character of an obsession and implies something that cannot be stopped, that flows inevitably towards catastrophe.

It has been said more than once that Malipiero had a

---

[6] Consisting of *Le Aquile di Aquileia* (1928), *Il Finto Arlecchino* (1925), and *I Corvi di San Marco* (1928); première of complete trilogy: Coburg, 15 December 1932 (at Mainz, in 1928, only Part II was performed).

[7] Fedele d'Amico finds no 'anti-Fascist' content in Malipiero's opera (based on the play by Pirandello) and maintains that Mussolini prohibited repeat performances because, like the majority of the audience who hissed the opera, he 'didn't understand it'. See *Cinquant'anni del Teatro dell'Opera 1928–1978*, ed. J. Tognelli, Bestetti, Rome, 1979, pp. 207–209.

difficult personality, almost constitutionally difficult. Life really did very little to ameliorate it. He was certainly not a man who could cherish illusions, neither in 1929 when composing this opera nor later. On every side they were carolling (as they would for many years to come) '*Giovinezza, giovinezza*', investing this word with elusive connotations.[8] But Malipiero, disillusioned and by nature pessimistic, set to music an admonition:

> *Il tempo fugge e mai non si rinverde*
> *E mena al fin le tue bellezze frale,*

> The moments flee, the green of Maytime never
> Comes again, and your frail charms must go. . . .

It shows his awareness of the human condition and contains a presentiment, perhaps, of the abyss into which mankind – and not only we Italians – would sooner or later fall. (Writing on another occasion about Gustav Mahler, a man just as free from illusions as Malipiero, I quoted Paul Claudel's aphorism 'Poets are like gulls: they sense the approach of the hurricane'.)

The melodic discourse of the '*Canzone del Tempo*' is most peculiar: very different from Bellini's enrapturing or Verdi's dramatic discourse, the antithesis of the habitually bombastic style of certain *verismo* composers. Not a single melisma appears in it; each syllable is hammered tragically, one note at a time, with absolute consistency. Malipiero adheres to this principle even at the beginning of the second stanza, a moment when he might have been tempted by lyricism – '*Pensa, Madonna, ben che 'l tempo fugge*' ('Remember well, Madonna, that time flies') – not to mention the third stanza, where the quickening pursuit of the syllables – two verses in the first two bars! – represents the fatal flow of time. Furthermore, the rests are just as deeply felt and carefully planned as the notes: three quavers' rest, including the initial one, in the nine bars of the first stanza; in the ten-bar second stanza, only one quaver's and one semiquaver's rest, apart from the inital rest of a crotchet. (Observe that in this stanza, not even

---

[8] '*Giovinezza*', Salvatore Gotta's song of youth which became the anthem of Fascism. See Mack Smith, *Mussolini*, pp. 47 and 133.

the full stop after the fourth verse suggested a rest to the composer!) And, in the eight bars plus one crotchet of the third stanza, apart from the initial rest of a quaver, there is but one semiquaver's rest. Thus we see a gradual process of acceleration from stanza to stanza, achieved by the diminution of the value both of certain notes and of the rests (four semiquavers' rest altogether in the first stanza, three in the second stanza, one in the third). The total effect of this 'Canzone' seems to me almost unique in the history of the Italian musical theatre.

*   *   *

In January 1959 I had an opportunity to spend entire days with Malipiero, at Rome, examining scores submitted to the first international contest of the Italian Society for Contemporary Music. The Maestro, despite his seventy-seven years, was the only judge of the seven who read the scores without glasses. In fact, he had to chide me more than once for reading too slowly! He himself proceeded expeditiously. On his head not a trace of baldness.

I recall that at the moment our task was completed Wladimir Vogel, the other 'doyen' of the jury (though fourteen years younger than Malipiero), informed him that a few closing remarks would be welcome. Here is exactly what he said: 'I came to Rome a bit hesitantly: everything's so rushed these days. . . . I was afraid of being too anchored to the mentality of my generation. . . . I asked myself if I could be sufficiently calm and fair in judging contemporary composition and experimentation. On the contrary, it happens that too many tonal or pre-dodecaphonic pieces have deeply offended me: if I experienced a few moments of joy, they came from reading the most advanced scores . . .'. It cannot be over-emphasized that these are the words of a man who is young at heart and, at the same time, almost unintentionally, a lesson to this and subsequent juries.

Indeed, it is by virtue of being young at heart that Malipiero could continue, well into old age, writing works of unmistakable personality and, in this case, one can honestly say, 'style'! The style – his and his alone – informs even a work as early as *Pause del Silenzio* [I] (1917), and it is reconfirmed by all his compositions up to the one-acts *L'Iscariota* and *Uno dei Dieci* (world premières at Siena during the 1971 Settimana Musicale). It culminates in his last flight, *Omaggio a Belmonte* (not the first time Schoenberg's name has been translated), first performed on 25 March 1972, one week after Malipiero's ninetieth birthday: a sublime work, indeed one of the loftiest in all his immense output.

With no other Italian composer have I conducted such a substantial correspondence over the decades as with Gian Francesco Malipiero. His letters, always extraordinarily lively, contain outbursts of anger and moments of tenderness, reflections on music as well as broader views on contemporary life. There are also intensely autobiographical passages, which some day will probably furnish interesting research material for anyone who wishes to understand certain reversals of character and *modus operandi*, the severity of some of his judgements but also his kindness of heart – in short, a portrait of the living composer.

How many times we met at Venice and Florence! (But of all our meetings, the one particularly stamped on my memory is that sinister 10 June 1940 at Padua, when we heard the declaration of war proclaimed from the 'historic balcony'[9] and sank into despairing silence for the rest of the evening.) The sight of a palace, a personal encounter, was enough to make him expatiate on his dreams of living at the time of the Venetian Republic, so ardently would he have desired it. Shall I ever forget the day my wife and I were invited to dine at his famous house in Asolo, and the conversation turned – I don't recall how – to Giacomo Casanova? At the mention of this name Malipiero seemed to grow excited and, visibly inspired, began relating facts and anecdotes with such vivacity and authenticity that we had the impression Cavaliere Casanova was right there in our midst.

While I will admit that Malipiero's character was psychologically complex and at times contradictory, the peevishness so many others noted was never revealed to me. On the

---

[9] The balcony of the Palazzo Venezia at Rome, Mussolini's personal headquarters.

contrary, his kindness was unstinting, and try as I might I can't remember a single flaw in our friendship.

His last letter is dated 19 June 1972: a brief letter, just one page, in a rather unsteady handwriting. ('Excuse the writing,' he said, 'my right hand isn't feeble – but almost.') To describe it as bitter would be an understatement; it is sad and disheartening. He closed with a question: 'Where is Annalibera?'

The Maestro had shown great affection for my daughter since he first met her (she might have been ten at the time). And I still recall that when I told him, twelve years later, she was in India, he seemed astonished, then said with great seriousness and a touch of reproof in his voice: 'I wouldn't have let her go'. To such an extent was the Maestro living in the past as regards everything not connected with art and, especially, music.

I answered at once, to calm him, that she was at home. So ended our correspondence.

Fortunately, there was the telephone to keep me posted on his condition: months of pain until 1 August 1973, when a friend from Radio Florence called to tell me he had received the devastating news at six p.m. The Maestro had passed away in the hospital at Treviso.

Useless to try to find a seat on the trains, at that time of year even more congested than usual. A fraternal friend wanted to be near me, and drove me to Treviso the next day. We went together the following morning to the mortuary chapel of the hospital, to view the beloved Maestro for the last time in the open coffin. He had always been handsome, but never more so than he seemed that morning. His suffering, his struggles were over. He looked stretched-out and serene. Finally at peace.

L'Enfant
et les Sortilèges [1]

If we close our eyes and think for a moment of the characters who have appeared to our imagination since we began attending the opera, we shall see around us such a throng of images that it will be difficult to recognize them and put them all in order.

Men madly in love, rejected at first – then loved; jealous men, incited to crime; men ruled by folly, who shiver with fright and whom fate finally crushes; men of boundless generosity. *Femmes fatales* who die by the knife, and women who poison themselves for love; female criminals, and women who weep and despair. Divers mythological gods in human form, with all the failings of mortals; heroes descended to earth 'to show a miracle',[2] yet always fatally human. Women with the aspect and soul of an angel; women with yellow, almond-shaped eyes; dark-skinned women with kinky hair. Demons still red from the fires of hell; men pale as chalk, who follow their sad destiny, tossed on its tides. Nervous wrecks like Wozzeck, who can no longer resist. People of essentially sound mind, like Lucrezia Borgia, who has the gall to sing – 'Look out, take care of yourself, Don Alfonso, my fourth husband!' – whether in a voice more of warning than abuse one scarcely knows. Rigid, unyielding men like Don Giovanni, who fear nothing and shrink from nothing. Men like Jacopo Fiesco, who change costume and name to make themselves

---

[1] Essay written on the occasion of the Italian première of Ravel's opera, at the fifth Maggio Musicale (Florence, Teatro della Pergola), 2 May 1939, directed by Fernando Previtali.

[2] '*Da cielo in terra a miracol mostrare*': Dante, *La Vita Nuova*, XXVI; the first quatrain of this sonnet is quoted on p. 151.

unrecognizable and succeed so well in their disguise that the audience itself, at a certain point, cannot guess their identity. Unhappy people, like Rosina, who complains about the strictness of her stern guardian. And folk happy with their lot and with their trade, like comrade Alfio, composer of the official hymn of the cart-drivers.

What do these characters do? It would take a list as long as Leporello's to account for them! Courtiers, noblemen, swindlers, eunuchs, pirates, music masters, monks, gypsies, doges, kings, conspirators, students, spies, sailors, warriors, prisoners, squires, cut-throats, priests, sorcerers, poets – they all pass before the mind's eye. And we cherish the memory of two adolescents. Cherubino, child of that period which preceded the French Revolution by a few years; twice-immortal Cherubino, in whom Beaumarchais thought he saw 'what every mother, in her heart of hearts, would want her son to be – even at the cost of suffering'; Cherubino, enamoured more of love itself than of a woman, who ends by marrying just any little maid, the gardener's daughter. The other adolescent is Octavian, in *Der Rosenkavalier*, belonging to the immediate pre-War era. Octavian, not truly in love with anyone – least of all the Marschallin von Werdenberg; the tiny egoist who marries Sophie, a silly little goose from a good family, daughter of the exceedingly vain Herr von Faninal – war profiteer[3] *ante litteram*. (To the moral parallel of the two adolescents corresponds, with absolutely geometric rigour, an artistic, musical parallel.)

In all this multitude we see not even a single child. Why . . . ? Perhaps because the composers who have so deeply probed the souls of men and women and adolescents considered the soul of a child too 'simple'? We of the War and post-War generations, who know on the contrary how complex and profound is the soul of the child, would not agree. More likely great artists, accustomed to dealing with the 'big emotions', haven't even noticed the *little world* that exists alongside the other, not superior but only more visible world. Let us now try to survey the rich musical literature of

---

[3] A colloquialism dating from World War I: *pescecane* means 'shark', dog fish.

childhood amassed in our time, and see how children have appeared as characters on the stage.

Casting a glance at the instrumental music of the past, we cannot help mentioning the name of Robert Schumann. Yet I believe that neither *Album für die Jugend* nor *Kinderszenen* should be over-estimated from a strictly psychological point of view. I rather think that after having explored the infinite technical and expressive possibilities of the piano, Schumann once felt an urge to simplify himself and his writing, wished for a moment to reduce his means to the minimum. Undoubtedly a rare case. Only Modest Mussorgsky, a few decades later, succeeded in giving us the first true interpretation of the soul of the child, in his song cycle *The Nursery* [1872] for voice and piano. And in *Boris Godunov*, Feodor and Xenia, the son and daughter of the Tsar, are historically the first children to act on the stage of the opera theatre.

Mussorgsky – Debussy: once more we must juxtapose the two great names. Not to exaggerate the derivations, as did so many critics at the turn of the century; but to establish a connexion between *The Nursery* by the Russian composer and the *Children's Corner* suite [1906–08] by the Frenchman, between the children of Tsar Boris and the tragic figure of little Yniold in *Pelléas et Mélisande*.

Feodor, the younger child of the murderous Tsar, is a mirror that reflects only the most superficial aspect of his father's figure: its greatness. And this mirror so distorts the vision that he doesn't even suspect how ephemeral Boris's greatness really is. Consider only the map scene. Feodor is sitting at the desk when his father enters, anxious and grim as always. 'What is that?' he asks his son, pointing to the map spread out on the desk. 'The map of Russia, your kingdom from sea to sea.' The expansive utterance, the interspaced chords befitting unequalled majesty, prove my point.

Little Yniold, son of Golaud, Mélisande's stepson, is likewise a mirror that reflects a single aspect of his father – but a very different, much more intimate and dreadful aspect. Golaud, jealous of Pelléas, has a conversation with his little boy [Act III, Scene 4] to determine exactly how things stand between Pelléas and Mélisande:

'What do they talk about when they're together?'

'Pelléas and Mama?'
'Yes. What do they talk about?'
'Me – always about me'.
'And what do they say about you?'
'That I'm going to be very big'.

The boy's answers are too vague to satisfy Golaud, who bursts out: 'Here I am like a blind man,[4] searching for his treasure at the bottom of the ocean!' He promises his son a quiver with arrows, big arrows, then lifts him up on his shoulders so that he can observe through the window what is happening within a room of the castle.

'Is Mama alone?' asks Golaud.
'Yes . . . No, no! Uncle Pelléas is with her. . .'
'What are they doing?'
'They aren't doing anything, Daddy.'
'Are they close to each other? Are they talking?'
'No, Daddy. . .'
'They're not moving nearer to each other?'

Suddenly the little boy's tone changes: 'I'm terribly afraid! . . . Daddy, let me get down!' Yniold, as the mirror of his father, reflects only his tragic doubt, the infinite misery of the jealous man.

If Mussorgsky and Debussy have interpreted the soul of the child, in *The Nursery* and the *Children's Corner* suite respectively, and if their operas brilliantly exploit the reactions of children to adults, Maurice Ravel's approach is different. In 1908 he composed a suite of five children's pieces for piano, four hands, and entitled it *Ma Mère l'Oye* (*Mother Goose*) – a genuine masterpiece of grace and refinement. This music, inspired by well-known fairy tales, is very remote from both the religious primitivism of Mussorgsky's 'Evening Prayer' and the static oriental trance of 'With the Doll'; very distant, too, from that civilized, artful European malice which permeates Debussy's 'Serenade for the Doll' and 'Golliwog's Cake-walk'. In *Ma Mère l'Oye* Ravel attained the highest degree of psychological simplicity and succeeded, within certain limits, in stepping outside of his own personality and becoming a little boy.

[4] See p. 100, n. 2.

Not an interpreter, a narrator of the soul of the child – in the manner of Mussorgsky or Debussy – but quite simply an *actor*. Ravel was therefore ready to bring the child on stage and make him the protagonist of an opera.

(Since I have dwelt on psychology up to this point and have mentioned only great composers, no one will be surprised that I have bypassed Engelbert Humperdinck's casual foray into the musical expression of childhood.)

*   *   *

The plot of *L'Enfant et les Sortilèges*, '*fantaisie lyrique*' on a text by Colette, can be briefly summarized.

The setting is a room that opens onto a garden, a room containing some big armchairs, a wide divan, a wooden grandfather clock with flowered dial, wallpaper in a pastoral motif, a squirrel's cage hanging near the window, a large fireplace with embers and boiling kettle, a purring cat.

The Child, six or seven years old, is sitting at the desk. He has homework to do, but a fit of laziness has overtaken him and the lessons aren't progressing. The boy bites his pen, scratches his head, and hums.

His mother enters and, little edified by her son's behaviour, scolds him harshly. When she asks if he is sorry for his laziness, the Child's only reply is to stick out his tongue an inch. His mother's anger reaches the boiling point. She leaves him some dry bread and tea without sugar. As punishment the Child must remain alone until dinner-time and think about his misconduct.

What a coincidence! This very afternoon the Child isn't hungry; he prefers solitude to company. He feels exactly like a naughty boy and delights in his mischievousness. With a slap of the hand he smashes the black Wedgwood teapot and Chinese cup. He climbs onto the window sill, opens the cage, and pricks the squirrel with his pen until it manages to escape into the garden. He jumps down from the window and pulls the cat's tail, then stirs up the fire with the poker and kicks over the kettle. Brandishing the poker like a sword, he tears the lovely Arcadian wallpaper to shreds. To finish the job, he takes the pendulum of the clock and slashes his school books and the fairy-tale book, and at last, with nothing left to destroy, drops exhausted into an armchair.

But at this moment the unexpected, the unforeseeable happens. The armchair moves away with a ponderous step and, bowing ceremoniously to a Louis XV bergère, invites her to dance. Now the chairs are rid of the naughty boy forever; no longer will they offer him hospitality for daydreams or pillows for repose. The clock, ashamed of its mutilation, goes and stands in a corner. The black Wedgwood teapot and china cup mutter insults towards the Child and plot their revenge. The fire informs us that its duty is to warm the good but burn the wicked.

It is already dusk. In an exquisite atmosphere of pipes and tabours, a procession of shepherds and shepherdesses winds its way from the wallpaper. As it recedes we glimpse first a slender hand, then golden tresses emerging from a page of the torn book. . . . It's the Fairy Princess! Of all the wonders the Child has seen, this is the most astonishing. Here in front of him is the enchanted Princess he had summoned in his dream the night before, who had kept him awake so long! The Child had murmured to himself: 'She is blonde/With sky-blue eyes'.[5] He had searched for her in the rosebuds and the fragrance of lilies; he considered her his first true love. Alas! Even the beautiful Princess goes away. . . . She has left a golden hair on the Child's shoulder, and it reminds him of a moonbeam.

Now our protagonist is roused from his melancholy meditations by the arrival of a sprightly old man with the appearance of a Greek *Pi*. It's the little old Mathematician, who with malicious glee reels off problems the unhappy Child cannot solve!

> Two taps run into a tank!
> Two slow trains leave a station
> At twenty minute intervals
> Val, val, val!
> A peasant-woman,
> Woman, woman, woman,
> Carries all her eggs to market!

[5] Libretto translated by Felix Aprahamian (1981), with the recording on HMV ASD 4167/Angel DS-37869 conducted by André Previn.

Once a haberdasher,
Dasher, dasher, dasher
Sold six yards of cloth!

The little old man is surrounded by Numbers, solving absurd equations: $4 + 4 = 18$, $11 + 6 = 25$, $7 \times 9 = 33$.

Two cats speak their amorous and tender language, and a bit later, in the garden, we find ourselves in the middle of a concert of toads and frogs. Here is the tree whose bark, where the Child had cut it, smarts like a wound. Here's the dragonfly the Child had pierced with a pin, and the bat whose mate he had stolen. And here, again, is the squirrel.

Overcome by fright, the boy cries out the only word that comes instinctively to his lips: 'Mama!' The animals seem to recognize this as the cry of the one who has teased and tormented them so often. They form a coalition and start attacking the little torturer, but in the *mêlée* a squirrel is wounded and falls at the feet of the Child. Filled with compassion, he snatches a ribbon from his neck and bandages the little creature's paw. The animals all remain silent for a long time.

Is the Child then good at heart? It seems so. Now he is finally worthy of uttering the name 'Mama!'

L'Enfant et les Sortilèges is an episodic opera, as a synopsis of the libretto makes clear; it abounds in closed forms. The dance of the two armchairs suggests a modern interpretation of the minuet. The duet of the teapot and china cup is quite a regular foxtrot. The fire's aria is a *rondò a capriccio*, and the scene of the little old Mathematician a rhythmic ostinato; while the form of the old madrigal has been recast in the choral finale. And yet, despite the derivations of the episodes, the opera has its own absolute unity and indisputable structure.

Ravel composed this 'lyric fantasy' during the period from 1920 to 1925, the year of its première at Monte Carlo. I am not aware of subsequent stage productions.[6]

---

[6] Staged at the Opéra-Comique, Paris, 1 February 1926; at Brussels, 11 February 1926; at Prague, 17 February 1927; at Leipzig, 6 May 1927; at Vienna, 14 March 1929.

When an artistically perfect opera, inspired by a subject full of grace and charm, an opera whose score is not excessively difficult to perform, doesn't 'go over' (as theatre people say), one asks why such an undeserved fate? There is always a misunderstanding when a work of art isn't repeated, and here I think it is due to the immense difficulty of the staging. Yet the solution to the problems of *mise en scène*, however inventive, will always be relative in this opera, which seems to me fifteen years ahead of its time. If Colette's fanciful story and Ravel's music had been conceived in 1935 rather than 1920, the ideal medium would certainly not have been opera but a great Walt Disney colour cartoon. Only in this form, I firmly believe, could *L'Enfant et les Sortilèges* find its definitive expression – free from compromise, open and clear.

Now let's take a slightly closer look at several episodes, beginning right with the foxtrot of the teapot and china cup. The teapot is obviously at home in very *chic* salons: it speaks English, spiced with a few French expressions. The cup articulates words and amusing puns with very peculiar spellings. It mentions Mah-jong, harakiri, the film actor Sessue Hayakawa . . . in short, the three or four things from the Far East that everybody knows.

And what is the composer's stance? His music is just as chic and stilted as the teapot's conversation. After a brief, essentially rhythmic introduction comes the first strophe, in the tempo of a 1920-style American dance. The ensuing *maggiore* for the china cup is very suave in melody, elegant in harmonization. But Ravel's intelligence demanded something more. To complement the banalities uttered by the cup, he felt obliged to embellish his music with equivalent banalities: a stream of high-pitched parallel intervals, mostly fourths, in the Chinese pentatonic scale. Debussy had used this device, with excellent evocative effect, in '*Pagodes*' (its first appearance in European music, to my knowledge[7]). Of course, it gradually became in the impressionist period – and, alas, even much

[7] Debussy actually used the pentatonic scale for the first time in '*Clair de Lune*', the third song of the cycle *Fêtes Galantes* (Set I, 1892). '*Pagodes*' is the first piece of the piano suite *Estampes* (1903).

later! – the cliché chinoiserie prized by amateurs dying to recreate exotic atmospheres.

The refrain should have followed the second strophe. But to Ravel's probing mind, a repetition pure and simple of what had already been said would have been tantamount to mental laziness. He does repeat the melody, to be sure, but superimposed exactly on the reprise of the theme of the first strophe and all its motifs. This superimposition is achieved with such astonishing bravura and lightness of touch that we don't even suspect the contrapuntal skill or the difficulty of the many problems solved. The episode ends with a short coda.

The other section we shall examine has an entirely different character. It is the 'pastorale' that winds its way through the voices and orchestra, while from the torn wallpaper issues the small procession of shepherds and shepherdesses lamenting:

Shepherds:	Farewell, Shepherdesses!
Shepherdesses:	Shepherds, farewell!
All:	No longer shall we pasture our green sheep On the purple grass!

Long harmonic pedals lend this piece the static quality of bagpipes, historically a feature of the pastorale genre from Bach to our time and one not even the ultra-modern Alban Berg disdained (see *Lulu*, Act I, Scene 2: the six bars in the duet between Lulu and Dr Schoen explicitly marked '*à la Musette*').

In Ravel's 'pastorale', the melodic arabesques are brief and expressive. Here, as in the choral finale of the opera – the part most closely related to the charming suite *Ma Mère l'Oye* and particularly to its last movement, '*Le Jardin Féerique*' – every humourous whim, every intellectual conceit is completely banished. Here, as I mentioned earlier, the composer has become a small boy again, the protagonist of his own creation. Here he is before us, inspired by and almost absent from the events that surround and overwhelm him. Here he is, alone, making the greatest effort our time has known to attain purity of heart.

Pages from a Diary
Salome

Berlin, 9 February 1930

I was lucky to have been able to see *Salome* a few evenings ago,[1] an opera with which I was shamefully unacquainted. For Alexander von Zemlinsky[2] directed, and this great artist (almost completely unknown in Italy) succeeded in making Strauss's dense score as transparent as that of *Così fan tutte*. From now on, if anyone tells me the score of *Salome* is muddled, I shall answer that the performance must have been inadequate.

The opera was finished twenty-five years ago. If it were merely a case of superficial 'modernity' – modernity seasoned with scandal at the première – probably no one would speak of it today. But *Salome* is much more than that. We hear it as an artistic success and, as such, part of our civilization: an opera that has now become classical, clear.

There is one point, however – a page, to be exact – which disturbed me for hours on end, perplexed and even mortified me a little. I was in fact unable to identify the instrument (undoubtedly a *solo* instrument) that played two notes in the low register: two very sweet, intense tones of distinctive timbre – a long A, followed by an even longer D – intended to support for several bars the delicate body of high strings and a few wind instruments. It wasn't difficult to exclude the brass

---

[1] At the Staatsoper am Platz der Republik, 4 February 1930.

[2] Zemlinsky (1871–1942), a prominent Austrian opera conductor and composer, was Schoenberg's only formal teacher and his brother-in-law. In the *Lyrische Suite*, Berg paid homage to Zemlinsky by quoting from his *Lyrische Symphonie*.

at the outset, but it seemed impossible to consider the low-pitched woodwinds or, finally, the strings, whose timbre would have been quite different. What then?

Promptly next morning I was the first customer in a music store. After making a very modest purchase of paper, I asked if I might glance at the score of *Salome*, and it wasn't difficult to find what I was looking for: page 330. A miracle, without doubt, a stroke of genius. And, at the same time, an admirable lesson in 'economy' (a word that might at first sound strange if applied to Richard Strauss). All differences granted, of course, it suddenly reminded me of Mozart's definitive lesson, when he reserved the entrance of the trombones for the last part of *Don Giovanni*.

With the gigantic orchestra at his disposal, Strauss had created in 329 pages many truly fascinating atmospheres and found instrumental mixtures quite unprecedented at the beginning of the 20th century. Clearly, he *desired* to postpone until the last moment (the entire score consists of 352 pages) the presentation of an isolated timbre that one could never expect to hear, so unrelated does it seem to the commonly understood possibilities of the orchestra; a timbre that apparently comes to us from a distant, yet-to-be-discovered world.

Furthermore, the surprising colour seems to have been planned to strengthen the meaning of the words – fortunately quite audible in this passage! It occurs at the precise moment when Salome, bent over the decapitated head of Jochanaan, sings:

> *und wenn ich Dich ansah, hörte ich* geheimnisvolle Musik
> and when I looked on thee I heard *a strange music*.[3]

At the beginning of the bar in which the protagonist utters the adjective '*geheimnisvolle*' enters the secret, mysterious instrument I couldn't identify: the organ, backstage, *pianissimo*.[4]

* * *

[3] Oscar Wilde, *Salome*, transl. Lord Alfred Douglas, Dover, New York, 1967, p. 65, emphasis added.

[4] In the opening storm scene of *Otello*, Verdi indicates three organ notes a semitone apart, 'to be played in the register of the basses and the timpani'. See Budden, *The Operas of Verdi*, Vol. III, p. 334.

March 1969

P.S.: A few years ago Italian Radio sponsored a series of discussions on a certain trend in contemporary music. During my exchange of views with Pietro Grossi,[5] I didn't fail to mention the passage that had prompted these thoughts thirty-nine years ago as a presentiment of electronic timbres.

---

[5] Pietro Grossi (b. 1917), electronic music composer and experimenter.

Letter to
Léonide Massine

137/81 75th Road
Flushing, New York
26 April 1957

Dear Monsieur Massine,[1]

Several days ago a kind letter from our mutual friend Igor Markevitch informed me of your project, and meanwhile I have received your friendly letter[2] together with the ballet scenario. While I thank you with all my heart for this latest

---

[1] In French; *LD: Saggi* . . . , pp. 90–91. Leonid Feodorovich Mjasin (1896–1979), celebrated Russian ballet dancer and choreographer.

In his contribution to a round-table at the Palazzo Strozzi, Florence, 30 April 1963, Dallapiccola acknowledged his debt to Massine 'for the experience of what can be achieved on the stage by means of *contradiction*. I am alluding to his interpretation of the "*Farruca*" in Manuel de Falla's *El Sombrero de Tres Picos*.*

'The other dancers I have seen act the part of the protagonist, the Miller – even very recently – began the dance obviously at the point where the music of the "*Farruca*" begins. Not Massine. He remained seated on the floor, legs crossed, with a flask in his lap. After several bars of the principal rhythm, he tossed the flask into the air and it was caught by an extra on the opposite side of the stage. Absolute immobility for several more bars (what an eternity it seems to the viewer!), then finally an unforgettable leap.

'Massine plunged into the music *in medias res*: one of the most startling surprise effects I have ever experienced in the theatre'.
            '*L'Arte Figurativa e le Altre Arti*', *Parole e Musica*, p. 161.
   * *The Three-Cornered Hat*, comedy-ballet based on a novel by Pedro de Alarcón, produced in London by Sergei Diaghilev's Ballets Russes in 1919, with décor by Picasso and choreography by Massine.

[2] Dated 19 April 1957, proposing a ballet based on the *Parsifal* legend, to be performed at the Paris Opéra in January 1958.

token of your esteem and friendship, I regret infinitely to say that I am unable to accept your kind proposal. There are two reasons for this decision: in the first place, I definitely intend to begin work next Summer on my new opera,[3] after so many years of contemplation and after so much hesitation. And then . . . I would never have the courage to attack the problem of the *Parsifal* legend after Wagner.

I can easily understand, of course, that it is certainly possible to interpret this legend quite differently . . . but *for me*, Wagner's treatment is very nearly definitive.[4]

Please forgive me for not being able to answer you in the affirmative, and remember that I am very faithfully yours,

LUIGI DALLAPICCOLA

[3] *Ulisse*, a project Dallapiccola seems *always* to have been considering. See 'Birth of a Libretto', pp. 232–262.

[4] 'The work of Wagner that I consider his greatest among all others and the most effective theatrically as opera is *Parsifal*. I put it even higher than *Tristan und Isolde*. Nothing seems to occur in the scene of the love feast [Act I], and yet the whole universe comes alive. . . .

'And the score of *Parsifal*! Its transparency makes it appear to me so thoroughly modern.'

'Luigi Dallapiccola: Fragments from Conversations', p. 311.

Letter to
Wolfgang Wagner

34 Via Romana, Florence
15 April 1968

Esteemed Herr Wolfgang Wagner,[1]

Please accept my apologies for not having answered until today, due to pressure of work, your very kind letter dated 12 March. And believe me, I am truly abashed by your request. To write about *Die Meistersinger* – how could I?

At the opera house of Graz, in May 1917 when I was thirteen years old, it was *Der Fliegende Holländer* that made me decide to devote my life to music. One month later, exactly on St John's Eve (was it a coincidence? I cannot be certain), I happened to hear *Die Meistersinger* for the first time.

For years this seemed to me the most sublime of Richard Wagner's operas – *Parsifal* is obviously not an opera for adolescents. I loved it profoundly then, as now. How could I forget the second-act entrance of Pogner and Eva at the end of the street, on the stage at Graz, as the music darkens and fades away? It would be apparent that night was falling, even if the stage lights weren't being extinguished one by one. That evening I realized for the first time what landscape in music could be;[2] I realized that the protagonist of Act II is St John's

---

[1] In Italian; *LD: Saggi . . .*, p. 104. Grandson of the composer and director of the Bayreuth Festival, Wolfgang Wagner had asked Dallapiccola to write an essay for the programme of a new production of *Die Meistersinger*.

[2] After hearing Mahler's First Symphony for the first time, Dallapiccola wrote in his diary (Vienna, 21 January 1930):

'Gustav Mahler impressed me at once as a great landscape painter, although that was no cause for astonishment. The landscape has always

Eve. (Sometime later I began to think that the protagonist of the third act of *Tristan* is the sea.) And on leaving the theatre after the musical miracle, another miracle: but this time, one of nature. The full moon (*Vollmond*) was shining – no longer on stage, but in the sky. (I dare not believe that this, too, had been anticipated by the Intendant, whose name, Julius Grevenberg, I still remember.)

Believe me, esteemed Herr Wagner, when so many recollections of life accumulate and become congested, a human being finds it difficult to achieve that cold detachment which seems essential today for writing the kind of critical essay you request of me. This is only a personal letter, dictated by the love I always feel for the music of Richard Wagner, and nothing more. With very cordial regards,

Yours,
LUIGI DALLAPICCOLA

---

exercised a great influence on Austrian composers. Haydn, Schubert, and in a sense Bruckner too, were great landscape artists. Nor can this observation be limited to Austrians, if we consider for a moment the very Teutonic second act of *Die Meistersinger von Nürnberg*. Above Pogner, Eva, Sachs, Walther and Beckmesser towers St John's Eve [Midsummer Eve, 23 June], the virtual protagonist of the entire act, from the precise moment Pogner and Eva appear at the end of the street, when the music fades and darkens with twilight, until, after the brawl, it shines in the glorious full moon and the Night Watchman slowly leaves the stage. It is St John's Eve, with its intense fragrance, that emboldens Walther and Eva; St John's Eve that turns the melancholy, profound Hans Sachs into a mocking joker'.

'*Primi Incontri con Gustav Mahler (Pagine
di Diario)*', *Parole e Musica*, p. 290.

Words and Music in
19th-Century Italian Opera

(1961-1969)

To Laura

Ladies and Gentlemen:
A century and a half had passed since Marco da Gagliano called *dramma in musica* 'truly the spectacle of princes'. The isolated aristocratic audience who attended performances of operas by Peri, Caccini, and Monteverdi had long since vanished. The musical theatre, having passed through various phases, had become a necessity for a different and wider public. At this moment the *melodramma*[1] burst on the

---

[1] 'Another word for opera in Italian was *melodramma*, which emerges mainly towards the end of the 18th century. *Melodramma* in Italian means simply what we call opera, and nothing else; it does not mean either *Melodram* (German), *i.e.* spoken declamation through a musical accompaniment [as in Jiří Benda's *Ariadne auf Naxos*, 1775], or *mélodrame* (French) with its modern English. equivalent "melodrama", so called because it was a romantic play with a good deal of incidental music – not really an opera at all.'

> Edward J. Dent, 'The Nomenclature of Opera', Part I,
> *Music and Letters*, XXV, London, 1944, p. 135.

Dallapiccola restricts the term *melodramma* to the early 19th-century operas of Rossini, Donizetti, Bellini, and Verdi through *Un Ballo in Maschera*. But 'a century and a half' after Marco da Gagliano's comment (in the preface to *Dafne*, 1608) would place the beginning of *melodramma* in this limited sense around the middle of the 18th century, while the gods and demigods disappeared from Italian opera only in the early years of the 19th.

In any case, the term is not translated here. According to *The Cambridge Italian Dictionary*,* *melodramma* 'must never be translated by the English "melodrama", for which the Italian equivalent is *melologo*', that is, 'speech

scene. It was undoubtedly a real explosion.

The earliest librettists were poets, literati, intellectuals. They had put gods and demigods on the stage and made them speak an elegant, patrician language. In the period of Italian *melodramma*, however, the gods and demigods were all cast aside. We shall see presently how the language of the libretto was transformed. Now only human beings appeared on the stage. To be sure, they were often men elevated to the rank of heroes, but men nonetheless: always and only human.

The *melodramma*, with its words, with its music, fills a lacuna in Italian literature. It compensates for the lack of a true Romanticism.

The Verdi phenomenon is inconceivable without the Risorgimento.[2] It makes little or no difference, for our discussion, whether or not Verdi played an active role in the movement. He absorbed its atmosphere and tone. At that time, religious feeling was definitely on the decline, but in its place was kindled a genuine love of country – genuine because without rhetoric.

It was the era when secret societies flourished, societies plotting against Austrian oppression. And how many conspiracies we see in Verdi's operas! Verdi, the authentic son of the Risorgimento, breathed ideals during his youth that influenced his entire life. Think for a moment of *Otello*, 1887. Austria had been driven out of Lombardy thirty years before; Italy had attained its unity. And yet Verdi, then an old man, still sang with the enthusiasm of his youth. Remember the chorus proclaiming, amidst the storm, on the shore of the island of Cyprus:

---

accompanied by orchestral music whether in a play or not'. However, the recommended translation, 'serious opera', is also misleading since it could be taken as a reference to 18th-century *opera seria*.

*Edited by Barbara Reynolds, Cambridge University Press, London, 1962, Vol. I, p. 471.

[2] 'Verdi's early life and the greater part of his operatic career fall within that phase of Italian history known as the *risorgimento*, a movement of renewal and revivification, a "rising-up-again" of the Italian people to nationhood, that stretched from the Italian conquests of Napoleon in 1796 to the unification of Italy in 1870'.

David R.B. Kimbell, *Verdi in the Age of Italian Romanticism*, Cambridge University Press, Cambridge (UK), 1981, p. 3.

Salva l'arca e la bandiera
Della veneta fortuna!

Save the vessel and the flag
Of Venetian destiny!

There is no other period in the history of Italian music comparable to that of the *melodramma*. Never before or afterwards were the people so profoundly, so decidedly at one with the composer. Something not unlike it occurred centuries earlier, in painting. We have all read how the people would genuflect when a painter carried his finished altarpiece into the church. I venture to say that not quite everyone knelt out of artistic appreciation: they worshipped the Mother of God as she entered the church. Likewise, in the 19th century, the people rejoiced, were moved and enraptured when scenes of conspiracy and conspirators were enacted, for they could recognize in them the sublimation of their feelings. And, too, their own destiny practically depended on the outcome of such conspiracies.

The era of the *melodramma* is the 'epic period' in the history of Italian music.

In that period, as a matter of fact, a style of libretto writing evolved which was by and large devoid of literary value, a style which never partook of the spoken language and was confined to the realm of opera. Only by virtue of the music did this style come to life.

From Trent, in July 1906, Busoni wrote to his wife: 'To keep me company for a few hours, I bought Verdi's *Un Ballo in Maschera*. . . . A strong work, brutal, yet of great power and plasticity. Some of its moments, I think, can be counted among Verdi's best. . . . But the libretto! And the verses! . . . *"Sento l'orma dei passi spietati"* – have you ever read anything like this? . . .'.[3]

---

[3] 'And Verdi? There has been a slight exaggeration of the horrors of the words he put to music. The sadly famous *"orma dei passi spietati"* does not move me to disdain. Woe be unto us if we read Shakespeare in this way: don't tell me, for God's sake, that a shadow is seen and not heard.* Besides, even the old libretti, which were written expressly to be set to music, confirm when they achieve certain successful expressions that

How could we fail to agree, at first glance? And yet, the truth is that Verdi was interested above all in making the words function as a sort of launch pad for the dramatic situation.[4] To Antonio Ghislanzoni, who was preparing the libretto of *Aida*, the composer wrote to justify certain radical alterations he had made in the text: 'I know very well you'll ask me: and what of verse, rhyme, stanza? I don't know how to respond, except that when the action demands it I would at once relinquish rhythm, rhyme, stanza. . .'.

Verdi was also interested in the singability of the syllables. We find an extremely probative example in the sketch for *Rigoletto*. At the outset he unhesitatingly accepts the original version: '*Diana,*[5] *Agnese per me pari sono*' [Act I, Scene 1]. Only when it comes time to elaborate the orchestral score does Verdi change the text to '*Questa o quella per me pari sono*' ('For me, this woman or that is the same'), and no demonstrations are needed to convince us that the second version is singable while '*Diana, Agnese. . .*' is not.

The language of opera librettos was a mixture of unimaginable negligence and misplaced affectation. Librettists seldom chose the simple *parole* ('words'), for instance, when they could use *accenti* ('accents') or even *detti*. To speak

---

poetry and music proceed on their own and that their conjunction remains in the realm of occasional serendipity. It is worse when they involuntarily enter the realm of the surreal'.

Eugenio Montale, 'Words and Music', *The Second Life of Art: Selected Essays*, edited and translated by Jonathan Galassi, Ecco Press, New York, 1982, pp. 232–233.

* The editor notes (p. 231) that this line has been criticized 'because it is impossible to hear a shadow. "*Sento l'orma dei passi spietati*" means "I hear the shadow of those despised steps"'.

[4] Verdi to Giulio Ricordi, 1–10 July 1870: 'By *parole sceniche* I mean those words that sculpt a situation or a character, which are always also most powerful in their effect on the public. I know that at times it is difficult to give them lofty and poetic form. But . . . (forgive the blasphemy) both poet and composer must have, when required, the talent and the courage to write neither poetry nor music . . . Horror! horror!'

Weaver, *Verdi: A Documentary Study*, p. 224.

[5] Diane de Poitiers, in Victor Hugo's drama *Le Roi s'Amuse*. In Piave's libretto the proper names have been changed (Triboulet becomes Rigoletto, etc.), so that the reference to 'Diana' is inappropriate as well as difficult to articulate at the indicated tempo, *allegretto*.

of *campane* ('bells') would have seemed too realistic, so instead they wrote *sacri bronzi* ('sacred bronzes'). They preferred *tempio* ('temple') to *chiesa* ('church') and a Gallicism frowned on by philologists, like *appressarsi*, to the Italian *avvicinarsi* ('to approach'). In librettos it wasn't *la mano* ('the hand') that grasped the sword, but *la destra* ('the right'). We sometimes read not *cannone* but *bronzo ignivomo* ('fire-vomiting bronze'), in the style of Fusinato;[6] and when a character is outside his own country, we are told he is *in stranio suolo* ('on foreign soil').

True, the Duke of Mantua exhorts Maddalena, '*Abbracciami*' ('Embrace me').[7] But we mustn't forget that Maddalena, sister of the sinister Sparafucile, is a kind of prostitute. To a woman of another class, the same Duke would have said, '*Stringimi al seno*' ('Press me to your bosom').

Thus the irrational charm of *melodramma*! A surrealist spectacle if there ever was one!

That opera runs the risk of absurdity we have known for some time. But we also know – and realized much earlier – that in certain cases, in art as in life, it is just this extreme risk which constitutes the crucial test for sublimity of style. (That is precisely what happens with Verdi.)

The word *donna* ('woman') rarely appears in librettos unless it is qualified by an adjective. And while Alfredo, in *La Traviata* [Act II, Scene 2], asks Flora's guests: '*Questa donna conoscete?*' ('You know this woman?'), it is typical of that irascible lover to refer to Violetta, a few moments later, as '*femmina*' ('wench'). More frequently librettists will write *beltà*, or even *beltade*, as if only beautiful women inhabited the earth.

This style was so rooted in the tradition of Italian opera that it was imposed even on translations. In Act I [Scene 3] of *Die Walküre*, Siegmund can rightly exclaim: '*Ein* Weib *sah ich, wonnig und hehr*' ('I saw a *woman*, dignified and lovely'); but the Italian version will unfailingly be: '*M'è apparsa sí diva beltà!*' ('A divine beauty appeared before me!'). And in

---

[6] Arnaldo Fusinato (1817–1888), poet and writer on patriotic themes.
[7] *Rigoletto*, Act III.

Guillaume Tell, where the original reads '*Nos frères* sur les eaux *s'ouvrent un chemin qui ne trahit pas*', and the German transla- tion '*Führt sie dem Bruderbund der stille* See *entgegen*', nothing should have stopped the Italian translator from writing *acqua* ('water') or *lago* ('lake'). Since the verse occurs in a recitative, there was no metrical problem to overcome. And yet the translator, rejecting the words *acqua* and *lago*, chose the grotesque locution *mobile elemento* ('movable element').

This absurd language is brought to life, as I suggested earlier, by virtue of the music and, in masterpieces, is fused with the music into a unified whole. In a good *melodramma* – even if not a masterpiece – it gives birth to that *dramatic eloquence* which, in the final analysis, is highly characteristic of and peculiar to an entire important period of music history. For me, a possible 'modernization' or even alter- ation of the librettos would be quite as inadmissible and irreverent as a transformation of the music itself.

I should now like to offer an example which better clarifies my ideas, although I will be the first to admit that it is an extreme case.

Several years ago I happened to attend a performance of *Simon Boccanegra*.[8] No doubt the majority of my listeners will remember the finale of Act I, the so-called 'revolt scene', the pearl of the opera. Simon, now the first doge, is seated on the dogal throne in the Council Chamber of the Palace of Abbots at Genoa. Surrounding him are twelve delegates of the patrician party and twelve of the plebeian. *Peace* seems to be the prevailing motif of the entire scene, despite its sudden, horrifying conclusion. In the libretto we read:

> *La stessa voce che tuonò su Rienzi*
> *Vaticinio di gloria e poi di morte,*
> *Or su Genova tuona.*
>   (Mostrando uno scritto)
>   *Ecco un messaggio*
> *Del romita di Sorga; ei per Venezia*
> *Supplica pace.*

[8] Teatro San Carlo, Naples, 19 April 1959, directed by Mario Rossi; a performance Dallapiccola did not actually attend, but heard on the radio.

The selfsame voice that thundered over Rienzi
A prophecy of glory and then of death
Now thunders over Genoa.
   (*Showing a document*)
                              Here is a message
From the hermit of the Sorgue, imploring peace
For Venice.

Paolo, a representative of the people, interjects drily:

Attenda alle sue rime
Il cantor della bionda Avignonese.

Let the minstrel of the blond from Avignon
Attend to his rhymes.

I can easily believe that in our day and age, when tabloids
and digests form the basis of 'culture', not exactly the entire
audience might instantly recall that the Sorgue is a river in
Vaucluse, a most important place in the life and art of a very
great poet. However, I do think that the allusion to 'the
blond from Avignon' should be sufficient to put the listener
on the right track, and so I was appalled to hear the
following variant:

               Ecco un messaggio
Di Francesco Petrarca; ei per Venezia
Supplica pace.

               Here is a message
From Francesco Petrarca, imploring peace
For Venice.

From the original version, with its veiled allusion, we have
arrived at a betrayal of the spirit of *melodramma*. For the very
name of Petrarch, just because it is such a great name, gives
us a realism in place of the surrealism that is one of the
postulates of musical theatre.

I said a moment ago that the music, and only the music,
pumped life into the language of librettos. And now it is
time to observe how this music, in its most diverse manifes-
tations, maintains a sort of 'common denominator' between
analogous dramatic situations.
   Think how every shock, every horror, every rape and
abduction, every surprise, every apostrophe, every curse –

and sometimes even desperate invocations – are underscored by the diminished-seventh chord. Remember that not only victories but also renunciations of victories are emphasized by trumpets or by the whole brass choir, as in Otello's desperate '*Addio vessillo trïonfale e pio!*' ('Farewell holy, triumphant banner!') [Act II]. Remember that agitated, accented staccato figurations accompany characters excluded from society, surprise attacks, conspiracies, and conspirators. From innumerable examples I shall select only five:

a)   from *Nabucco*: Ismaele is cursed by the Levites [Act II, Scene 2].

Ex. 1

b)   from *Rigoletto*: the courtiers prepare to abduct Gilda [Act I, Scene 2].

Ex. 2

c) from *Il Trovatore*: entry of Count di Luna's guards [Act II, Scene 2].

Ex. 3

d)   from *Macbeth*: the hired assassins lie in wait for Banquo [Act II, Scene 2].

Ex. 4

e) from *Un Ballo in Maschera*: beginning of the terzetto in Act II; in the background, the conspiracy.

Ex. 5

This 'formulaic style' offered the Italian people a key for comprehending the dramatic situation and identifying themselves with it. This style, which I should like to call 'fixed epithet', proved as helpful to listeners in the 19th century as – *mutatis mutandis* – the Gregorian chant or the Protestant chorale had been in other periods of music history.

Formulaic style and fixed epithet: thus have commentators on Homer described such tropes as '*nimble-footed* Iris', '*white-armed* Helen', 'Argos, *breeder of horses*', 'Achaea, *of the very beautiful women*', '*rosy-fingered* Dawn'. . . . And this is

not the least of the reasons why, at the beginning of my
lecture, I wished to define *melodramma* as the 'epic period' of
Italian music.

In 1939 the great English musicologist Edward J. Dent
asked me whether I knew an Italian treatise, or chapter of a
treatise, that described the structural principles of the aria
in *melodramma*. My answer was negative, although I couldn't
help wondering why so formidable a scholar as Dent should
have asked me, a layman, for such information.

Today I believe I can say that there was a tradition,
transmitted verbally or by example. I should now like to
consider what the *poetic quatrain* has given composers of
melodramma, and I shall specify at once that my investigation
will focus upon arias, ariosos, and cavatinas. To begin with
an elementary example, let us take four verses from one of
the best known and loved of all scenes in *La Traviata* [Act II,
Scene 2]:

> *Ogni suo aver tal femmina*
> *Per amor mio sperdea. . .*
> *Io cieco, vile, misero,*
> *Tutto accettar potea.*

> This woman squandered
> All she owned for love of me. . .
> Blind, cowardly, wretched,
> I could accept it all.

The widest vocal range in the first verse is a major sixth; in
the second verse, a minor seventh. We observe no appreci-
able metrical differences between the two verses: the slight
thrust towards the high note, so admirably underscored by
the harmony, is what strikes us most. The drama occurs in
the third verse, where the emotional crescendo[9] is attained
by means of a discontinuous and agitated syllabification,
suitably balanced by the agitation of the accompanying
figure. The fourth verse, with its emotional diminuendo –

[9] To be distinguished from the 'structural crescendo' which Dallapiccola perceives in *Wozzeck*, *Pelléas et Mélisande*, and *Christophe Colomb*. See pp.
79–80 and 100.

completely independent of the dynamics of the music –
concludes the quatrain.

Ex. 6

At this point it will be interesting to see how Verdi solved
his compositional problem when the poet added two verses
to a quatrain. We find an example in the quartet from
Rigoletto [Act III]:

Bella figlia dell'amore,
Schiavo son de' vezzi tuoi;
Con un detto sol tu puoi
Le mie pene consolar.

Beautiful daughter of love,
I am the slave of your charms;
With a single word you can
Console my sufferings.

This quatrain is set to music almost exactly in conformity
with the plan just described. There is no melodic difference

between the first and second verses, and in both the widest
vocal range is a major sixth. The emotional crescendo is
attained in the third verse, where the voice spans an octave;
the emotional diminuendo follows in the fourth. But here
the librettist has added two extra lines to the quatrain:

Vieni, e senti del mio core
Il frequente palpitar. . .

Come, and feel the quick beating
Of my heart. . .

Verdi accepts them but, for reasons of musical structure,
adds two others by repeating the third and fourth verses of
the preceding quatrain: '*Con un detto sol tu puoi/Le mie pene
consolar*'. Thus the original six verses of the libretto have
become eight. While Verdi has respected the traditional
structural plan in the first quatrain, with eight verses now at
his disposal he does not fail to regard verses 5 and 6 in turn
as the culminating point of the pair of quatrains. And in fact
if the voice reaches A flat in the crescendo of the first
quatrain, in the *overall crescendo* of the quatrain-pair it goes
up to B flat; and the diminuendo is accomplished by
repeating the music of verses 3 and 4 of the first stanza.

Ex. 7

In Leonora's cavatina in *Il Trovatore* ['*Tacea la notte*', Act I, Scene 2], the libretto presents two stanzas of ten verses each. The metrical articulation of the first two couplets is identical; at the end of the second, a rising tendency (minor third). Verses 7 and 8 function in the second quatrain as do verses 3 and 4 in the first: the big emotional crescendo comes on the penultimate verse, the diminuendo on the last. Verses 5 and 6 represent an interpolation, and this is the structural innovation of the piece –

Ex. 8

– an innovation we shall meet again in Leonora's aria '*D'amor sull'ali rosee*' [Act IV, Scene 1], where the librettist once more offers the composer a stanza of ten verses. Observe the last two verses (sections *C* and *D* of the second quatrain), Verdi's greatest melodic miracle, so different from all the rest (Ex. 9). Where else has he made such frequent use of wide intervals?

I should like to re-emphasize that the emotional crescendo is always found on the third verse of a quatrain, or on the third couplet of a quatrain-pair. It can be effected by means of rhythmic excitation, harmonic surprise, or an upward thrust of the vocal line. More often than not the end result is achieved through the collaboration of two, or even all three, of these elements; rarely will a fourth element contribute to the crescendo, namely an absolutely novel twist of instrumentation. I shall return to this topic presently, in connexion with a passage from *Otello*.

A highly significant example of the voice's upward thrust occurs in the duet from *Un Ballo in Maschera* [Act II], where the tenor sings '*O qual soave brivido*' ('Oh, what sweet thrill'). There is a fermata, in fact, at the beginning of the third couplet. Here, for the first time in our examples, we

Ex. 9

encounter a coda, and since it is based on reiterations of words previously heard, this coda is totally independent of the plan of the aria.

While up to this point I have quoted exclusively from the operas of Verdi, one shouldn't infer that the same structural plan was not used by Rossini, Bellini, and Donizetti as well. In Mathilde's aria 'Sombres forêts', in Act II of *Guillaume Tell*, where the third verse lacks a contrasting metrical articulation, the harmony assumes the responsibility for emphasizing the climax of the first quatrain. And the classic example of Italian melody, '*Casta diva*',[10] provides the most abundant confirmation of the plan I have been illustrating. Indeed, so important has the third verse become that even its duration is affected. If the first verse comprises sixteen units of three quavers, and the second verse fifteen (including the rests), the third verse contains no fewer than twenty-two units and the fourth verse only four.

We should not assume that in his last creative period Verdi decisively renounced the traditional plan. An example from Act I of *Otello* will suffice to demonstrate it. At the climax of the 'storm scene', where the chorus and orchestra are marked *ff*, *tutta forza*, Boito wrote the following verses:

[*Dio, fulgor della bufera!*
[*Dio, sorriso della duna!*
[*Salva l'arca e la bandiera*
[*Della veneta fortuna!*
[*Tu, che reggi gli astri e il Fato!*
[*Tu, che imperi al mondo e al ciel!*
[*Fa che in fondo al mar placato*
[*Posi l'àncora fedel.*

    God, lightning in the storm!
    God, the smile of the shore!
    Save the vessel and the flag
    Of Venetian destiny!
    Thou, who rulest the stars and Fate!
    Thou, who governest world and sky!
    Grant that the faithful anchor
    Rest on the bottom of the calmed sea.

There is greater complexity here, perhaps, than in the cases cited previously. However, it will not pass unnoticed that in the third verse, '*Tu, che reggi gli astri e il Fato! Tu, che imperi al mondo e al ciel!*', the emotional crescendo is effected by means of the harmony and by two incredible cymbal crashes on the weak beat of bars 4 and 8, marked *Soli*.

At the beginning of this lecture, I alluded to the sketch of

---

[10] Bellini, *Norma*, Act I.

Rigoletto. Let's glance now at its last page, containing a rough draft of the canzone '*La donna è mobile*' – obviously nothing more than a note jotted down in haste. In the definitive version – the one we know, also found in the complete sketch – the music for the first and second verses corresponds (even if not in key) to that of the note hastily scribbled on the last page. Not so the music for the third verse which, in the rough draft, completely disregards the 'rule'; there is, in fact, neither rhythmic animation nor the possibility of harmonic surprise. What is more, the melody, instead of pushing upwards, descends.

Ex. 10

With the aim of underlining once more the fundamental importance of the third verse, it may be useful to dwell on a rather special case. We all know that most of the variants in the original text of Italian operas are due to the ambition of singers. There is one, however, that not only convinces me but seems more beautiful than the written text. Unfortunately, I haven't been able to ascertain whether this variant is long-standing or recent, and whether it was approved by Verdi himself.

In the aria '*Ah sí, ben mio, coll'essere*' from Act III [Scene 2] of *Il Trovatore*, Manrico sings the same quatrain twice: in section *A* (Ex. 11) the highest note is D flat, in section *C* it is A flat. The second time, in section *A* the top note is E flat (although very short), to which I think the B flat often sung in place of the A flat as written in section *C* corresponds marvellously: it is the fulcrum of the entire quatrain.

The performer cannot but thoroughly examine the third verse before establishing the general tempo of the aria.

Was there a poetic tradition that consciously or unconsciously governed the structure of the aria in Italian *melodramma*? I can't say. But certainly, the perusal of an immense number of closed, rhymed hendecasyllabic quatrains in

Ex. 11

Italian and French poetry, from Dante to Baudelaire, makes us realize that the second verse is simply a continuation of the first on a slightly higher emotional level. The culminating point is *the third*, and the last verse concludes 'diminuendo'. I shall offer just four of the innumerable examples.

From Dante:[11]

Tanto gentile e tanto onesta pare
La donna mia, quand'ella altrui saluta,
Che ogne lingua deven tremando muta,
E gli occhi no l'ardiscon di guardare.

So deeply to be reverenced, so fair,
My lady is when she her smile bestows,
All sound of speaking falters to a close
And eyes which would behold her do not dare.

From Petrarch:[12]

---

[11] *La Vita Nuova*, XXVI; transl. Barbara Reynolds, Penguin Books, Harmondsworth, 1969, p. 76.
[12] *Rime*, XCI; editor's translation.

La bella donna che cotanto amavi
Subitamente s'è da noi partita,
E, per quel ch'io ne speri, al ciel salita;
Sì furon gli atti suoi dolci e soavi.

The lovely lady whom you so adored
Went suddenly and left us unattended;
To heaven now, I hope, she has ascended,
Her grace and gentle nature to reward.

Observe the participle *salita* in the third verse, a verb form clearly denoting ascent. From Victor Hugo:[13]

Ruth songeait et Booz dormait; l'herbe était noire;
Les grelots des troupeaux palpitaient vaguement;
Une immense bonté tombait du firmament;
C'était l'heure tranquille où les lions vont boire.

Ruth mused and Boaz slept; the grass was black;
The bells of the flocks were tinkling vaguely;
A boundless benevolence fell from the sky;
It was that calm hour when the lions go to drink.

In the third verse, the verb *tomber* denoting descent is altogether cancelled by the adjective *immense* and the noun *firmament*. Finally, from Baudelaire:[14]

C'est la mort qui console, hélas!, et qui fait vivre;
C'est le but de la vie, et c'est le seul espoir
Qui, comme un élixir, nous monte et nous enivre,
Et nous donne le coeur de marcher jusqu'au soir;

Death? Death is our one comfort! – is the bread whereby
We live, the wine that warms us when all hope is gone;
The very goal of Life. That we shall one day die:
This is the thought which gives us courage to go on.

Observe in the third verse *two* verbs denoting ascent, *monter* and *enivrer* ('to intoxicate', 'to elate'), not to mention the noun *élixir*!

Could the *melodramma*, 'popular' theatre par excellence, have evolved – unbeknown even to its creators – from

---

[13] '*Booz Endormi*' in *La Légende des Siècles*; editor's translation.
[14] '*La Mort des Pauvres*' in *Les Fleurs du Mal*; transl. Edna St Vincent Millay, Washington Square Press, New York, 1962, p. 143.

something primitive, elementary? If we examine that part of the 13th-century liturgical drama *The Play of Daniel*[15] in which the protagonist tells the King the meaning of '*MANE, THECHEL, PHARES*', we cannot help being impressed by its structural resemblance to the majority of the arias in *melodramma*.

Ex. 12

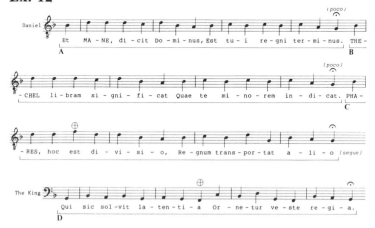

But I wouldn't want anyone to believe that I consider the emotional crescendo in the penultimate section of a musical quatrain the exclusive property of Italian *melodramma*, for it can also be found in other kinds of music. The first name that comes to mind is Schubert – above all the 'popular' Schubert, certainly not the composer of *Nacht und Träume*, where the musical structure is totally different. Here we may aptly recall that Alban Berg, with great penetration, pointed out the 'instrumental' characteristics of the voice in Schubert's Lieder.[16] Now in my view, the supreme originality of *melodramma*, its uniqueness, is due to its having overlooked – indeed, quite deliberately disregarded – the Italian instrumental tradition.

[15] Although the only surviving manuscript (British Museum, Egerton 2615) dates from the 13th century, it was almost certainly written a hundred years earlier. See Noah Greenberg, *The Play of Daniel*, Oxford University Press, New York, 1959.

[16] Berg advanced this idea in the talk '*Was ist Atonal?*', broadcast on Vienna Radio, 23 April 1930.

Another name that should be mentioned is Beethoven, and one of the most important examples in this regard is the rondo of the Piano Sonata in E minor, Op. 90. We have it on Schindler's testimony that Beethoven entitled this movement '*Conversazioni con la Diletta*' ('Conversations with the Beloved'): hence, a dramatic situation without staging.

But what happens in the composition of an aria in *melodramma* is rather different; the third section is a 'gesture'. And to illustrate this, I could do no better than to quote two examples virtually identical in melody yet completely contrasting in effect (Ex. 13): on the one hand, a passage from the second subject of the *adagio* of Mozart's Violin Concerto in A major [K.219]; on the other, a passage from the sextet in *Lucia di Lammermoor* [Act II]. In the former, the third and fourth sections develop according to the logic and rules of instrumental dialectic. In the latter we find the 'gesture', which I think we may consider one of the *dramatic conditions* of *melodramma*.[17]

*   *   *

While I have tried until this point to demonstrate the analogy between the structure of the poetic quatrain and that of the aria in *melodramma*, I should now like to broaden my scope and attempt to show how Verdi applied such a structural principle to a large form, like the terzetto in Act II of *Un Ballo in Maschera* [1859].

Let's begin by examining the libretto. Each of the characters is given eight verses. In the older editions, which we

---

[17] 'But every one of Mozart's operas is a pure symphonic score and there is something of an opera scene in each quartet. The gifted theorist Momigny* made the experiment of putting words in the style of an aria in *opera seria* to the first movement of Mozart's D minor Quartet; through this experiment, when listening to the piece thus newly interpreted (and otherwise not changed by a note) we experience the effect of being thrown suddenly into the middle of a Mozart opera.'

Busoni, *The Essence of Music*, p. 3.

*Joseph-Jérôme de Momigny (1762–1842), scholar and music editor, is chiefly remembered for a theory of phrasing important in the 19th century.

Ex. 13

must assume correspond to Antonio Somma's manuscript, just as in those more recently printed (see the libretto accompanying the recording Toscanini made at New York in 1954), the characters enter in the following order: Amelia, soprano; Riccardo, tenor; Renato, baritone.

My first observation – a fairly exciting one – is that in setting this terzetto to music, Verdi reversed the order of the male voices established by the librettist. He shifted the entry of the baritone from third to second place, vice versa that of the tenor. This observation alone is sufficient to document the remarkable lucidity of Verdi's approach. The climax of the terzetto is now reserved for Riccardo, the tenor. To the three stanzas provided by the librettist, the composer has added a fourth by way of a musical reprise, in which the characters repeat some (tenor) or all (soprano and baritone) of the words they have previously sung. Verdi, with his formidable dramatic instinct, could hardly fail to realize that the remorse – almost a guilt complex – expressed by the tenor represented the culminating point of the piece. What we have, then, is a total success.

If, more than a century after its composition, we listen to this terzetto with contemporary ears (the only ones we can use), if we read it with contemporary eyes (again, the only valid ones), we shall perceive things which until yesterday we should have overlooked. And so we will talk about macrostructures and microstructures with no fear of being tagged 'sophisticates'. The terzetto from *Un Ballo in Maschera* has been called beautiful, even ravishing. Many are content with such assessments. The terzetto will remain beautiful, ravishing, even after my attempt at analysis, for analysis can neither detract from what is aesthetically perfect nor add to what is artistically worthless.

May I remind you of a famous aphorism of the Doctor Angelicus, St Thomas Aquinas, concerning the components of beauty? '*Ad pulchritudinem tria requiruntur: integritas, consonantia, claritas*'. We may interpret this as follows:

Unity – namely, the design as a whole;
Harmony – the equilibrium among the constituent parts;
Clarity – the essential expression of what one has to say.

Let us examine the first *macro*structure, *A*, corresponding to the soprano's stanza (see Figure 1, pp. 158–9). Each of the *micro*structures *a*, *b*, *c*, *d*, represents four bars; *e*, a codetta of eight bars. Codettas of equal duration are found also at the end of the second and fourth *macro*structures, *B* and *D*. (Please don't forget that the codettas and the coda, *macro*structure *E*, are unrelated to the stanzas in the libretto but have a strictly musical importance: in them the characters repeat the words they have previously sung.)

First *micro*structure, *a*:

Odi tu come fremono cupi
Per quest'aura gli accenti di morte?

Do you hear how grimly resound
In this air the accents of death?

35.

Ricordate una famosa frase del dottore Angelico, San Tommaso d'Aquino, circa gli elementi costitutivi della Bellezza?

<u>Ad pulchritudinem tria requiruntur:</u>
<u>integritas, consonantia, claritas.</u>

Nel nostro caso, dunque:

<u>Integrità</u> — cioè il disegno nel suo complesso;

<u>Consonanza</u> — cioè l'equilibrio tra le parti che lo costituiscono;

<u>Chiarezza</u> — cioè l'espressione essenziale di quanto si ha a dire.

Esaminiamo la prima <u>macrostruttura</u>; corrispondente alla strofa del soprano. Ciascuna delle <u>microstrutture</u> a) b) c) d) rappresenta 4 battute; la <u>microstruttura</u> e) rappresenta la <u>Codetta</u>, della durata di otto battute. Una <u>codetta</u> della stessa durata si trova alla fine della seconda e della quarta <u>macrostruttura</u>. (Non si dimentichi, per favore,

From the manuscript of 'Parole e Musica nel Melodramma (1961–1969)'.

C (tenor)

$d]$ *Son colui che nel cor lo ferì.*

$c]$ *Ah! l'amico ho tradito pur io . . .*

$b]$ *Che minacciano il vivere mio?*

$a]$ *(Traditor, congiurati son essi,*

B (baritone)

$d]$ *Va, ti salva, del popolo è vita*
Questa vita che getti così.

Climax of $A + B$
(baritone and soprano)

$c]$ *Va, ti salva, o che il varco all'uscita*
Qui fra poco serrarsi vedrai;

$b]$ *Allo scambio dei detti esecrati*
Ogni destra la daga brandì

$a]$ *Fuggi, fuggi: per l'orrida via*
Sento l'orma de' passi spietati.

A (soprano)

$d]$ *Al tuo capo già volser la mira . . .*
Per pietà, va, t'invola di qui.

Climax of first stanza: the voice
reaches high F; dynamic crescendo
followed by diminuendo; weak beat
accented by two horns, violas, cellos.

$c]$ *Ne' lor petti scintillano d'ira . . .*
E già piomban, t'accerchiano fitti . . .

$b]$ *Di lassù, da quei negri dirupi,*
Il segnal de'nemici partì.

$a]$ *Odi tu come fremono cupi*
Per quest'aura gli accenti di morte?

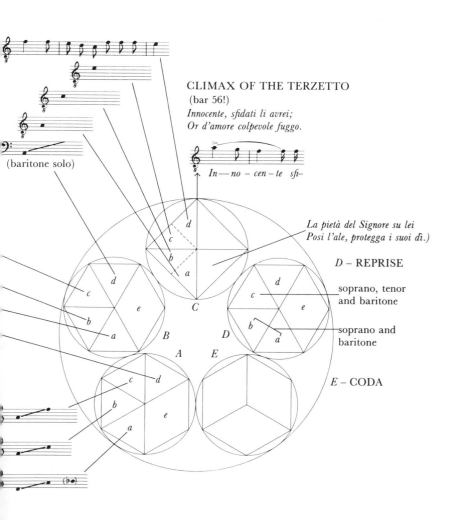

CLIMAX OF THE TERZETTO
(bar 56!)
Innocente, sfidati li avrei;
Or d'amore colpevole fuggo.

In — no – cen – te sfi–

(baritone solo)

La pietà del Signore su lei
Posi l'ale, protegga i suoi dì.)

D – REPRISE

soprano, tenor
and baritone

soprano and
baritone

E – CODA

Figure 1

The vocal range is D to A (with B flat as a neighbouring tone).

In the second *micro*structure, *b*, we find the same metrical pattern:

Di lassù, da quei negri dirupi,
Il segnal de' nemici partì.

From up there, from those black crags,
The enemies' signal was fired.

The melody begins its upward thrust. Instead of the fifth D–A, we have the fifth F–C.

The third *micro*structure, *c*–

Ne' lor petti scintillano d'ira. . .
E già piomban, t'accerchiano fitti. . .

In their bosoms they flash with rage. . .
And they already plunge down, encircle you, closely. . .

–represents the apex of the first *macro*structure, *A*. Three elements contribute to this effect: the vocal range reaches high F; there is a dynamic crescendo, followed by a dynamic diminuendo; and, as if this weren't enough, the weak beat of the bar is unexpectedly accented by two French horns, violas, and 'cellos.

The fourth *micro*structure, *d*–

Al tuo capo già volser la mira. . .
Per pietà, va, t'invola di qui.

They have already turned their aim at your head. . .
For pity's sake, go, flee from here.

–is the conclusion of the quatrain-pair and, compared with the previous section, represents an emotional diminuendo. We shouldn't be deceived by Amelia's high A on the word *qui*, merely a note of resolution that does not in the least minimize the importance of the high F, the climax of the third *micro*structure (*c*) in terms of vocal range. On the contrary, I would say that this A is totally independent of the three subsequent A's, repeated almost as cries of anguish. The vocal scores of the opera do not show an accent on the first A (not even the first edition, which obviously must have been based on the original manuscript score), but the three subsequent A's *are* accented.

The second *macro*structure, *B*, given to the baritone, is identical in form with the first. The variant in the concluding verses 7 and 8 is due only to the necessity of arriving at the dominant at the end of the stanza. One further disparity is the entrance of the soprano, an octave above the baritone, in the third *micro*structure (*c*), producing a double crescendo.[18]

We now come to the third *macro*structure, *C*, formally the climax of the whole terzetto.

> *(Traditor, congiurati son essi,*
> *Che minacciano il vivere mio?*
> *Ah! l'amico ho tradito pur io. . .*
> *Son colui che nel cor lo ferì.*

> (Traitors, conspirators are they,
> Who threaten my existence?
> Ah! I too have betrayed my friend. . .
> I am the one who wounded him in the heart.

Whereas in the two preceding *macro*structures, verses 1 and 2, as well as 3 and 4, are joined by the musical phrase, here the first four verses are divided from each other by quaver rests. Already there is one element which contributes to the emotional crescendo, and the composer will add two others: the first verse is based on the note A, the second on C, the third on E, and the fourth begins on F – as you see, the necessary upward thrust is rigorously observed (triple crescendo). Note, moreover, the very striking interjections '*Va, fuggi*', '*Ti salva*' ('Go, flee', 'Save yourself') by the soprano and baritone.

Without a rest the tenor begins verses 5 and 6, at once the climax of the third *macro*structure (*C*) and of the whole terzetto:

> *Innocente, sfidati li avrei;*
> *Or d'amore colpevole fuggo.*

> Innocent, I would have defied them;
> Now guilty of love, I flee.

[18] The soprano again joins the baritone in the codetta (*e*) to reinforce the words '*Va, va, va*'.

After the high A is attained on the first syllable ('In-*nocente*'), the vocal line gradually descends: the linking of verse 5 with 6 and 7 with 8 marks the beginning of the emotional decrescendo, both of the *macro*structure and of the entire piece.

Here, at verse 7, and not before, Verdi placed the indication *poco allargando, col canto*. Unfortunately, it is too often anticipated, seriously interrupting the rhythmic force of the composition.

I must now count the bars of the five *macro*structures in order to clarify their proportional relationships. The first, *A*, comprises 24 bars; the second, *B*, also 24; the third, *C* – for dramatic reasons the most concise (there's no codetta) – 16 bars; the fourth, *D*, again 24; and the coda, *E*, 23. There is a fermata on the last chord of the coda which, according to 19th-century practice, simply doubles the note values. So the coda, too, may be counted as 24 bars. The total is therefore 112.

The tenor's verse '*Innocente, sfidati li avrei*', the climax of the composition, begins precisely at bar 56: arithmetically the centre of the piece. This seems to me marvellous, all the more since Verdi certainly did not count the bars. It was sheer intuition that led him to work this miracle of proportions.

Thus we have reached the concluding part of the terzetto. The fourth *macro*structure, *D*, is musically similar to the first. Observe, however, that two voices (soprano and baritone) – not a single voice, as before – take part in the first eight bars of this 'reprise'; and that starting from the third *micro*structure, *c*, the tenor also participates. Therefore, *three* voices are heard in the fourth *macro*structure (*D*), two voices in the parallel passage of the second (*B*).

Concluding the terzetto is the coda of 24 bars: that is, the sum of the bars in the three codettas of *macro*structures *A*, *B*, and *D*. A coda of merely conclusive character and, if you like, a trifle 'commonplace'. This adjective is not intended as a *criticism*: it is only a matter of comprehending (which means justifying) a dialectical and stylistic procedure that characterized an entire era. Everyone is perfectly free to accept or reject it. But to argue from the '1964 perspective', to take an anti-historical position, would be tantamount to judging the 29 bars of C major at the end of Beethoven's Fifth Symphony 'too long', or the *ottava rima* of *Orlando Furioso* formally 'monotonous', or the proportions of Wagnerian opera 'excessive'. And especially unjustified is an eight-bar cut in the coda sometimes made in performances of the opera – ridiculous, considering that these eight bars last scarcely ten seconds! This cut disturbs the balance of the whole composition.

Ladies and Gentlemen:

Before taking leave, I should like to have the honour and pleasure of listening with you to the scena and terzetto from *Un Ballo in Maschera*. Concentrated in this excerpt we shall find several elements of the formulaic style and some famous pearls of libretto language.

A lonely field at night. On the stage, Amelia and her lover. Another person approaches – or rather, 'draws nigh' (*s'appressa*) – whom the lover recognizes as his best friend and Amelia, her husband. Instead of calling him 'husband' (*marito*), which would really have been a little too 'bourgeois', she uses the word *consorte*, much more in keeping with the language of *melodramma*. And the recognition on the woman's part is underscored by the diminished-seventh chord: Amelia covers her face with a veil to avoid being recognized by her husband. He had come to warn his friend of the conspirators lying in wait for him on the surrounding hills, who had already spotted him in the lonely field accompanied by a veiled woman – naturally described as a *beltade*. The lover could still save himself by escaping down a pathway, but he is unwilling to leave the veiled woman alone in the company of her husband.

Three souls oppressed by anguish, each for a different reason; and in the background, the conspiracy. The composer's genius – the 'genius of the dramatic accent', in Busoni's felicitous definition[19] – triumphs over the absurd situation, the grotesque language, the rickety syntax, and the pathos of the formalistic style.

---

[19] Translated as 'genius for climaxes' in *The Essence of Music*, p. 9; *cf. Lo Sguardo Lieto*, p. 123.

Pages from a Diary
Rigoletto

Florence, 23 January 1962

Yesterday I heard *Rigoletto* once more.[1] And so I've had a further demonstration of the meddlesomeness of certain producers who, whatever their knowledge of music, seem to consider it a factor of minor importance. Must opera then become mere 'pageantry'? Too many producers have obviously forgotten Busoni's fundamental dictum:[2]

> The theatre all too quickly swallows the nourishment which makes it capable of living, and is always greedy for new food. Only the soundness and cleanness of the score is able, after its short existence on the stage is over, to preserve an opera as an artistic monument for posterity. Many an opera which passed for dead has been brought to light again by the excellence of the score.

Opera, today, is no longer heard but *seen* – as if the cinema weren't quite sufficient for seeing![3] An evening at the opera appears to be steadily descending to the level of 'entertainment'.

The curtain rises on Scene 1, 'a magnificent hall in the

[1] At the Teatro Comunale, Florence, conducted by Bruno Bartoletti; Tatiana Pavlova, producer; Aldo Calvo, scene designer.
[2] *The Essence of Music*, p.14
[3] 'After all, the sets are really nothing but a scenic abridgement. Forest, Church, Knight's Hall. And in this case (without our missing it) there is no connecting context. We do not see the path which leads through the town to the church and on to the forest and up to the castle into whose knightly hall we step. Those are the tasks and crafts of the cinematograph and in no way belong to the opera.' *Ibid.*, p. 13.

ducal palace'. The splendour of the hall can be suggested by a thousand visible signs: murals, tapestries, statues, exotic plants, ottomans, greyhounds. . . . Yes, we get the picture. The producer wants to portray, as compellingly as possible, the sybaritic character of the rakish Duke of Mantua. Such is the lack of confidence nowadays in the power of music. Yet for those who still attribute some importance to the music, for those who *listen* and don't merely *watch*, the character of the Duke is already apparent – and perfectly delineated – a few minutes after the opera begins. The ballata '*Questa o quella per me pari sono*' is all we need to understand him completely.

The first act comprises two scenes: after the one in the 'magnificent hall', we are transported to 'the most deserted end of a blind alley'.

At the conclusion of Scene 1, Verdi writes: 'The curtain falls for a moment to permit a change of scene'. But if the 'moment' Verdi prescribed stretches into an interval of ten or fifteen minutes, as too often happens when the stage must be cleared of the bric-à-brac and junk accumulated there to emphasize what the music, by itself, has already made explicit, the audience can no longer understand the marvellous architecture of the work nor comprehend it dramatically. (In Florence there was an actual intermission, longer than the first scene, so that the opera grew to *four acts!*[4])

One observation about the comprehension of *the drama* will be sufficient. Monterone curses both the Duke and Rigoletto at the outset. Afterwards, at the end of his invective, the malediction is addressed to Rigoletto alone, and his response is '(What do I hear? Oh, horror!)'. The first words the protagonist will utter at the beginning of Scene 2

---

[4] In a letter of 29 June 1853 to Antonio Somma, who had just finished a first outline of the *Re Lear* libretto, Verdi wrote:
'The one thing that has always kept me from using Shakespearean subjects more frequently has been precisely this necessity of changing scenes all the time. When I went to the theatre it was something that made me suffer immensely, it was like watching a magic lantern. In this the French are right: they arrange their dramas so that they need only one scene for each act'. Weaver, *Verdi: A Documentary Study*, p. 191.

and twice pronounce, terrified, a little later are '(That old man cursed me!)'. Now if Verdi's indication – the 'moment' I alluded to – is ignored, the audience will have the impression that Rigoletto is evoking a distant memory rather than venting the recently experienced terror which still obsesses him.[5]

Regarding *both the music and the drama*, I would mention that after the curse comes the concluding episode of Scene 1, in which the Duke, his three courtiers, and the chorus take part:

> *Oh tu che la festa audace hai turbato,*
> *Da un genio d'inferno qui fosti guidato.*

> Oh, you who have boldly disturbed the festivity,
> Were led here by a demon from hell.

Rigoletto interjects the parenthetical '(Horror!)' once, in bar 9, then participates in the ensemble from bar 36 on: from the moment Monterone starts cursing him again.

Finally, concerning *the music*: if there is a prolonged break, or – worse – if the opera is divided into four acts, the subtle structural connexions between the openings of the first and third acts will no longer be perceptible; not to mention the quasi-thematic relationship between the first-act episode Liszt would have called '*tempestuoso*'[6] (Ex. 14) and the storm (*tempesta*) in Act III (Ex. 15).

It seems to me unacceptable that the practices of scene designers and producers, however inventive, should hinder

---

[5] 'What Verdi was most interested in was the effect of the curse on Rigoletto's mind – that is the real psychological crux – so it is only as Rigoletto broods over the incident on his way home that the curse motif is actually formulated'.

Kimbell, *Verdi in the Age of Italian Romanticism*, p. 439.

See also Kerman, *Opera as Drama*, p. 156.

[6] Liszt employs the expression '*tempestuoso*' repeatedly in all his piano music, to indicate a nuance, a subdued chiaroscuro verging rather on *piano*. It evokes the menace of an advancing but still distant thunderstorm: a painterly idea, often misconstrued or even interpreted in the opposite manner. See *Réminiscences de Don Juan*, critical edition by Ferruccio Busoni, Breitkopf & Härtel, Leipzig [1918], p. 6.   —LD

Ex. 14

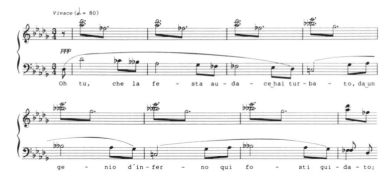

Ex. 15

rather than facilitate the public's understanding of the opera.

* * *

Florence, 26 January 1962

The notes taken a few days ago suggest a re-reading of Massimo Mila's 'Open Letter to Arthur Honegger and Modern Music', dated Turin, 26 February 1950, and published as an appendix to his *Giuseppe Verdi* (Laterza, Bari, 1958). A most civilized essay, one that states its case with uncommon equilibrium. I regret that I must limit myself to quoting a few sentences, because the whole 'Letter' deserves thought.

Honegger, in his introduction to the *Almanach de Musique 1950*, felt obliged to protest 'against the encroaching commercialism in music and against the exclusion of all innovation from musical life'. (I think he intended to comment on the commercial spirit in associations, not in the sphere of composers, where in 1950 it was still a very isolated though much discussed phenomenon.)

Mila's first question for Honegger is this: '. . .why then was it necessary for you to be unjust to a masterpiece like *Rigoletto*, in order to lodge a justified complaint about the commercialization of musical life?' And he goes on to quote the composer: 'Is the applause for the "*piuma al vento*", whose vulgarity would throttle any accordion in the rue de Lappe, really enough to exalt this story about a mistake in packaging?' Here Mila asks a second, no less pointed question: 'Is it possible that a musician like you discerned nothing in this masterpiece except the "*piuma al vento*", that harmless bagatelle?'

Mila concludes with the hope that Honegger was writing in 'a fit of pique' and would repudiate his own words if he spoke of Verdi's masterpiece 'from first-hand knowledge'. In polemics such fairness is hard to find.

Mila didn't think to inquire whether, by chance, Honegger might have suspected that the notorious travesty staged at the Paris Opéra under the title *Rigoletto* – perhaps an unintentional parody – bore no resemblance to Verdi's text. Furthermore, out of courtesy for a famous composer with whom he was personally acquainted, Mila seems quite inclined to concede that '*La donna è mobile*' is a 'harmless bagatelle'.[7]

---

[7] In a letter to Dallapiccola dated Asolo (Treviso), 20 November 1970, Gian Francesco Malipiero writes:

'. . .I understand Honegger's resentment. At that moment in Paris, the operas of the "Italian Risorgimento" were condemned *en bloc*, and perhaps it was due to their success on Parisian stages.

While I am certainly not disposed to defend something that needs no defence, I shall comment on a couple of passages. Let's examine the first ten pages of Act I (in the vocal score, published by Ricordi). This episode can be divided into three clearly differentiated sections: Preludio/ Introduzione/Ballata. The preludio is an instrumental rendition of the phrase '(That old man cursed me!)'. In the introduzione, the Duke is talking with his courtier Borsa amid the sumptuous revelry. First he refers to Gilda, whom he doesn't yet know by name but is determined to possess. A bit later he couches his admiration for his guest, the Countess Ceprano, in elegant, restrained language. Then follows the ballata '*Questa o quella per me pari sono*'.

Now let's look at the first seven pages of the third act. This episode also consists of three sections: Preludio/Scena/ Canzone. After the succinct and sombre orchestral introduction, Rigoletto converses with his daughter on the street. Next, inside the squalid tavern, the Duke, dressed as 'a regular cavalry officer', engages Sparafucile in repartee. The following exchange is found in both the sketch and the autograph score:

Duca:	*Due cose, e tosto...*
Sparafucile:	*Quali?*
Duca:	*Tua sorella e del vino...*
Duke:	Two things, and quickly...
Sparafucile:	What?
Duke:	Your sister and some wine...

'In July 1920 my *Sette Canzoni* had its première at the Paris Opéra, on the same bill as *Rigoletto*: a disaster. What a strange fate, mine. Maybe I deserved no better.

'From childhood, remember, I heard Verdi spoken of at home as the cause of our family catastrophe. The story goes that the success of my grandfather's* *Attila* infuriated the publisher Ricordi, because Verdi's *Attila* [1846] was a fiasco. The publisher bought my grandfather's opera, changed its title [to *Ildegonda di Borgogna*], and prevented further performances. My grandfather then put himself into the hands of an impresario. Villa, property, everything was consumed – and in my childish imagination, the catastrophe was called Giuseppe Verdi.'

LD: Saggi..., pp. 104–105.

*Francesco Malipiero (1824–87).

Except that in the autograph, the Duke's rejoinder is emended; a variant written with different ink doesn't strike me as being in Verdi's handwriting. Did the original version seem too ribald for the audience of 1851? Or did the moralizing censor, vigilant as always and never more so than when dealing with Giuseppe Verdi, interfere? In fact, the published edition, the one that is performed, reads: '*Una stanza e del vino*. . . ('A room and some wine. . .'). All the same, it would be well to remember the first version and consider that after three bars of recitative, the Duke launches into the canzone '*La donna è mobile*'. (Significantly, Verdi entitled it 'canzone'.[8])

We needn't dwell on the degree of structural correspondence between the two passages just examined, but it will be worthwhile to compare the two entrances of the Duke of Mantua. In the 'magnificent hall', where lords and ladies of noble lineage are assembled, he sings the ballata '*Questa o quella*. . .', full of patrician elegance and froth. Awaiting his assignation with the harlot Maddalena in Sparafucile's squalid tavern, he could only be expected to strike up the plebeian air '*La donna è mobile*'. There is nothing scandalous in this vulgarity (luckily for us, Verdi never regarded *goût* as an essential ingredient in artistic creation), but rather a perfect portrayal of the Duke. When in Rome. . . . A *fickle* man, no less inconstant than the heroine of his proverbial song – and more so.

At the end of this song the Duke addresses his first words to Maddalena, who has meanwhile come downstairs in gypsy costume:

> *Un dì, se ben rammentomi,*
> *O bella, t'incontrai. . .*

> One day, if I remember right,
> I met you, O beauty. . .

Listen to Toscanini's courageous performance – the bravest and most convincing of all I have heard. Toscanini doesn't shrink from the so-called vulgarity. If, in this sense, the

---

[8] To distinguish it, as a popular song (*canzone di strada, canzone popolare*), from the serious aria.

orchestral opening of the canzone is exceedingly decisive, bordering right on the controversial, in the dialogue between the Duke and Maddalena the orchestra is converted into a sublime, enormous hurdy-gurdy.

Sparafucile had already managed to introduce us indirectly, nonetheless clearly, to Maddalena, a character who moves into the foreground of the drama during Act III.[9] When Rigoletto asks him [in Act I, Scene 2] how he can murder people so casually in his own house, Sparafucile replies:

È facile. . .
M'aiuta mia sorella. . .
Per le vie danza. . . è bella. . .

It's easy. . .
My sister helps me. . .
She dances in the streets . . . she's beautiful. . .

In Alban Berg's *Lulu*, the orchestral variations (*grandioso, grazioso, funèbre, affettuoso*) composed as a link between the two scenes of Act III were intended to encapsulate the crucial moments in the life of his heroine. Frank Wedekind's theme is heard in its final, fragmentary form at the end of the fourth variation: only four bars, with the comment '*wie eine Drehorgel*'. Lulu has sunk to the nadir of degradation: she's a whore in the East End of London. And so, more than eighty years after *Rigoletto*, Alban Berg still regarded the hurdy-gurdy as the most suitable instrument for the dramatic and musical portrayal of a prostitute.

In light of that the accordions of the rue de Lappe may do as they wish – choke or blush. It's all the same to us.

---

[9] In fact, it is Maddalena's tearful entreaty that her brother wait before slaying the Duke which makes Gilda realize something new to her and completely unanticipated: 'What! such a woman weeps!. . ./And I will not give him aid!' So Gilda is moved to sacrifice herself by the weeping of Maddalena, the key character in the scene. –LD

Reflections on
Simon Boccanegra
(1969)

'Stupid criticism and praise more stupid still! Not a single elevated or artistic idea! No one has wished to point out my intentions; absurdities and stupidities all the time. . . .' Such were Verdi's sentiments in a letter to Tito Ricordi,[1] after the performances of *Aida* at La Scala. Several years later he answered Countess Clarina Maffei, who was urging him to write another opera: 'Why on earth should I write music? What should I succeed in doing? What have I to gain from it? The result would be wretched. I should be told all over again that I *don't know how to write*, and that I have become a *follower of Wagner*. A fine sort of glory! After a career of almost forty years to end up as an *imitator*!'[2]

Clearly, if Verdi was sensitive to unfavourable reviews, he was hypersensitive to insults. His estrangement of sixteen years from Arrigo Boito, whom he first met in Paris, in 1862, and who was destined to play such an important part in the last period of Verdi's creative activity, stemmed from a crude attack the twenty-one-year-old poet had launched against him in 1863. At a reception following the première of *I Profughi Fiamminghi* by his bosom friend Franco Faccio, Boito, with drinking glass in hand, recited his 'Sapphic Ode':

---

[1] Dated 2 January 1873; translation in Frank Walker, *The Man Verdi*, J.M. Dent, London, 1962/University of Chicago Press, Chicago, 1982, p. 469.

[2] Letter of 19 March 1878; *ibid.*, p. 471.

Forse già nacque chi sovra l'altare
Rizzerà l'arte, verecondo e puro,
Su quell'altar bruttato come un muro
Di lupanare.[3]

Verdi took this as an affront and wrote to Countess Maffei, his and Boito's patroness: 'I know there has been much talk about this opera – too much talk, in my opinion – and I have read some articles in the newspapers, where I've found big words about *Art, Aesthetics, Revelations*, the *Past* and the *Future*, etc., etc., and I confess that (great ignoramus that I am) I understood nothing of all that'.[4]

The Countess tried in vain to calm the irate Maestro, to convince him that while Boito was hot-tempered, he could also be generous and exceedingly noble. Vainly did the publisher Giulio Ricordi defend him, speaking of Boito's 'exuberance, naïveté, harmless impudence'. If Verdi had talked it over with Manzoni, he, in his infinite wisdom, would have reminded him that Boito took part in the movement called 'Scapigliatura',[5] a group of artists based in Milan whose platform disavowed all tradition, who resolved to write, paint, live *extra legem*. Manzoni would have advised him to re-read a certain paragraph in the first chapter of *I Promessi Sposi*: 'The man who is always on the offensive, or

---

[3] '. . .Boito rose to recite a curious ode, *All'Arte Italiana*, expressing in drastic form his views on the debased state of Italian music since the days of the "holy harmonies of Pergolesi and Marcello", and his hopes that it would be reformed and revivified by a younger generation of composers. "Perhaps the man is already born", he declared, "who will restore art in its purity, on the altar now defiled like the wall of a brothel".'

Ibid., p. 449.

[4] Letter of 13 December 1863; *ibid.*, p. 450.

[5] 'They wore Bohemian clothes, congregated at the Caffè Martini, read Baudelaire and Hugo, and drank absinthe; they raged against the established order with a fury worthy of the German *Sturm und Drang* movement of a century earlier; and like the *Sturm und Drang* their movement took its title from a work by one of its members: Cletto Arrighi's novella *La Scapigliatura e il 6 Febbraio*. As so often happens the iconoclasm of the "scapigliati" was all the more violent for having occurred late. "Christ has died again!" cried the poet Emilio Praga in a blasphemous attack on Italy's literary "saint", Manzoni.'

Julian Budden, *The Operas of Verdi*, Vol. II, Cassell, London/
Oxford University Press, New York, 1978, p. 14.

afraid of being offended at every turn, naturally looks for
allies and comrades'. He would also have informed Verdi
that while the 'Scapigliati' advanced as the primary goal of
their art an unparalleled originality and eccentricity to
which they ascribed new and revolutionary ferments, they
were lapsing into the driest academicism, into a quite
extrinsic, exasperating, and superficial novelty of expression. But Verdi didn't ask Alessandro Manzoni.

Grey and almost inactive – the years following *Aida*,
except for those that gave the world the *Requiem* [1873–74].
Did Verdi doubt himself at a particular moment? Certainly,
some of his remarks from this period give us pause. The
statement, for example, that only when people stop talking
about harmony or melody, German music or Italian music,
will the era of music perhaps begin.[6] Or the one we find in a
letter of 1875 to Count Arrivabene: '. . .the *music of the future*
does not frighten me'.[7] Verdi lives quietly at Sant' Agata
and composes nothing. In 1876 the temple devoted to the
glory of German music is inaugurated at Bayreuth. For
anyone who urges him then to resume work, Verdi has an
answer: 'I, too, have been an artist'. Three years later he
tells Giulio Ricordi: 'I'm too old. I leave my place to the
young'.

The publisher, anxious about Verdi's prolonged silence
and eager to propose some new projects – perhaps even
more, to rouse him from apparent apathy or undue resig-
nation – the publisher solicits and receives the aid of the
Maestro's devoted wife. By an odd coincidence, one evening
at the hotel where Verdi usually stops when in Milan, who
should join the composer and the publisher in conversation
but Boito's old friend Faccio! Ricordi knows quite well that
Shakespeare is the poet Verdi loves and reveres above all
others. He attacks indirectly, as Cassius does with Brutus in
Julius Caesar, and hints at a possible *Otello*. 'Excellent subject
for opera, Shakespeare,' he says. To Verdi's question 'Yes,

---

[6] In a letter to Arrivabene dated 16 July 1875; see Budden, *ibid.*, Vol. II,
pp. 55–56.
[7] See p. 108, n.2.

but who could write the libretto?', Ricordi and Faccio respond in unison: 'Arrigo Boito'. The next day Boito brings Verdi a draft of the *Otello* libretto prepared in advance. But the Maestro hesitates. He is afraid his strength and health aren't equal to such an arduous undertaking. Then the publisher suggests, as a diversion and make-work, that Verdi revise *Simon Boccanegra*, an opera not well received at its Venetian première in 1857, and after performances two seasons later in four other Italian cities, dormant for twenty years. Verdi had once conceded that the story of *Boccanegra* was 'too sad, too depressing'; however, he added immediately, 'it's sad because it must be sad – but it is gripping'.[8] And so he accepts Ricordi's proposal. Boito is commissioned to revise the libretto.

* * *

The Prologue to the 1857 version opens with a brief, traditional prelude which foreshadows the themes to appear later, in the course of the opera. After a short introduction consisting mostly of dry, staccato chords, there are eight bars of melody – melody we shall hear again (also, with the proper transformations, in the 1881 version) at the moment when the Doge, sedated by the poison Paolo has administered, murmurs in his sleep: 'Oh Amelia, oh Amelia, you're in love with an enemy!' These bars are followed by the choral motif '*All'armi, all'armi, o Liguri*' which closes Act II. Of this no trace is found in the 1881 version of the prelude. Instead there is a remarkable introductory page whose sombre hue will strikingly colour the indirect presentation of the protagonist a little later, with the words of Paolo (an Iago *ante litteram*, as so many have aptly described him):

> *Il prode che da' nostri*
> *Mari cacciava l'african pirata,*
> *E al ligure vessillo*
> *Rese l'antica rinomanza altera.*

---

[8] Letter to Arrivabene, 2 February 1881.

> The brave man who drove
> From our seas the African pirates,
> Who restored the Ligurian flag
> To its proud, ancient fame.

True, the second act of the new version ends with the chorus 'To arms, to arms, men of Liguria', set to 'agitated, accented staccato figures'.[9] But then in a purely instrumental guise, embellished by the tempestuous motion of the basses already present in the prelude of the early version, it opens Act III. (Wagner, by not dissimilar means, achieved a miraculous unity in the three acts of *Der Fliegende Holländer*.[10])

In another passage of the Prologue, where 'Sailors, Workmen, and Pietro enter gradually', Verdi removes some ornamental details and delineates the scene with the most appropriate clarity. At times he will add: as in the instrumental episode following Fiesco's aria '*A te l'estremo addio, palagio altero*' ('A last farewell to you, proud palace'), almost a lament for the death of his daughter Maria, underscored by the chorus. Here a few notes and several very subtle dynamic shadings are enough ineffably to enhance the brief passage, already so beautiful in the first version. This episode seems a presentiment of certain melodic-harmonic procedures cherished by Gustav Mahler. An invocation of peace for a dead woman, it is written, by the way, in the

---

[9] See p. 140.

[10] In an unpublished lecture on *Wozzeck*, given for the Amici della Scala of Milan, 7 March 1952, Dallapiccola compares the unity of Berg's opera with that attained by Wagner in *The Flying Dutchman*:

'Berg, therefore, conceived his opera as a *unified whole*; the intervals between acts are nothing more than a nod to operatic convention and a respite for the audience. I know of only one other three-act opera with a comparable structure: *The Flying Dutchman*.

'*In the memory* of the listener, Act II of this youthful and extremely sensuous Wagner opera begins, in fact, with the chorus of the spinners, and Act III with the sailors' chorus. In the memory, I repeat: for the brief introduction to the second act resumes the atmosphere of the orchestral conclusion of the first, while there is an analogous relationship between the beginning of the last act and the end of the second. I don't know if, or to what extent, Berg might have contemplated the Wagnerian model. But certainly, in both operas a total unity reigns supreme'.

Parole e Musica, p. 224.

same key – F sharp major – as the great invocation of peace for the living in the finale of Act I.

Lastly – and this happens quite often in the second and third acts – there are points at which the old and new versions coincide. The episode in Act III, for instance, where the protagonist sings, looking out to sea, '*Oh refrigerio! la marina brezza!*' ('What relief! The sea breeze!'): one of the greatest examples of landscape painting, or 'the voice of nature', to be found in the history of Italian opera. Nor are there noteworthy alterations in the final meeting between the Doge and Fiesco, both characters of iron will:

Fiesco:	*Simone,*
	I morti ti salutano!
Doge:	*Gran Dio!*
	Compiuto è alfin di quest'alma il desìo!

Fiesco:	Simon,
	The dead greet you!
Doge:	Great God!
	My soul's desire fulfilled at last!

It recalls, does it not, the Students from Cracow in Busoni's *Doktor Faust*, at the end of the penultimate scene, and the protagonist's words after their exit:

Vorbei, endlich vorbei!
Frei liegt der Weg, willkommen
Du, meines Abends letzter Gang,
Willkommen bist Du!

All is over at last; the way is free; the evening's end is welcome.[11]

I shall not discuss the various transpositions to different keys which Verdi made in the revised version, nor certain apposite – if sometimes very brief – interpolations in the libretto, such as these distinctly Shakespearean lines in the penultimate scene of Act II:

Perfin l'acqua del fonte è amara al labbro
Dell'uom che regna!

---

[11] See p. 102, n. 5.

Even spring water tastes bitter to the lips
Of the man who reigns!

Regarding the declamation in general, and its influence
on the characterization of the major roles, I refer the reader
to Wolfgang Osthoff's valuable essay '*Die beiden "Boccanegra"-
Fassungen und der Beginn von Verdis Spätwerk*'.[12]

Verdi, as we see, had pinpointed equally the passages he
still considered completely valid after twenty years and the
weak spots in the early version. He knew above all that an
entire scene must come under the axe: the finale of Act I,
music and text. (Basevi[13] declared that he had had to read
F.M. Piave's libretto SIX TIMES [his capitals] before he
could understand it. Boito would say only that it doesn't
hold up.)

In the 1857 version, the introductory chorus '*A festa, a
festa, o Liguri*' can remind us of the worst pages of *Attila* or
Alzira or *Giovanna d'Arco*. The 'Hymn to the Doge' is empty,
noisy, and conventional – and, as if that weren't enough, its
prosody is often defective. The 'Ballet of the African
Corsairs' is rubbish. Nor does Amelia's aria '*Nell'ora soave*'
('At the sweet hour'), with its excessive choral interjections,
characterize her more successfully than the very weak
Gabriele Adorno.

Though profoundly altered after the ninth bar, this aria is
all that remains, in the 1881 version, of the first-act finale of
the early version. Three of the five choral interjections are
eliminated; all the rest is new. The character of Amelia is
fully clarified during the ensemble and, beginning with the
invocation of peace she addresses to Fiesco, her role comes
to the fore. This is a conquest of immense significance: no
longer are there two pale characters, but only one – Adorno.

Even before he thought of collaborating with Boito on the
revision of the *Boccanegra* libretto, Verdi had expressed his

---

[12] In *Analecta Musicologica*, I, Cologne, 1963, pp. 70–89.
[13] Abramo Basevi (1818–95), Italian music critic, author of the first
serious study of Verdi's music: *Studio sulle Opere di Giuseppe Verdi*, Florence,
1859.

view of the Council Chamber scene in a letter to Ricordi:[14]
'How? With a hunt, for instance? It wouldn't be theatrical. A
celebration? Too commonplace. A pitched battle with the
African pirates? Not very entertaining. Preparations for war
with Pisa or Venice?'

We are unexpectedly moved, after this last sentence, by
the Maestro's epiphany as he describes his conception of
this finale. At the same time, we observe that he remained
the most authentic son and heir of the Italian Risorgimento,
years after it had passed into history.

> On this point [continues Verdi], I recall two superb letters of
> Petrarch's, one written to the Doge Boccanegra, the other to
> the Doge of Venice, telling them they were about to engage in
> fratricidal strife, that both were sons of the same mother,
> Italy, etc. How wonderful, this feeling for an Italian father-
> land in those days! All this is politics, not drama; but a man
> of resource could make drama out of it. For instance,
> Boccanegra, struck by this thought, would like to follow the
> poet's advice; he convokes the Senate and the privy
> council. . . . Horror all round, recriminations, fury even to the
> point of accusing the Doge of high treason, etc. The quarrel is
> interrupted by the seizure of Amelia. . . .

I dare say that few times, even in a careful study of
musical manuscripts by the most disparate composers, can I
have observed the moment of conception of an artistic
creation so clearly, directly, and impressively as in the
excerpt quoted from this letter.

Boito suggests that the finale of Act I take place either in
the Senate or the Church of San Siro; Verdi chooses the
Senate and gives the poet his reason. It is interesting to note
how subtly, how astutely the composer communicates his
views to the poet. Verdi's sole concern was to impose what
his infallible sense of musical theatre dictated, and he
writes as his characters speak: that is, by indirections finds
directions out. 'Your criticisms are justified, but you,
immersed in more elevated works, and with *Otello* in mind,

---

[14] Dated 20 November 1880; translation in Budden, *The Operas of Verdi*,
Vol. II, p. 256.

are aiming at a perfection impossible here. I aim lower and, more optimistic than you, I don't despair'.[15] This, I believe, was the only time in all his long life that Verdi called himself an 'optimist'. Hardly a sign of optimism, the supreme contempt with which he set to music the Doge's exclamation '*Ecco le plebi!*' ('Here comes the rabble!'). Yet, with apparent deference, he succeeded in making a real dramatic poet accept ideas and verses framed in his own words, just as he had done with that humblest of versifiers, Francesco Maria Piave.

Regarding this finale, I should like to quote a paragraph from the essay by Professor Osthoff mentioned above: 'The text it is based on goes back to an idea of Verdi's, one which lends the whole a new ethical stance and which, by releasing this work from the limits of the conventional *opera seria*, brings it close to a dramatic chronicle on the order of Mussorgsky's *Boris Godunov*'. Also, several lines by Massimo Mila: '. . .the political forces are approached with Machiavellian clarity, while the private passions of the characters are implanted naturally and grow a hundred times more resonant when projected onto the widest screen of public life. The people as a political force have never enjoyed a more vigorous musical characterization, except in the Passions of Bach'.[16]

About the impact of the opera, Verdi writes to Count Arrivabene after the première: 'In the second act, the effect seems to diminish. But it wouldn't be surprising if, in another theatre where the first finale was less successful, Act II gained as much applause as the others'.[17] The first finale could never be 'less successful'. That strange, mysterious, indefinable entity we are accustomed to calling 'the public' – in which each individual feels something different, but eventually finds himself in harmony with others – the public at the première already recognized the greatness of

[15] Letter of 11 December 1880; translation in Walker, *The Man Verdi*, p. 480.

[16] *Cf.* Mila's essay in the booklet accompanying the recording of *Simon Boccanegra* conducted by Claudio Abbado (Deutsche Grammophon 2709 071), p. 12.

[17] See p. 175, n. 8.

the first finale of *Simon Boccanegra*, not the least bit inferior to the loftiest scenes in *Otello*. And the public began to glimpse for a moment, if still vaguely, the deepest meaning of this vast fresco. They sensed that it symbolized the resurrection of Giuseppe Verdi.

Thoughts on a Passage in
Falstaff
(1969)

The revisions Verdi made in his *commedia lirica*, probably after the first performances, are always very interesting and highly instructive. Sometimes they affect the musical substance, at other times the instrumentation.[1] One which seems to me particularly noteworthy, since it involves not only the music but the dramatic situation as well, is found in Act I, Scene 2.

There are five characters on stage. Fenton, Dr Caius, Bardolph, and Pistol are 'all talking softly but excitedly to Mr Ford' – according to the stage directions – anxious to expose the plots Sir John Falstaff is hatching to spoil his conjugal bliss. While he doesn't understand their words, Mr Ford has the impression of hearing 'a hum of conspiracy' around him. (Once again we are presented with 'agitated, accented staccato figures'.[2]) Each of the characters is given twelve verses, verses that are shining testimony to Boito's profound knowledge and love of 17th-century Italian burlesque poets. In the whole passage, only one verse is clearly

---

[1] Concerning one of his own works, *Preghiere* (1962) for baritone and chamber orchestra, Dallapiccola writes in a letter of 11 January 1965 to the American musicologist Asher G. Zlotnik:

'. . .a change of *orchestration* (apart from the correction of actual "mistakes") cannot in fact be made without altering the music itself. In other words: the orchestration is not something abstract, rather it is one of the elements of the composition. A change of orchestration must "involve" the other dimensions as well'. *Parole e Musica*, p. 509.

[2] See pp. 140 and 176.

perceptible: the penultimate, sung by Pistol in a grotesquely martial manner–

State all'erta! all'erta! all'erta!

Be on guard! On guard! On guard!

–and reinforced at the unison, surely not accidentally, by the three trumpets, *forte*.

In the first edition of the vocal score (G. Ricordi & Co., 1893), a few bars before the end of the episode, we see that all five characters have a rest of four crotchets against the silence of the entire orchestra.

Ex. 16

In subsequent editions of the vocal score and, more importantly, in the orchestral score (1912), the stage directions quoted above are amplified: 'they enter from the right as a group, talking softly but excitedly among themselves, with the effect of much grumbling (*un gran brontolamento*)'.

If I said a little earlier that the words are distinctly audible neither to Mr Ford nor to the audience, we learn from the augmented stage directions that this is precisely what the composer intended.

But Verdi would never, for any reason, fail to bring the utmost clarity to the dramatic situation. He is aware that Mr Ford is the double of Otello, transported to the realm of comedy.[3] One couldn't imagine a character (even the loyal Emilia) asking Desdemona if Otello is jealous, yet it is quite natural for Meg to ask Alice 'Is Ford jealous?' and for her to answer 'Very!'

Did the pause noted in the first edition strike Verdi as being too long, thus creating a void rather than a tension towards the end of an episode that is all movement? Certainly, in the revised, definitive version, at the point where the first printed edition had four crotchets' rest between the *pp* and *pppp* of the voices – without orchestral support – Mr Ford, solo, bursts out angrily, *forte* (observe the accent on each of the eight quavers):

Ex. 17

[3] By the same token, Felix Krull is the double of Joseph [in *Joseph and His Brothers*]. In Thomas Mann's last book, unfortunately never completed [*Confessions of Felix Krull, Confidence Man*, 1955], we witness the de-idolization and debasement of his other characters: Mr Houpflé is the double of Potiphar, Pharaoh's Eunuch and Captain of the Guards; Diane Philibert, married to Houpflé, is the double of Potiphar's wife, Mut-Em-Enet ... Rozsa, in her turn, is the double of the Haetera Esmeralda (*Doktor Faustus*).   –LD

Se parlaste uno alla volta...

If you spoke one at a time...

From a musical and dynamic standpoint, this *forte* is the marvellous counterpoise to Pistol's '*State all'erta! all'erta! all'erta!*' It is also very important from a dramatic point of view, inasmuch as we now clearly perceive two verses rather than one. Nor is that all: in this bar Mr Ford evinces a desire to know, 'without veils and without/Ambiguous words',[4] the secret of what appeared to him 'a hum of conspiracy'. Another correspondence, therefore, between this Otello transported to the realm of comedy and his tragic predecessor.

Verdi needs no more than a single bar to attain perfection. After which the jealous Ford can address Pistol in the most realistic manner imaginable: 'Repeat'.

---

[4] *Otello*, Act II, Scene 3 ['*Dunque senza velami/T'esprimi e senza ambagi*'].

–LD

Notes on the Statue Scene in
Don Giovanni

(1949-1969)

To Professor Hans Heinz Stuckenschmidt[1]

'Above and beyond the absolute, intrinsic greatness of artists, in certain cases one would like to emphasize a rather special trait of character. There are some, endowed with particularly acute vision, who not only created aesthetically perfect works but were able to glimpse the future – even the distant future – in a flash and throw out bridges towards it. . . .'

These lines I wrote in my diary, at Venice, around the middle of September 1937, a few days after the Italian première of the Suite, Op. 29, by Arnold Schoenberg:[2] so clearly did the first variation in the third movement seem to issue from the *vivace alla marcia* of Beethoven's Piano Sonata in A major, Op. 101!

I happened to re-read this paragraph purely by chance about eight years later, at the end of the War, when contacts with international culture could gradually be restored. At the same time I discovered, in the October 1944 issue of *The Musical Quarterly*, an article by Heinrich Jalowetz entitled 'On the Spontaneity of Schoenberg's Music'. Dr Jalowetz

---

[1] H. H. Stuckenschmidt (b. 1901), critic and professor of music history at the Technical University of Berlin, author of books on Busoni and Schoenberg.

[2] At the fifth International Contemporary Music Festival, Venice (Teatro Goldoni), 9 September 1937, the day following the world première of Dallapiccola's *Tre Laudi*.

observed that Mozart, at the beginning of the development section in the finale of the Symphony in G minor [K.550], had used a series of ten different notes (different, except for the triplet leading into bar 5) and treated them as independent tones – not according to the rules of traditional chromaticism.[3]

Ex. 18

Naturally, I hadn't been waiting for Heinrich Jalowetz's penetrating comment to convince me of the matchless audacity of Mozart's genius. Even as an adolescent I was astonished by the striking asymmetry of the initial thirty-two bars of the overture to *Die Entführung aus dem Serail*, obtained by a succession of phrases of 8 + 6 + 8 + 10 bars.[4] Later, while studying Schoenberg's *Harmonielehre*, I found some surprising passages from the G minor Symphony strongly underscored and duly annotated:

Ex. 19

[3] 'What makes the example from Mozart so unusual,' Jalowetz continues, 'is the ruthless, overlapping sequence, which appears four times and contains a three-note group (made of a diminished fourth and diminished seventh) that has no diatonic point of support. . . . In Mozart's remarkable passage, the harmonic dissolution is further intensified by the rhythmic dissolution' (p. 387).

Heinrich Jalowetz (1882–1946), a Czech composer, conductor, pianist, and music critic, was among Schoenberg's first students. He emigrated to America in 1939 and taught at Black Mountain College, North Carolina. Dallapiccola met him in Prague, at the thirteenth ISCM festival, September 1935.

[4] 'He is a friend of Order: miracle and sorcery preserve their sixteen and thirty-two bars'.

Busoni, 'Mozart: Aphorisms' [*The Essence of Music*, p. 105]. –LD

Nor had I myself failed to notice Mozart's idiosyncratic approach to traditional versification, an approach I shall now try to summarize.

Everyone knows that the poetic verse, with its syllabic structure, its accents, its fixed metrical pattern, has given composers of all periods suggestions – sometimes good suggestions, sometimes very unfortunate ones. Verses of eight syllables (*ottonari*), accented principally on the third and seventh, and verses of ten syllables (*decasillabi*), accented on the third, sixth, and ninth, were especially prized by composers of *opera buffa* and *dramma giocoso*.[5] With a handful of rhythmic formulas at their disposal, with a musical declamation often based on a limited number of notes (sometimes a single note), even the great masters vastly exploited the gaiety of these verses – a gaiety that seemed innate. As a matter of fact, the verses achieved their full effect when accepted just as they were, without the need for further invention by the composer.[6]

In the '*Calunnia*' aria,[7] Rossini initially divides two

[5] According to Dent, '*dramma giocoso* is the normal term for all Italian comic operas of the second half of the 18th century. . . . What the title-pages called *dramma giocoso* was nothing more or less than what ordinary people in ordinary conversation called *opera buffa*'.
                         'The Nomenclature of Opera', Part I, pp. 132 and 135.
On the classification of metres in Italian verse, see Budden, *The Operas of Verdi*, Vol. II, pp. 17–19.

[6] One is reminded that even later, when *opera buffa* had passed into history, the ottonario was considered an 'easy' verse to set to music. As the sketch of *Rigoletto* [Act III] makes clear, Maddalena's entrance in the quartet was written, already in the first draft, without hesitations or corrections:

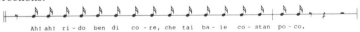

Ah! ah! ri - do   ben di   co - re, che tai ba - ie   co - stan po - co,

Not so the entrance of the protagonist—

Ta - ci,   il pian -ge - re   non va   -   le,

—which reveals four erasures, all in the rhythmic notation. This indicates that Verdi himself had to make a considerable effort to achieve such a highly dramatic formulation, with that pause after the first word which sounds like a whiplash. The convention of the ottonario was a burden even on him.   –LD

[7] *Il Barbiere di Siviglia*, Act I.

ottonari into four metrically identical units, each hemistich separated by rests of five crotchets' duration.

Ex. 20

We soon encounter another formulation, among the most typical octosyllabic patterns, and again repeated four times.

Ex. 21

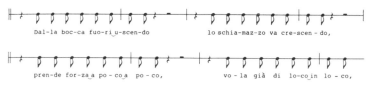

Here the rests between the individual verses are shorter (four crotchets) than those in the preceding example. Finally, a third formulation, in which four ottonari follow one another without any rests.

Ex. 22

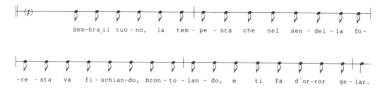

Now let's see how Mozart meets the challenge of the ottonari and decasillabi offered him by Lorenzo Da Ponte, in the *allegro* of the aria '*Madamina, il catalogo è questo*' [No. 4]. So far as the ottonari are concerned, the composer adopts two of the metrical formulations found in Rossini: four verses divided by rests of four crotchets, in the passage—

V'han fra queste contadine,
Cameriere, cittadine,
V'han contesse, baronesse,
Marchesane, principesse,

> There are peasant girls among them,
> Chambermaids and city women,
> Countesses and baronesses,
> Marchionesses, princesses,

–followed without interruption by two additional verses having no rest between them:

> *E v'han donne d'ogni grado,*
> *D'ogni forma, d'ogni età!*

> Women there of every station,
> Every shape and age!

The immediately ensuing codetta, which repeats the last verse, is of a strictly instrumental nature. And in the coda that closes the *allegro*, there is a reprise (bars 71–77) of the six ottonari just quoted, but without the rests; then the real conclusion [bars 77–84].

But this famous aria contains other passages of an altogether different interest. In a succession of four decasillabi, Leporello, catalogue in hand, first enumerates his master's conquests for Donna Elvira. Da Ponte doesn't seem to have anticipated, in the libretto, that this inventory would have to be repeated: a very important repetition from a musical standpoint, as we shall see.

> *In Italia seicento e quaranta,*
> *In Almagna duecento e trentuna,*
> *Cento in Francia, in Turchia novantuna,*
> *Ma in Ispagna son già mille e tre!*

> In Italy six hundred and forty,
> In Germany two hundred and thirty-one,
> A hundred in France, in Turkey ninety-one,
> But in Spain already a thousand and three!

Ex. 23

In I - ta - lia sei-cen - to e qua - ran - ta,

in Al - ma - gna due-cen - to e tren-tu - na,

cen - to in Fran-cia, in Tur-chia no - van - tu - na, ma...

The first three verses are divided from each other by rests of eight crotchets. Between the first and second there are no differences of rhythm or pitch; not so the third verse, which transforms the concluding crotchets of the preceding verses into quavers (at ·*ʃ*.). Thus Mozart makes the adversative *ma*, which begins the fourth verse, fall on the weak beat of the bar – for the listener, something totally unexpected.

But he would have considered a literal repetition of Leporello's list too easy. With Mozart, the process of composition becomes ever more subtle, the elements of surprise more numerous. This time the first and second verses are each divided into two units of 4 + 6 syllables by a rest of seven quavers; the rest between the two verses (four crotchets) is only half as long as its counterpart in the first inventory. And, at the third decasillabo, '*Cento in Francia, in Turchia novantuna*', a stroke of genius: Mozart begins *on the strong beat of the bar*!

Ex. 24

The whole page seems to take on a fresh appearance, as though a new light were projected upon it (especially if Leporello's E is executed *sf*). And such is the surprise that the adversative *ma* in the fourth verse must be repeated no fewer than three times, always on the weak beat, in order to restore the necessary equilibrium.

Lest anyone think at this point that I am merely splitting hairs, allow me to mention how strongly impressed I was by a page of André Gide's *Journal 1939–1942*. Searching one day for his daughter, who took elocution lessons, the writer found her practising the pronunciation of vowels in a verse from *Phèdre* by Racine: '*N'était qu'un faible essai des tourments que j'endure*'. The first hemistich contains six repetitions 'of one sound, *è*, almost identical yet subtly distinguished'. Gide concludes: 'The charm of French classical poetry arises from just such a play of imponderables'.

I shall have occasion to return to the problem of the ottonario.

*   *   *

Although I am by no means a Mozart scholar, the observation of Dr Jalowetz's quoted at the beginning of this essay prompted me to jot down some notes on the role of the Commendatore in the finale of *Don Giovanni*. This episode can only be considered, both on the written page and in the opera house, an anticipation of 20th-century 'expressionism'.

Ex. 25

It is superfluous to relate how very many contributions to the evolution of writing and language and expression have had their remote origins in necessities of a technical, organizational nature. And it would be just as gratuitous to insist that, in art, every stroke of the pen depends upon the most diverse conditions. Suffice it to recall a passage – much quoted, yet never quoted enough! – from the final volume of Proust's *À la Recherche du Temps Perdu*:

> I had arrived then at the conclusion that in fashioning a work of art we are by no means free, that we do not choose how we shall make it but that *it pre-exists us* and therefore we are obliged, since it is both necessary and hidden, to do what we should have to do if it were a law of nature, that is to say to discover it.[8]

Thus, if Domenico Scarlatti wrote the following passage in one of his sonatas–

[8] *Time Regained*, translated by Andreas Mayor, in *Remembrance of Things Past*, Random House, New York/Chatto & Windus, London, 1981, Vol. III, p. 915, italics added.

Ex. 26

–that still does not mean that he consciously used the whole-tone scale (for the first time in the history of Western music, to my knowledge[9]). It is the fundamental rhythm, clearly established at the beginning of the piece, which required the composer to write these notes and not others, in order to fill the existing interval between the D flat and the C. Of course, having pointed out the supreme interest of such an extraordinary passage, having indicated its absolutely superior aesthetic effect, I am at a loss to ascertain whether Scarlatti weighed the significance of his daring. Personally, however, I am inclined to believe that he was at least vaguely conscious of it.

Let us take another look at the passage in the *Harmonielehre* where Schoenberg, with his inimitable perspicacity, comments on the beginning of the fifth movement of the *Pastoral* Symphony, so controversial for the boldness of its harmony:

> And that Beethoven quite certainly sensed this singularity is proved by his sense of form, which pressed him to answer this singularity with another, congruent singularity, to resolve as it were this singularity: with the *rhythmically remarkable entry* of the tonic harmony on the second half of the measure (·ƒ).[10]

(The importance of the indication *sf* can never be sufficiently stressed!)

[9] Sonata in F major, Kk. 106 (L. 437).
Commenting on the Italian edition of *Harmonielehre* (Milan, 1963), Dallapiccola observed that Schoenberg heard the whole-tone scale, 'with the greatest surprise', in Liszt's *Réminiscences de Don Juan*. Alfredo Casella thought that Liszt had used it for the first time in the '*Sursum Corda*' of *Années de Pèlerinage*, Book III, and H.H. Stuckenschmidt found it in Mozart's *Dorfmusikantensextett*. (See *Parole e Musica*, p. 244.)

[10] Arnold Schoenberg, *Theory of Harmony*, transl. Roy E. Carter, University of California Press, Berkeley, 1978, p. 402.

Ex. 27

Applying the same method of analysis – already used implicitly in the comment on Ex. 24 – to the Scarlatti quotation, we see that the first liberty, the employment of the whole-tone scale, is directly offset by another: the three notes which follow this scale are completely independent of it, so that we have a succession of *nine* different notes. The second liberty is intended to counterbalance the first.

There is no need to demonstrate that the episode in *Don Giovanni* where the Commendatore asks his host the two most demanding questions a man can be asked (Ex. 25) is fully justified by its aesthetic result. But before proceeding, I must clarify one point. The Commendatore, in my view, is *the protagonist of the opera*. One understands very well why Søren Kierkegaard had not the slightest doubt that the protagonist is Don Giovanni himself. In his remarkable essay on Mozart's masterpiece we read:

> With the exception of the Commandant, everyone stands in a kind of erotic relation to Don Juan. Over the Commandant he can exercise no power, for the Commandant represents reflective consciousness; the others are in his power. Elvira loves him, her love puts her in his power; Anna hates him, so she is in his power; Zerlina fears him, which puts her in his power; Ottavio and Mazetto go along for the sake of relationship, for the blood bond is strong.[11]

[11] S. Kierkegaard, *Don Giovanni. La Musica di Mozart e l'Eros*, [Denti], Milan, 1944.   –LD

Translated by David F. Swenson and Lillian M. Swenson, in *Either/Or*, Princeton University Press, Princeton, 1971, Vol. I, p. 124; subsequent quotations from pp. 111 and 122.

Kierkegaard also perceived 'something erotic in Leporello's relationship to Don Juan; there is a power by which Don Juan captivates him, even against his will' (p. 124).

In any case, it is noteworthy that the Commendatore is recognized as having a place apart. Even more significant is the following passage: 'The music immediately makes the Commandant something more than a particular individual, his voice is expanded to the voice of a spirit'. Yet the Commendatore is the protagonist not only because he represents spirit or conscience. From a *musical* point of view he is the protagonist because, appearing in the introduction and the finale, he fixes the two points on which that great arch, the structure of *Don Giovanni*, is erected. His two menacing utterances–

> *Di rider finirai pria dell'aurora!. . .*
> *Ribaldo audace! Lascia a' morti la pace!*

> You shall cease laughing before dawn! . . .
> Brazen rascal! Leave the dead in peace!

–and his 'Yes!' in the graveyard scene are nothing more than a preface to the finale, just as the *andante* that follows the fall of the mortally wounded Commendatore is but a pendant to the introduction. Protagonist, then, chiefly because he establishes the architecture of the entire opera. At this point it must be noted that the Commendatore falls *to the same diminished-seventh chord* which we hear again at the moment when the Statue makes its entrance. (See Figure 2, page 196.)

'But what of Donna Anna's aria?' someone will rightly object – the aria '*Non mi dir, bell'idol mio*' [No. 23], inserted between the graveyard scene and the finale. Yes, it was precisely this aria that moved Berlioz to pen words of fire:

> It is an aria of intense sadness, full of a heartbreaking sense of loss and sorrowing love, but towards the end degenerating without warning into music of such appalling inanity and vulgarity that one can hardly believe it to be the work of the same man. One has the impression that Donna Anna has suddenly dried her tears and broken out in ribald clowning.[12]

And in a footnote:

[12] *Mémoires*, Vol. I, Chapter XVII, Calmann Lévy, Paris, 1878.   –LD
The Memoirs of Hector Berlioz, translated and edited by David Cairns, Gollancz, London, 1975, p. 93.

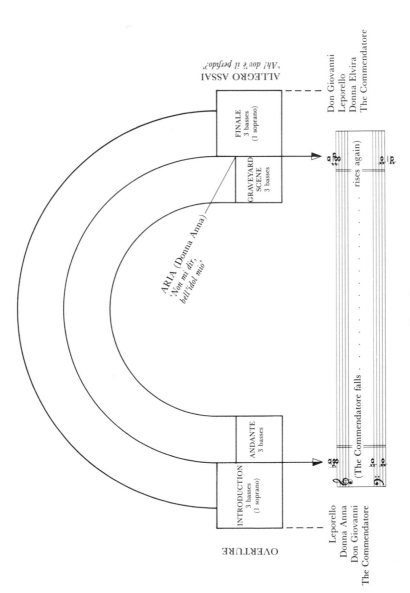

Figure 2

Even shameful seems to me too light a word. Mozart in this passage has committed one of the most odious and idiotic crimes against passion, taste and common sense of which the history of art provides an example.

For all the abundant evidence Berlioz's restless spirit gave us of his irascibility, he seldom expressed himself with quite so much vehemence. I am convinced, nevertheless, that Berlioz found excessive fault with Donna Anna's vocalises, although I will admit that they stand in the greatest contrast to the state of mind of the woman who loves – and at the same time hates – Don Giovanni. I think I can guess what seemed so intolerable, without his actually realizing it: not so much the aria itself as the point in the action at which it is inserted. Berlioz didn't even ask himself if Mozart's 'error' was one of *construction* and if the aria '*Non mi dir. . .*', placed elsewhere in the opera, would have had a less jarring effect. But inserted between the graveyard scene and the finale, it certainly does interrupt the action, driving towards its inevitable conclusion, and seriously unbalances the total architecture of the opera.

We heard Berlioz speak with sanguinary violence against Donna Anna's aria, while offering no solution to the problem. Kierkegaard takes a step forward. In the essay quoted above, he expresses himself with affectionate, touching hesitancy:

> And yet I here approach a precarious point; for I admit that there are two arias that must go, that however perfect they are in themselves, they still cause an interruption, retard the action. I would willingly keep this a secret, but that would not help, the truth must out. If one takes these two away, then all the rest is perfect. One of these is Ottavio's, the other Anna's. . .

And so Kierkegaard desires, he almost proposes – speaking in the conditional – that Donna Anna's aria be eliminated. (Personally, I can't agree with the philosopher about Ottavio's aria. How could we give up '*Il mio tesoro intanto*' [No. 21], musically one of the most adventurous arias and metrically one of the freest, beginning with that incredible seven-bar period: a necessary moment of stasis after the great sextet and the *allegro assai* '*Ah, pietà! Signori miei!*'?)

After the unanimous reactions of a great composer and a great philosopher, here is the response of a great conductor. On the evening of 23 October 1956, at Toscanini's house in New York, the conversation turned by chance to *Don Giovanni*. And apropos of the aria '*Non mi dir, bell'idol mio*' the old Maestro told me only this: 'In my performances I simply omit it'. Now even those who sometimes disagree with Toscanini's performances of Mozart have always had to acknowledge his unique sense of musical theatre. I will admit how pleased I was to learn that Toscanini agreed, indirectly and instinctively, with the viewpoints expressed above and that he had solved the structural problem in the only possible way.

The Commendatore, as I pointed out, falls to the same diminished-seventh chord that we hear again when he re-appears on stage in the guise of the Statue. What happens within the great arch supported by the two columns, namely the principal action of the opera, is conditioned by the Commendatore's invisible presence. *Don Giovanni* is designated *dramma giocoso*. What the drama is, and how it is conditioned by the presence of the Commendatore, I shall try to explain later. For now, in order to give a few points of reference, I would only mention some of the occasions when the dramatic quality is ascendant: Donna Anna's tragic outburst '*Don Ottavio! son morta!*' [No. 10]; the scene of the masks, at the summit of the arch; and the sextet '*Mille torbidi pensieri*'. About the sextet I would like to make one observation, as though in parentheses.

We learn from the recitative which closes Act II, Scene 1 that Don Giovanni wants to exchange clothes with Leporello. Since it *is* a recitative, we hear each word distinctly; and what is more, at the end of the recitative we witness the stratagem. We, the audience, are thus perfectly informed about the goings on. One cannot say as much for the five characters who take part with Leporello in the great sextet. When circumstances force Leporello to reveal his true identity, they express their amazement by addressing each other the question '*Dèi! Leporello? Che inganno è questo?*' ('Ye Gods! Leporello? What trick is this?'). And straightaway begins the *molto allegro*.

Leporello sings the following quatrain:

Mille torbidi pensieri
Mi s'aggiran per la testa.
Se mi salvo in tal tempesta
È un prodigio in verità.

A thousand muddled thoughts
Are whirling through my head.
To save myself in this storm
Will truly take a miracle.

Donna Anna, Zerlina, Donna Elvira, Don Ottavio, and Masetto are also given four verses – the first two corresponding to Leporello's, the others quite different:

Che giornata, o stelle, è questa!
Che impensata novità!

What a day this is, oh my stars!
What a bolt from the blue!

For these five characters it really is 'a bolt from the blue', since they could never have guessed that Leporello was hiding under his master's attire; but not for us, who were in on the ploy from the beginning. At this moment the composer intervenes personally, to focus our attention on a purely musical detail (one of those 'imponderables' Gide spoke of).

When the five exclaim '*Che impensata novità!*' for the second time, homophonically, after four bars in E flat major there is a sudden shift of key to D flat major: a real 'bolt from the blue' in the music of Mozart's time and still surprising today. Without taxing my memory, I could cite a dozen cases in literature where the author seems to suspend the narrative for a moment and engage in a dialogue with his reader. In music, this is the only example I have happened to notice.

Ferruccio Busoni – what a profound student of Mozart! – once remarked that the character of Don Giovanni already seems somewhat cold in the libretto. Unfortunately, Busoni failed to elaborate on this point, and we have no way of knowing if he suspected that Don Giovanni himself is not the protagonist. One who must have thought so, in the mid-19th century, even if to my knowledge he never expressed it verbally, was Franz Liszt: perhaps not the greatest composer of his time, but certainly the most intelligent of all.

Let us briefly examine his most important transcription, *Réminiscences de Don Juan* [1841]. 'Reminiscence': a word we should bear in mind and consider carefully. 'Something that recalls another thing, intentionally or not,' according to a famous dictionary.[13] Liszt begins his piece with the verse '*Di rider finirai pria dell' aurora!*', followed immediately by '*Ribaldo audace! Lascia a' morti la pace!*' Then come the two chords that announce the entrance of the Statue, chords made all the more strident by the pianistic 'gusts' so typical of Liszt. Throughout the entire first part of the *Réminiscences*, it is the figure of the Commendatore alone which looms before us.

Part II presents Don Giovanni and Zerlina, but their encounter is abruptly interrupted by the Commendatore's re-appearance. His verse '*Tu m'invitasti a cena*' ('You invited me to dinner') receives a tempestuous interpretation. And again, in the transition to the final part, based on the so-called 'Champagne Aria' ('*Fin ch'han dal vino calda la testa*' [No. 11]), here is the mysterious protagonist, who returns once more in the conclusion, evoked by the same verse heard at the beginning.

If Don Giovanni is not the leading character of the opera, it is due to the fact that he is subject to the will of the Commendatore – the one who, as Kierkegaard wrote, represents conscience. Don Giovanni is damned at the very instant he slays the Commendatore. From that moment, not one of his amorous exploits reaches a happy end. We see him as the prey, around whom a circle of pursuers draws closer and closer.

Don Giovanni is the most moral of all operas. Long before the hero's final chastisement, it lives up to the promise of its original title, *Il Dissoluto Punito, ossia: Il Don Giovanni*. And so we find it hard to understand why Beethoven never forgave

---

[13] *Nuovo Dizionario Italiano della Lingua Italiana* by P. Petrocchi (1887–91).

Mozart for having put such an immoral character on the stage.[14]

It shouldn't be surprising that the Commendatore, the mysterious protagonist, expresses himself in a manner so exceptional for his time (Ex. 25), at the climax of the great drama, in the scene never surpassed nor equalled by any of the master opera composers. The Commendatore is a being from beyond the grave; his mode of expression cannot be that of other men. But perhaps it wasn't only considerations of an artistic or transcendental nature that led Mozart to his prodigious invention: perhaps it will be necessary to appeal to *technical* and *practical* considerations.

Mozart has arrived at the culmination of the drama, which is rushing headlong to its conclusion. The characters must now, more than ever, be drawn with the utmost precision. At this point, the slightest imperfection would cause the failure not only of the scene in question but of the whole opera. Mozart, as we know, believed that in opera the delineation of character must be based above all on the human voice. But in the Statue scene the three characters are *three basses*, so the composer lacks that fundamental and principal means of psychological characterization: diversity of vocal timbre.

Everyone knows what this diversity meant to the great masters of musical theatre. If we examine the sketch of *Rigoletto* [Act II], we see that Verdi, having fully noted the baritone melody and reached Gilda's entrance in the duet '*Sì, vendetta, tremenda vendetta*', limited himself to writing:

Ex. 28

---

[14] '[Mozart] never passes judgement on a protagonist, not even when most of the other characters have nothing but judging on their minds (as in *Don Giovanni*). Free of value judgements, beyond all morality, he presents both positive and negative attributes (if we can speak of positive attributes at all, for nearly all the characters' qualities are revealed in relationship to the negative hero, Don Giovanni, who controls them).'

Hildesheimer, *Mozart*, p. 152.

He left the phrase unfinished, with the simple indication 'repeat the motif'. Verdi's formidable craft as a man of the theatre told him that the change of key (Rigoletto, A flat major; Gilda, D flat major), and especially the change of vocal timbre, would be enough to infuse the page with that sense of a sharp blade thrust into the flesh – an effect more than sufficient for the perfect musical and dramatic realization of the scene.

But for Mozart it was a matter of differentiating three characters at the most delicate and crucial moment of his work, without being able to count on the perspective that different vocal timbres establish *naturally*. A desperate problem if there ever was one in opera. Let's see how he came to grips with the problem and solved it.

Of the three characters, the one who causes least anxiety is Leporello. Here Mozart relies on the *parola intonata*,[15] which had already rendered inestimable service to the composers of *opera buffa*.

Ex. 29

During this entire scene, neither Don Giovanni nor the Commendatore sings in triplet rhythm. By this means Leporello is differentiated from the other two basses, and his part stands out effortlessly.

Don Giovanni, much more than his servant, needs the orchestra for his characterization. In the whole opera there is only a single moment when the usually imperturbable and dominating Don seems to waver: the moment the Statue appears. What has happened to Don Giovanni, confronted with the apparition of the SPIRIT? What has he become, this man who assailed and conquered 2,065 women – if Leporello's catalogue is accurate? Don Giovanni scarcely manages to stammer '*Non l'avrei giammai creduto*' ('I would never have believed it'), but it is the orchestra, with

---

[15] That is, a vocal delivery closer to ordinary speech than to true singing.

its syncopated rhythm, with semiquavers in the second violins, with the trumpets' cold octaves, which gives us the idea of fear – the fear that freezes, not that which is resolved, *operatically*, in a cry.

Ex. 30

Don Giovanni is conscious of his momentary weakness, and ashamed of it. This will be clear if we observe that the passage just quoted, heavy with anguish, is repeated by the orchestra in transposition (but the vocal declamation has a quite different accent!) towards the end of the dialogue with the Commendatore, precisely at the words

A torto di viltate
Tacciato mai sarò!

I shall never be falsely accused of cowardice!

Ex. 31

Don Giovanni needs to re-assert himself, to cancel out his shame. And he isn't slow to do it (Ex. 32):

Ho fermo il core in petto:
Non ho timor; verrò!

I have taken heart:
I am not afraid; I'm coming!

If I just now alluded to the sudden weakness of a usually cool and undaunted man, confronted with the apparition of the Spirit, it must be recognized that his fresh metamorphosis is equally – if not more – surprising. The 'young, extremely licentious nobleman', as Da Ponte described him, is suddenly transformed into a hero. Don Giovanni has never been so great as at this moment. Don Giovanni, a man moulded of clay, has never understood anything that wasn't

Ex. 32

of this world. Perhaps he has succeeded in dominating the earthly scene so completely only because the spiritual realm has remained, as it were constitutionally, beyond his ken.

At his table the musicians perform three operatic excerpts to brighten the meal. First, a couple of trivial numbers from *Una Cosa Rara* and *Fra i Due Litiganti*,[16] followed by a self-quotation from the aria which ends Act I of *Le Nozze di Figaro*. It has been said that the first two quotations, which practically invite comparison with the third, should be considered Mozart's revenge against 'successful' opera composers of his day. (Revenge is hardly rare in the history of art. Did Michelangelo not depict his rival Bramante in 'The Last Judgement' – to credit a tenacious popular myth – taking pains to place him among the damned?) Even if we accept this view, it constitutes, in my opinion, only a small and insignificant part of the problem.

---

[16] *Una Cosa Rara, ossia Bellezza ed Onestà* (1786) by the Spanish composer Vicente Martín y Soler (1754–1806), on a libretto by Lorenzo Da Ponte; *Fra i Due Litiganti il Terzo Gode* (1782) by Giuseppe Sarti (1729–1802), on a libretto by Carlo Goldoni.

'*Non più andrai. . .*' play the musicians. But no longer in the brilliant key of C major! Leporello, who is competent in musical matters – otherwise Don Giovanni wouldn't have asked him '*Che ti par del bel concerto?*' ('What do you think of this lovely concert?') – Leporello knows every piece on the programme and delights in rattling off its source. At the beginning of the quotation from *Figaro*, he claims he knows this strain only too well. (*Figaro* is also a 'hit', he would emphasize: indeed, a bigger success than the other two operas quoted.)

Non più andrai, farfallone amoroso,
Notte e giorno d'intorno girando. . .

Now your days of philandering are over. . .

is the musicians' burden. But the man moulded of clay doesn't even suspect that he, Don Giovanni, might be the 'lovesick butterfly'. He fails to grasp that the players are repeating, in purely musical terms, the Commendatore's solemn prophecy in the graveyard scene: 'You shall cease laughing before dawn!' Don Giovanni does not recognize the sign that comes to him from the beyond, the sign that the musicians are writing on the wall with an invisible hand: the first of three warnings which once appeared to Belshazzar during his impious banquet. But if their admonition is somewhat cryptic, Donna Elvira's is much more obvious because expressed in words. She doesn't ask Don Giovanni to love her or beg him to return to her; she only implores him – and with what tenderness! – to change his way of life. Vain entreaty. As she exits, the desperate woman seems to write the second warning on the wall. The Commendatore then substantially repeats Donna Elvira's appeal and further exhorts Don Giovanni to repent. In vain.

The proportions and importance of the three episodes progressively increase, almost as if to underscore the crescendo of the words '*MANE, THECHEL, PHARES*'.[17] With the last terrible utterances of his 'No!', Don Giovanni stains himself with the unpardonable sin. He has persevered deliberately in final impenitence. He is damned. But his gesture 'I have taken heart: I am not afraid; I'm coming!'

[17] The Book of Daniel, Chapter V, 25–28. See p. 153.

(Ex. 32) is such that, in damnation, he will not be alone. A great brother awaits him: Capaneus.[18]

Here it is necessary to clarify, from a strictly musical point of view, the relationship between Don Giovanni and his servant. What thoughts flashed through Leporello's mind at the moment he met the Statue and saw it heading towards the banquet hall! And how he expresses them in music! The libretto presents six ottonari:

> *Ah! Signor! . . . per carità!*
> *Non andate fuor di quà!*
> *L'uom di sasso, l'uomo bianco. . .*
> *Ah! padrone! io gelo, io manco.*
> *Se vedeste che figura,*
> *Se sentiste come fa. . .*

> Ah! Sir! . . . for pity's sake!
> Don't leave the room!
> The man of marble, the white man. . .
> Ah! master! I'm freezing, I'm fainting.
> If you had seen that shape,
> If you'd heard the sound it makes. . . .

In the music there are four distinctly different metrical articulations of the first four verses, different both in terms of declamation and – in three cases – duration.

Ex. 33

---

[18] Dante, *Inferno*, XIV, 43–75.   –LD

'This is Capaneus, who took part in the war of the "Seven against Thebes". While scaling the city wall, he boasted that not even Jove could stop him, and was struck with a thunder-bolt.'

The Divine Comedy, translated by Dorothy L. Sayers, Penguin Books, Harmondsworth, 1978, Vol. I (*Hell*), p. 160.

I could cite no more subtle and multifarious example of
the ottonario in music.

The articulation of the fifth and sixth verses seems to
approach the traditional setting of ottonari, in order to
avoid a glaring discrepancy between Leporello's declamation and that of Don Giovanni.

Ex. 34

At this point Da Ponte provided an extra verse consisting
of several repetitions of the syllable 'ta', preceded in certain
editions by the indication 'imitating the footsteps of the
Commendatore'.

Ex. 35

This brief passage suddenly blocks the ostinato motion of
quavers which had begun seventeen bars earlier. And here
is how Don Giovanni reacts to his servant's baffling story:

> *Non capisco niente affatto.*
> *Tu sei matto in verità!*

> I don't understand a single word.
> You are truly out of your mind!

Clearly, the man moulded of clay cannot comprehend: he
says so himself. No wonder the music for these two verses
obeys the most regular, traditional rules for the setting of
syllables.

Ex. 36

The Commendatore is differentiated equally from Don Giovanni and from Leporello by the *arioso* quality of his vocal lines, abounding in octave leaps and unusual intervals, becoming ever more extraordinary with the continuous crescendo of dramatic tension throughout the scene (Ex. 37), until it arrives at the passage I believe to be the first example of expressionism in opera (Ex. 25). Expressionistic music resorts habitually to wide intervals, and this practice led to the discovery of the peculiar *tension* that exists between the most distant notes. Needless to say, we now hear the tenth as an interval independent of the third. Anyone who doubts it should try substituting thirds for the Commendatore's two tenths: the tension contained in the wider interval will be immediately pulverized.

Ex. 37

Finally, there is one other detail that must be clarified. During the Statue scene – from the *andante* (bar 433) to the *più stretto* (the point where the Statue clasps Don Giovanni's hand) – the Commendatore's declamation is always underscored, with a *precision* I find hard to believe is purely fortuitous, by the inexorable rhythm which resounds in the orchestra.

Ex. 38

I have stressed the word *precision*, because the sole exception to my statement (bars 483–484, where the principal rhythm continues even during Don Giovanni's declamation: something that hadn't occurred in the parallel passage at bar 478) is only an apparent exception. In this case the 'principal rhythm' is completely masked by the flute-oboe chords on the weak beats of the bar, and even more by the triplet rhythm of the violins and violas. Since these are *the only triplets* to appear in the orchestra during the entire scene, the listener's attention is obviously concentrated on them.

Ex. 39

While certain typically expressionistic composers have conceived of using a 'principal rhythm' as an essential musical element throughout an entire composition (for example, the *Hauptrhythmus* in Alban Berg's *Lulu* and Violin Concerto), we should remember that this *Hauptrhythmus* had already found a complete and most convincing artistic and technical application in the Statue scene. And so I believe it isn't entirely by chance that this very scene offers the first example of expressionism in opera. Expressionism, the culmination and ultimate experience of Romanticism, is already encapsulated in that utterly romantic scene, the finale of *Don Giovanni*.

*   *   *

P.S.: Here my discussion of *Don Giovanni* would have ended. But some years ago the Statue scene afforded me yet another surprise.

Roger Sessions and I[19] had gone to have dinner with Darius Milhaud in Oakland, California. Milhaud had seen a

---

[19] The two composers met in 1951 at Tanglewood, and each subsequently dedicated a work to the other: Sessions, in 1954, his *Idyll of Theocritus* for soprano and orchestra; Dallapiccola, two years later, *Cinque Canti* for baritone and eight instruments.

performance of *Don Giovanni* in San Francisco the previous evening, and several details so strongly impressed him that he was eager to re-examine the score next morning. His ear hadn't deceived him. Concentrated in a very small space he found the twelve tones possible in our tempered system.[20]

Ex. 40

I don't wish to draw any conclusion from that. Milhaud's observation is a further contribution to the study of this problematic opera and of the inexhaustible scene where Mozart's intuition seems to have reached its zenith, where the genius of Mozart was able to glimpse the future in a flash spanning more than a century and throw out towards it one of the fundamental bridges.

[20] In '*Lettre Ouverte à Luigi Dallapiccola*' Milhaud, pointing out the twelve-tone series in Ex. 40, remarked: 'I think this will amuse you, especially coming from a musician like me, so little inclined to the twelve-tone system, but who – as you know – admires you and wishes you well'.

La Rassegna Musicale, Vol. XXIII, No. 1, Turin, January 1953, p. 41. (A preliminary version of Dallapiccola's essay had appeared in the same journal, Vol. XX, No. 2, April 1950. See p. 24.)

Milhaud used this twelve-tone series in *David* (1954).

III
The Ulysses Theme
Pieces of a Myth

Monteverdi's
Il Ritorno di Ulisse in Patria
Notes on a Practical Edition
(1942)

I shall not start with the 'descent into hell'. However, it will
be useful to recall now the beginning of a great literary work,
one very close to my heart. Two propositions: the first
affirmative, the second interrogative. 'Very deep is the well
of the past. Should we not call it bottomless?'[1]

To be sure, anyone who wants to plumb the abysses
carved out by the millennia will be obliged to descend into
hell; not we ourselves, separated from the death of the great
Claudio Monteverdi by only three centuries. And yet three
centuries represent an aeon to us, whose entire musical
experience spans five hundred years at most.

In all the arts, the history of attributions is long and
varied. The issue of *Il Ritorno di Ulisse* is rather complex, but
let us see if it can be summarized in a few words. Until 1881
only one fact was known for certain: that Monteverdi had
composed an opera on a libretto by the Venetian nobleman
Giacomo Badoaro, entitled *Il Ritorno di Ulisse in Patria* ('The
Homecoming of Ulysses'). When August Wilhelm Ambros
found it at the National Library of Vienna, the score lacked a
title-page and was classified as an 'unknown opera'. Raphael
Georg Kiesewetter had actually recognized it even earlier as

---

[1] Thomas Mann, *The Tales of Jacob (Joseph and His Brothers*, Book I),
translated by H.T. Lowe-Porter, Secker & Warburg, London/Alfred A.
Knopf, New York, 1976, p. 3.

an opera by Monteverdi, although for some reason – perhaps the extreme modesty of a musicologist – he failed to bring his important discovery to light. The score is the work of a copyist but contains several emendations in another hand, such as the witty directive in Act III, Scene 2: '*la si lascia fuora per esser maninconica*' ('leave it out because it's sad').

In 1887, six years after Ambros's announcement, Emil Vogel contested his attribution,[2] only to be refuted in turn by Hugo Goldschmidt, who maintained in 1902 that the controversial opera was written in pure Monteverdian style and who wrote a detailed critical study several years later, pointing out all of these stylistic traits in the music.[3] He was supported by Charles van den Borren, by Louis Schneider, by Henry Prunières. . . . At any rate, it is sufficiently indicative that no scholar took issue with Goldschmidt.

These highly authoritative views were further corroborated in 1922 by Robert Haas, who published the Vienna manuscript with realization of the figured bass in the great collection directed by the eminent musicologist Professor Guido Adler;[4] in 1925 by Vincent d'Indy, who made a 'practical' edition of the opera for performance at the Petite Scène, Paris; and in 1930 by Gian Francesco Malipiero, who had the manuscript with realization published by 'Il Vittoriale degli Italiani',[5] then included this opera in the Monteverdi Collected Edition. I have closely examined these three editions (unfortunately, it was impossible to track down van den Borren's) and feel deeply grateful for what I have learned from Haas, d'Indy, and Malipiero, even if in practice my edition agrees with none of theirs.

I should add that through a meticulous comparison of texts – those of Haas and Malipiero based directly on the

[2] Emil Vogel, '*Claudio Monteverdi: Leben, Werken im Lichte der zeitgenössischen Kritik*', *Vierteljahrsschrift für Musikwissenschaft*, III, 1887, pp. 315–450.

[3] Hugo Goldschmidt, '*Monteverdi's "Ritorno d'Ulisse"*', *Sammelbände der internationalen Musikgesellschaft*, IV, 1902–03, pp. 671–676; '*Claudio Monteverdi's Oper: "Il Ritorno d'Ulisse in Patria"*', *SIMG*, IX, 1907–08, pp. 570–592.

[4] *Denkmäler der Tonkunst in Oesterreich*, XXIX Jahrgang, Vol. 57, Vienna, 1922.

[5] 'The Victory Monument of the Italians', Gabriele d'Annunzio's villa at Gardone on Lake Garda, was also the name of a firm that published his literary works (before they were taken over by Mondadori) and Malipiero's edition of Monteverdi.

manuscript or photocopies, d'Indy's completed '*à l'aide d'une copie scrupuleusement exacte du manuscrit original qui se trouve à la Bibliothèque impériale de Vienne*' (as his preface expresses it) – through this careful comparison I have noticed several discrepancies, and while they may be insignificant they make me all the more eager to consult the controversial manuscript No. 18.763 at the National Library in Vienna. I have left no stone unturned: it has not been possible to see either the manuscript, removed from the city because of the War, or photocopies. Therefore I hope as soon as possible to correct those doubtful points where, in preferring one reading to another, my taste may have misled me.

When Mario Labroca asked, in October 1940, if I would undertake the grave responsibility of reworking Monteverdi's opera for the 1941 Florentine Maggio Musicale, I declined. Six months didn't seem sufficient time to 'translate' (*tradurre*) such a masterpiece with the care I felt it deserved. I accepted later, when my friend agreed to postpone his original project provided he could count on my collaboration in 1942, and I should like to thank him publicly for his confidence.[6]

It seems that after nearly forty years of silence, new doubts are being raised concerning the authorship of the opera.[7] For my part I have nothing against it. If Maestro Labroca's idea and my own hard work have helped revive a dispute (although we considered it settled long ago by the most serious scholars), we don't believe the cultural traditions of the Maggio Musicale have been betrayed. We ourselves are convinced that the opera is very beautiful, as fresh today as if three centuries had never passed. The rest may be discussed elsewhere.

Opposition is always possible – I might even say desirable. And we welcome it, so long as the opponent's

---

[6] First performance: Florence, Teatro della Pergola, 23 May 1942, directed by Mario Rossi. The opera was originally produced 301 years earlier, at Venice, Teatro di San Cassiano.

[7] This question has now been definitively settled by the work of such important Monteverdi scholars as Leo Schrade, Anna Amalie Abert, Wolfgang Osthoff, and Claudio Gallico.

credentials can stand comparison with those of an Adler, a
van den Borren, a Goldschmidt; so long as the adversary can
prove his point, either on stylistic or historical grounds, and
isn't content to protest that *Ulisse* could not be Monteverdi's
work if only because it is less beautiful than, say, *L'Incoronazione di Poppea.*

Let me repeat that this entire issue is the province of
music historians. Like every effort to discover the truth, it
should of course be considered a sacrosanct task. We all
recognize its towering significance, but for the practicing
musician it isn't supremely important. Just as painters had a
certain interest some years ago in determining whether 'The
Concert' was by Titian or Giorgione, so for musicians today
it is not a matter of life or death to ascertain Monteverdi's
authorship of *Il Ritorno di Ulisse.*

The artist is interested in the work, not in the name of its
creator. Do you remember the scene where Faust abruptly
asks Mephistopheles his name? And the reply:

> *Die Frage scheint mir klein*
> *Für einen, der das Wort so sehr verachtet,*
> *Der, weit entfernt von allem Schein,*
> *Nur in der Wesen Tiefe trachtet.*

> For one so down on the word,
> Who, so remote from everything external,
> Past all appearance seeks the inmost kernel,
> This question seems a bit absurd.[8]

On a more mundane level you may recall that in Paris,
thirty years ago, concerts devoted mostly to new music were
given without divulging the composer's identity, and after
the performance the audience was invited to vote its attribution. Now I ask if this procedure, applied on a large scale,
wouldn't represent progress? (And here I am not speaking
only about new music!) What an incentive to the listener's
attention! No longer would the audience supinely applaud
or censure names rather than works, as is the custom
nowadays.

And think how cautious the journalists would be! Faced

---

[8] Goethe, *Faust*, Part I, Arndt translation, p. 32.

with imminent danger, perhaps they would take their job more seriously. Granted: a batch of phrases scribbled between midnight and one o'clock does no grave harm to anyone, especially considering that a newspaper lasts only for a day and therefore has an even briefer existence than Mallarmé's vase '*D'une verrerie éphémère*'.[9] But it would take an experiment like the one I just mentioned to prove that when a newspaper editor appoints the court reporter or racing columnist as music critic, 'cloven tongues like as of fire' really don't descend from the editor's mouth, filling the journalists with the Holy Spirit and inspiring them 'to speak with other tongues'. Such an experiment would at once prove that the miracle of the Pentecost is not repeated so often as they would have us believe.

The Venetian nobleman Giacomo Badoaro, author of several librettos besides *Il Ritorno di Ulisse*, was anything but an exceptional figure in his time. 'My studies, dictated only by what pleases me, have suggested this work,' he writes in the preface to *Ulisse Errante*, set to music by Francesco Sacrati one year after Monteverdi's death. An amateur, if you like, but an amateur in the old and best sense of the word. (We shouldn't forget that Gesualdo, too, considered himself an 'amateur'.)

Giacomo Badoaro, a man of culture and taste, wrote Monteverdi an interesting, attractive poetic text, faithful enough to the final cantos of *The Odyssey*. An excessively long text no doubt, one the composer had to prune to a considerable degree; a text that perhaps made too many concessions to the taste of the period, but which was executed in masterly fashion and was linguistically more than respectable.

In a recent article entitled '*Il Ritorno di Ulisse in Patria*',[10] Alberto Savinio, writing with characteristic vitality and spirit, could allude to a certain 'Ibsenian' quality in Homer's hero. He observed that Ulysses, 'in order to die as he preferred, would have to wait for Dante to make him cross

[9] 'Of an ephemeral glassware': from *Autres Poèmes et Sonnets* II.
[10] In *Illustrazione Toscana*, Series II, No. 2, Florence, April 1942, pp. 25–27.

the Pillars of Hercules and be engulfed by a whirlwind in view of the mountain of Purgatory'. An altogether legitimate concept, one I myself endorsed a few years ago when Léonide Massine asked me to write him a ballet based on several episodes from *The Odyssey*. Indeed, I told him then very firmly that a Ulysses who hadn't been filtered through Dante's thought would be inconceivable for an Italian today. I added that I wouldn't permit the work to conclude with a triumph in the royal palace, either because of dramatic exigencies or to gain a so-called 'success'; but rather I should want Ulysses to be alone in the final scene, fleeing towards the ocean.

But could this idea, which now seems so elementary, have occurred to a man of the 17th century, a man certainly nourished much more by the culture of Ariosto than by the culture of Dante? And can we forget the advent of Romanticism, which has sanctioned and transformed so many things? Before Romanticism would it have been possible to end an opera with that profound question mark Busoni placed at the conclusion of *Doktor Faust*? Certainly not, nor could even less daring strokes be imagined.

Let's glance at Mozart – his name will satisfy everyone. It is remarkable that the librettists and the composer are anxious never to let the audience leave the theatre in the grip of an overpowering emotion. How else can we explain the rather insignificant little chorus inserted after the sublime quartet which, to all intents and purposes, ends *Die Entführung aus dem Serail*? How otherwise account for the *allegro assai* in *Le Nozze di Figaro*, following the very moving '*Contessa, perdono!*' that soars almost to the heights of a religious chorale? As for the finale of *Don Giovanni*, I shall let E.T.A. Hoffmann have the last word:

> . . .the enormous marble colossus enters; beside him Don Juan stands there like a pygmy. The ground shakes under the thundering footsteps of the giant. Don Juan shouts through the storm, through the thunder, through the howling of the demons, his terrified '*No!*' The hour of his destruction has come. The statue vanishes, thick smoke fills the room, out of it horrible masks emerge. Don Juan writhes in the torments of hell; from time to time one catches sight of him among the demons. An explosion, as though a thousand bolts of light-

ning struck–: Don Juan and the demons have vanished, one does not know how! Leporello lies unconscious in the corner of the room. – How beneficial is the effect produced by the appearance of the other persons who look in vain for Don Juan who has been removed from earthly vengeance by the infernal powers. It is as if one had only now escaped from the fearful circle of the hellish spirits.[11]

'Beneficial,' writes Hoffmann. Nothing, I think, need be added on this subject.

*   *   *

Since we are all well informed about the birth of opera, it will not be necessary to elaborate on the experiments of Jacopo Peri and Giulio Caccini in opposition to 16th-century counterpoint or to recall the advent of Claudio Monteverdi, whose interpretation of words was the most nearly complete and perfect in the history of music. Before I try to focus attention on particular passages in *Ulisse*, permit me a general observation. What should most strongly impress us is not the beauty of individual numbers but the level of the opera as a whole, consistently so high that it couldn't be imagined except during a period of absolute 'civilization' – I would almost say a time when civilization was in the very air.

The characters are musically delineated with perfect clarity, and that applies to the peripheral as well as the central figures. Furthermore, both the principal and secondary characters are drawn with exemplary coherence from beginning to end. This clarity of characterization never fades in certain episodes that may remind us of patches of colour. One example among many: the 'Chorus of the Phaeacians aboard Ship' [Act I, Scene 6], where the rascally, piratical note is struck so forcefully as to be unforgettable after a single hearing. (In this case, the extreme brevity of the episode only heightens its effectiveness.)

The musical interpretation of words culminates in the

---

[11] From '*Don Juan*' in *Fantasiestücke in Callots Manier* (1814–15); translated by Harry Steinhauer, in *German Stories*, Bantam Books, New York, 1961, p. 55.

roles of Ulysses and Penelope. The Queen's monologue, which begins the opera, is certainly one of the great pages in music history and worthy of comparison with it is the scene 'Ulysses awakes', also in Act I. In the opening monologue, the profound expression of muted sorrow is unbroken except by a fleeting ray of hope, when Penelope yields to an instant of rapture and contemplation:

> *Torna il tranquillo al mare,*
> *Torna il Zeffiro al prato. . .*

> Calm returns to the sea,
> The zephyr returns to the meadow. . .

In contrast to this prevailing immobility, Scene 7 expresses the thoughts of one awakened to everyday reality. Behold the man Ulysses, lost and alone on the deserted seashore, who feels that he is still very far from the end of his tribulations. He isn't afraid to complain about the cruelty of the gods and invokes a terrible curse on the Phaeacians, who he believes have broken their word:

> *Sia delle vostre vele, falsissimi Feaci,*
> *Sempre Borea nemico:*
> *E sian qual piume al vento o scogli in mare*
> *Le vostre infide navi,*
> *Leggere agli Aquiloni, all'aure gravi.*

> May the north wind buffet your sails,
> False-hearted Phaeacians:
> May your treacherous ships
> Lie becalmed in fair weather
> And be tossed by the gale like a feather.

I should now like to comment briefly on several scenes containing more than one character. Compare Act I, Scene 8, between Minerva and Ulysses, with Act II, Scene 3, between Telemachus and Ulysses. Minerva appears in the guise of an Arcadian shepherd, and Ulysses asks her the name of the beach where he has awakened:

> *Itaca è questa, in sen di questo mare,*
> *Porto famoso e spiaggia felice avventurata. . .*

> This is Ithaca, in the bosom of this sea,
> Famous port and shore of happy fortunes. . .

answers Minerva. Ulysses then relates how he was sheltered by the Phaeacians and how the storm had afterwards cast him up on the beach. As the scene continues, each of the two characters speaks with a distinctive voice: Minerva's words are never superimposed on those of Ulysses. In the drama, as in the music, a distance is always maintained between the man and the god. How different is the demeanour of the characters, how different the whole musical expression, in the scene between Telemachus and Ulysses. When the father is reunited with his son and reveals his identity, Telemachus expresses heartfelt joy – but joy still confined to the minor mode! – and their ensuing dialogue grows increasingly agitated. At a certain moment, however, the two voices are heard in unison, now in the bright key of *C major* to celebrate the dignified jubilation of reunion. Between father and son there are no barriers like those which separated the hero from the god.

A few additional words about Penelope's suitors: Amphinomus, Pisandrus, and Antinous. Charles van den Borren correctly perceived that of the three, only Antinous was distinctly characterized. But if we don't find the other two odious either in poetic or musical terms, as their role would imply, they nevertheless have that knightly bearing typical of *cavalieri antiqui* ('knights of old') without which even the sullen disposition of Antinous could not be brought into the necessary relief.

In physique and musical characterization, Irus, the fat buffoon who sponges on the suitors, seems to anticipate Falstaff by two and a half centuries. This is certainly interesting and worthy of thought. Having weathered the storms of a long career and attained the utmost serenity, Giuseppe Verdi, who couldn't have known *Ulisse*, overleapt 18th-century *opera buffa* and was led by his formidable instinct back to the wellspring of the Italian musical spirit. A coincidence which reminds us that history is rich in such ideal meetings.

Not even in *Ulisse*, with its bold musical language, did Monteverdi abandon that word-emphasis the madrigalists had used so tellingly. In the monologue of the shepherd Eumaeus [Act I, Scene 11] or in the suitors' terzetto [Act II, Scene 8], when the noun *sospiro* ('sigh') or the verb *sospirare* appears the melodic line is broken by a rest. The noun *dolore* ('grief'), the adjectives *dolente* and *discordante* ('sorrowful', 'discordant') – how can we forget Penelope facing the gravest decision of her life? – are expressed by dissonances. When Ulysses tells Minerva about his having been swept onto the shore at Ithaca by the *vento infido* ('fickle wind'), the music portrays the word *vento* with agitated figurations.

In my teaching I once hit upon the term 'ideogram' as a definition of such devices.[12] I am not aware if others have used it previously in the same sense, but in any case it does seem precise enough to express the idea. ('Eternity', in Chinese calligraphy, is represented by a bridge with water flowing beneath it.) I hope, at least, that others will not be inclined to interpret what I have called 'ideograms' as an expression of 'realism' (*verismo*) or 'naturalism' in music!

*   *   *

In the first part of this lecture, where I spoke about the Vienna manuscript, I used the term *partitura*. A precise term, since a score is nothing more than an assembly of 'parts'. Even in appearance, however, 17th-century scores differed greatly from those of later periods. With the exception of brief instrumental episodes designated *sinfonie* and *ritornelli*, in which the bass and four upper parts were fully noted, the scores of the 1600s were generally written on only two staves: one for the vocal line and one for the bass – the harmonic bass note, sometimes figured. Such scores have an almost stenographic appearance. Everything that lies between the vocal part and the bass must be completed, or, to use the technical term, 'realized'.

And here arise two parallel problems: the problem of interpretation and that of transcription, both widely discussed in Italy a few years ago. I shall not quote extensively from this debate, for the sake of brevity but especially because of an arrant display of empty verbiage by some who are more skilful in dialectics than in musical practice. Is it worth using weighty words and tangled syntax to describe

---

[12] See pp. 20–21, n. 17; p. 72, n. 3.

Grieg's ridiculous 'To the Spring'?[13] The lack of proportion is only too obvious. Such sterile disquisitions – I will not even call them 'displays of ingenuity' – can but remind us of certain conclusions Miguel de Unamuno reached in Chapter 2 of *The Tragic Sense of Life*. The philosopher, wrote the great Spaniard,

> philosophizes in order to live. Usually he philosophizes so as to be able to resign himself to life, or to seek some end-purpose, or to distract himself and forget his woes, or by way of sport and games. A good example of this last is that terrible Athenian ironist who was Socrates, of whom Xenophon in his *Memorabilia* relates that he was so skillful in describing to Theodata, the courtesan, the artifice she should employ in luring lovers to her house that she invited the philosopher to be her companion in the chase. . . : in a word, her pimp. The truth is that philosophy oftentimes tends to become a pimping art, albeit spiritual. And sometimes it is used as an opiate to alleviate pain.[14]

Among those who have reached positive conclusions on the problem of interpretation, I shall mention Alfredo Parente. He insists that the interpreter's task is 'to restore the physical conditions indispensable for the communication *of the work of art*; to revive the music of the past in its most authentic form and, therefore, in the spirit of greatest fidelity to the text; and to re-invest the written symbols with the values nearest those the composer intended by his use of graphic notation'.[15] Ferdinando Ballo rejoined that in this way 'the interpreter sacrifices every subjective value in order to become a cold scholar, bent on reconstructing with abstract fidelity the precious fragments of an incomplete notation; and one then thinks there can exist a perfect, absolute interpretation that must only be copied forever'.[16]

---

[13] *Lyric Pieces* (Series III), Op. 43, No. 6.
Dallapiccola alludes to an article by Edmondo Cione, '*Ancora a Proposito dell' Interpretazione Musicale*', in *La Rassegna Musicale*, Vol. V, No. 4, Turin, July 1932.

[14] Kerrigan translation, p. 34.

[15] An inexact quotation by Ferdinando Ballo (see following note) from Parente's book *La Musica e le Arti*, Laterza, Bari, 1936, p. 220.

[16] '*Interpretazione e Trascrizione*', *La Rassegna Musicale*, Vol. IX, No. 6, Turin, June 1936, pp. 190–191.

The results achieved, for example, by Arturo Toscanini might be said to support Parente's view. My impression, both in live performances and from recordings, has consistently been that Toscanini maintains a certain distance from the work of art in order to master its broadest perspective before recreating it in detail. Ballo's thesis, on the other hand, is close to certain ideas outlined earlier by Ferruccio Busoni in the *Sketch of a New Aesthetic of Music*: '"Notation" ("writing down") brings up the subject of Transcription'; and further, 'the performance of a work is also a transcription. . .'.[17]

It is absolutely certain that Busoni was referring to the period from J.S. Bach to post-Romanticism. We have only to read the preface of *The Well-Tempered Clavier* to realize that this great musician never thought of examining the music of previous centuries. No doubt Busoni profoundly loved Palestrina and Monteverdi, as many of his letters attest; but both were outside his field as an executant, and at the moment we are interested in performance practice. 'The performance of a work is also a transcription': I repeat and insist upon this proposition. And make no mistake about it, Busoni was speaking of music completely written out in all its parts, not of 'shorthand' notation. Did he therefore vindicate the rights of the interpreter? Certainly. Nor did he boast lightly of them.

Allegro deciso is the tempo marking Busoni proposes for the two-part fugue in E minor [Book I], which lacks an original indication. And in a footnote he expresses all his agony as a performer and a pedagogue, reminding us that Hugo Riemann ascribes a 'rather contemplative' character to the same piece, while Karl Tausig suggests an *Allegro con fuoco* and Hans Bischoff, an *Allegro capriccioso*. If the mere lack of tempo indications in Bach's music offers four unimpeachable authorities such a latitude of interpretation, who then will question the validity of Busoni's dictum, par-

---

See also G. Alberto Mantelli, '*Compositore e Trascrittore*', *La Rassegna Musicale*, Vol. VII, No. 2, March-April 1934, pp. 97–108.

[17] *Entwurf einer neuen Ästhetik der Tonkunst* (1907), translated (1911) by Theodore Baker, in *Three Classics in the Aesthetic of Music*, Dover, New York/Constable, London, 1962, p. 85; *cf. Lo Sguardo Lieto*, p. 52.

ticularly with regard to a work like *Il Ritorno di Ulisse* that specifies no instrumentation?

It seems likely that the Teatro di San Cassiano, at Venice, could muster only a very small orchestra: harpsichord, theorbo, and strings. Vincent d'Indy adheres to this scoring in his edition of *Ulisse* for the 1925 Paris production, and the preface informs us that his work has no musicological pretensions but simply aims to facilitate the performance of a masterpiece. Since the text as Monteverdi left it can be understood only by exceptionally competent musicians, my work too should be considered essentially 'practical': a *musical translation*. And this is necessary, since not even a discerning amateur – much less the general public – can realize what the original manuscript implies between the vocal part and the bass or imagine the voice-leading, the *drama of sound*, which must re-inforce the fundamental drama always expressed by the human voice.

At this point someone will ask: who has the right to undertake such projects? It is not for me to say, as after many months of passionate work I could hardly answer objectively. I *can* say, however, that during the long period devoted to my labour of 'translation' I always kept in mind the beautiful words Busoni wrote in August 1914, on releasing his edition of Bach's *Goldberg* Variations:

> In order to rescue this important composition for concert programmes, so that the thousands who are not able to perform it can at least hear it, the editor must make it more accessible by selectively abridging and retouching (more so than in other works by Bach) – accessible as much to the intellectual powers of the listener as to the faculties of the performer.

Before I explain my editorial method, it is necessary to clarify one other point.

Should transcription of old works be the province of musicologists or practicing musicians? Both parties frequently exhaust themselves debating this issue, and at Siena a couple of years ago the discussions became rather animated.[18] While I was not present, I could infer from what

[18] During the 'Scarlatti Week' (15–20 September 1940), organized by the Accademia Musicale Chigiana.

was reported that there was a little right and a little wrong on each side. Today I am more convinced than ever that both scholars and performers can and should make their own editions. These editions will co-exist and complement one another, in the same way that the various popular translations of Homer and Virgil complement the countless pure philological studies which elucidate doubtful points and compare texts.

Just as literary translations (with very rare exceptions) have a limited life span, because they more or less reflect the taste of their times and disappear to make room for others more in conformity with the taste of later generations, so it is and so it should be with musical translations. And no one will deny that a similar fate is reserved for interpretations. The work of the philologist and the historian, on the other hand, seems to suffer from far fewer limitations than that of the 'free' translator. This is natural, for the historian is not pre-occupied with the taste of a particular epoch; he has other aims and other aspirations. Because his work is restricted to a small circle of specialists and adepts, he doesn't have to make concessions to a wider, less accomplished public.

Among the concessions I felt compelled to make, let me first mention the many long cuts, always designed to keep alive the dramatic interest. I haven't followed the example of Vincent d'Indy, who eliminated the whole mythological apparatus except the character of Minerva, because he considered it extraneous to the plot. Indeed, I made a point of preserving Neptune's splendid monologue and his dialogue with Jupiter in Act I. But like d'Indy I preferred to dispense with a long mythological scene in Act III, a mere concession to the taste of an era that liked to see gods on the stage for the lavish theatrical display their appearance warranted.

I have lightened the dialogue, thereby reducing the exceedingly long opera (originally four-and-one-half hours of music) to a more normal length. I have added several brief instrumental episodes, derived from Monteverdi's thematic material, at the beginning and end of certain scenes which lacked a sinfonia, and sometimes at the end of scenes to accompany the exit of a character. I have also appended things of no musical importance: for example, a chord [in Act I, Scene 6] where Neptune (Poseidon) changes the Phaeacian ship into a rock, to avoid an inconsistency unacceptable to the audiences of today – that of seeing such an important event take place on stage without hearing the slightest orchestral comment.

Observing bass progressions of ascending fourths in Neptune's monologue and [in Act I, Scene 8], where Ulysses tells Minerva–

Ma dal cruccioso mar, dal vento infido
Fummo a forza cacciati a questo lido

But the fickle wind and the fierce sea
Impelled us towards this lee

–and also analogous progressions [in Act I, Scene 13], where the shepherd Eumaeus speaks of '*cielo irato*' ('Heaven enraged'), I concluded that chance could not account for them all. There seemed to be a principle at work here not unlike an embryonic Leitmotiv. And with the intention of making the *musical unity* more readily apparent to the audience of today, I have tried to develop the leading theme by applying it to the characters of Ulysses and Penelope as well, while always respecting Monteverdi's bass. Only in this way can my realization of the sinfonia preceding Neptune's monologue be explained, a realization which capitalizes on the original picturesque stage direction: 'Here the Phaeacian ship carrying Ulysses puts out to sea. Ulysses sleeps, and in order not to awaken him the following sinfonia is played very softly, always on one string'.

In Monteverdi's time, orchestral musicians were expected to improvise on a given bass. Undoubtedly they were proficient in the use of a certain number of formulas, much as jazz musicians are today – though, of course, with very different results. I felt that the harmonization should maintain great simplicity and dignity. If I have broken this rule, the very rare exceptions will be noted just at those points where the character, in a transport such as the 'awakening of Ulysses', renounces words and bursts into a cry more expressive than any gesture or any word.

I have used the large modern orchestra, for a very simple reason: old instruments aren't available, nor are performers skilled in 17th-century bowing technique. And apart from such practical considerations, only with the large orchestra could I characterize the principal roles, by using particular groups of instruments. This, too, is part of my concept of 'musical translation'. Since my work is addressed to the public, I have tried through instrumental characterization to differentiate the recitatives as clearly as possible. In the 17th century, after all, with the resources then at hand, each scene was given its own special instrumental colour.

In my 'translation' the character of Penelope is commented on by the chamber orchestra; the duet between Melantho and Eurymachus, by the small classical orchestra with the addition of harpsichord and harp; Neptune, by the brass, low woodwinds, violas, and double-basses; Jupiter, by the high woodwinds, violins, and cellos. Ulysses is accompanied by the large orchestra, which of course participates in the ensemble scenes. For dramatic – not exclusively musical – reasons, I have occasionally doubled the parts of the three suitors with the chorus. And the suitors are also characterized instrumentally.

I recall once hearing a marvellous orchestral transcription of several toccatas by Girolamo Frescobaldi.[19] Balance, flair for timbre, fidelity to the style – all completely realized. Yet my admiration for this arrangement was not transformed into love, because it sought to imitate (or, if you like, interpret) the organ by means of the orchestra. I know: Frescobaldi wrote for the organ. But the orchestra has *its own* voice, very different from all others. I think that once he has accepted this new and different voice, the transcriber should no longer imitate or interpret the original voice but should rather intensify the individual parts of the musical composition with the new means at his disposal, almost as though it were a matter of 'absolute music'.

In his version of the six-part Ricercare from Bach's *Musical Offering*, Anton von Webern gave us, I believe, the greatest model of artistic transcription of absolute music. And in the case of a work written for no particular instrument, a work

---

[19] Transcription for string orchestra by G.F. Malipiero (Ricordi, 1930).

that is music and only music, transcription is more justified than ever. 'Tradition. . . ,' someone will whisper. Ferruccio Busoni – much quoted, but never enough – Busoni defined tradition as 'a plaster mask taken from life which, in the course of many years, and after passing through the hands of innumerable artisans, leaves its resemblance to the original largely a matter of imagination.'[20] Even those who cannot fully accept this definition would admit that tradition is an internal matter and, therefore, very difficult to define.

*   *   *

In speaking of *Il Ritorno di Ulisse in Patria*, first performed in 1641 at the Teatro di San Cassiano, Venice, I have always used the generic designation 'opera'. For love of precision – and with the hope that no wise guy of the moment will declare it isn't an opera because it has no introductory chorus of Penelope's maid-servants, no 'brindisi' of the suitors, no 'improvisation' by Ulysses, no eulogy by Amphinomus – I will add that Giacomo Badoaro and Claudio Monteverdi called *Il Ritorno di Ulisse in Patria* a '*dramma in musica*'.[21]

---

[20] *Sketch of a New Esthetic of Music*, p. 77, n. 1.

[21] Dent points out that 'the Italian word *opera* is hardly ever to be found at all on any Italian title-page, although *opera* was a colloquial word for musical drama at Rome as early as 1644, and it appears quite frequently in Italian critical and theoretical writings. . . . Commercial opera begins at Venice in 1637, and from that time onwards the favourite category-title is *dramma per musica*'.

'The Nomenclature of Opera', Part I, pp. 132 and 134.

Birth of a
Libretto
(1967)

Ladies and Gentlemen:
My long years of teaching have presented me with ample opportunity to offer my students these words of advice: 'Memory, memory, and again memory. Take careful notice of everything around you: none of you can know *a priori* how important your brief notes might later be to your work'.[1] And how many times have I told my students what assistance I received, at a very important moment of my

---

[1] 'Convinced as I am that nothing in the world happens by chance, I have advised my students to look around them and take notes – for the purpose of documentation. And I never fail to mention that in most cases certain impressions appear *more beautiful* with time, but in every case *different*. I also advised them to accept the results of this distorting power of memory, since it is obvious that what one's memory has stored up will become fatefully *something else* on the day it assumes artistic significance'.

'*L'Arte Figurativa e le Altre Arti*', *Parole e Musica*, p. 160.

'It has always been my habit to copy out the poems I might one day set to music, keeping them in my wallet (sometimes for many years) and committing them to memory. Only by memorizing a poem can I truly appreciate it – by turning it over and over in my mind as I walk the streets, savouring every word and every syllable. Without such a process of gradual absorption, I don't believe I could possibly find a musical equivalent for the poem. And I have never hesitated to suggest this method to my students, at least as a first approach to the work of composition. At the same time, I have always recommended that they memorize their twelve-tone rows and the transformations of the rows, however complex and complicated they may be'.

'*A Proposito dei "Cinque Canti"*', *Parole e Musica*, p. 491.

232

formation, from the two great poets of memory – Marcel Proust and James Joyce.[2]

I have also emphasized, especially with my more advanced students, the problem of reciprocity between the author and his work, often quoting in this regard an enlightening sentence by Friedrich Nietzsche: 'And when you look long into an abyss, the abyss also looks into you'.[3]

I would like to ask that my audience please keep these introductory words in mind, as I speak today for the first time about the libretto of my soon-to-be-completed opera *Ulisse*.

Some years ago, when *Il Prigioniero* was performed at La Scala Theatre of Milan,[4] the music critic Massimo Mila wrote in his programme notes: 'From Puccini forward, we witness the common and rather depressing phenomenon of composers desperately searching for a "good libretto" with the same indifference and sense of detachment with which, on the eve of a friend's wedding, one would window-shop for a "nice present"'. Mila concluded that I, who have the honour of speaking to you today (and on such a special occasion), am not one of these composers, since 'librettos were always within him, demanding to be set to music'. It would seem that Mila, together with Proust, believes in the *pre-existence* of the work of art.[5]

May I add that during my years as a teacher, I have often pointed out that it is not always we who choose our texts; but at times it is the texts themselves which, coming to meet us, choose *us*. And so we have our first reference to Nietzsche's 'abyss'.

As I embark on this new voyage into my *temps perdu*,[6] I would like to establish three dates corresponding to three

---

[2] See 'On the Twelve-Note Road', *Music Survey*, October 1951, pp. 323–329.

[3] *Beyond Good and Evil*, Aphorism 146 [translated by Walter Kaufmann, Vintage Books, New York, 1966, p. 89].   –LD

[4] 17 February 1962.

[5] See p. 192.

[6] See p. 37.

events. The first two will probably seem, and rightly so, more odd than important; the third I consider fundamental.

May 1938: Léonide Massine suggested that I compose a ballet based on *The Odyssey*. The contract was duly signed by both parties, but a few months later the choreographer abandoned his original project and proposed another subject of mythological character: *Diana*.[7] The outbreak of World War II abruptly interrupted our negotiations.

Spring 1941: Mario Labroca, Intendant of the Florentine Maggio Musicale, commissioned me to edit Claudio Monteverdi's opera *Il Ritorno di Ulisse in Patria* for the contemporary theatre and to adapt its score for modern orchestra.

(I won't deny that these periodical appearances of Ulysses in my path aroused my curiosity and, with it, a certain sense of wonder. I began to feel that it wasn't simply a question of coincidence. In the meantime, images were rising from the depths of my unconscious – images so lost in the distant past I thought I had forgotten them.)

August 1912: I was on holiday with my parents and my brother in Ala, a small town in the Trentino. I remember that my brother and I were astonished one afternoon when our father, a humanist who had seldom shown any interest in or sympathy for what was then called 'the tenth muse', said that it would be better to have an early supper so that we could all go to the movies. A few hours later we understood our father's unexpected interest in this form of entertainment, to which he was constitutionally alien, when the title of the film appeared in bold white letters against the scarcely darker background of the screen of an open-air theatre:[8]

HOMER'S *ODYSSEY*.

---

[7] With stage design by Henri Matisse, who wrote to Dallapiccola on 13 June 1939, shortly before the composer's departure for Paris, to arrange a meeting. See *LD: Saggi. . .*, p. 64.

[8] Directed by Giuseppe de Liguoro, for the Milan Film Company, 1911.
                                                                                                    –LD

At a round-table on the interrelationship of the arts (Florence, 1963), Dallapiccola spoke about what he had learned from the cinema:

'In *Crime et Châtiment*, with Pierre Blanchard and Madeleine Ozeray, and music by Arthur Honegger (1937, I believe [1935; the director was Pierre

We all know how embarrassing it is – at least if one isn't a poet – to try to put a dream into words. Embarrassing because we are aware that, even though it might be easy to relate what happened in the dream, it is exceedingly difficult to render the flavour and especially that sense of distance always so characteristic of dreams. By the same token, I realize the near hopelessness of any attempt to speak today about a film I saw once, exactly fifty-five years ago. Nevertheless, I must take this risk.

At that time, as you know, films were in black and white. However, for special effects, and perhaps in order to obtain a greater visual variety, a particular device was sometimes used which I wouldn't be able to explain technically. The film was tinted an even, pervasive colour that varied according to the scenic requirements and the character of the action.

I can still see Penelope, bathed in a pale yellow light, as she weaves the shroud. I still see her gesture of disappointment and her desperate expression the night she is surprised by the suitors in the act of undoing her day's work.

Chenal]), I was impressed more strongly than I had ever been in the opera house by how vision can condition one's perception of musical dynamics, in certain very special cases. In this case: Raskolnikov leaves the chambers of Judge Porfiry after having been interrogated for the third time. The music has been silent for several minutes. Raskolnikov moves a few steps along the gallery; below, in the portico opposite him, appears Sonia, deathly pale, wearing a black scarf. Precisely at this moment the music bursts in with a strident *fortissimo*. Only a second viewing reveals that the apparent *ff* is actually a mere *mf*. It was Sonia's unexpected appearance that deceived our ears.

'Renoir's *La Grande Illusion* taught me the effect of perspective that different languages can give in dialogue. I am alluding particularly to his very restrained use of Oxford English, and of what the English language signified in the early decades of the 20th century. (For those who might not remember, *La Grande Illusion* is set during World War I.) This accounts for the surprising effect of the last words Major von Rauffenstein – Erich von Stroheim – shouts at the lieutenant who is about to escape, before killing him with a shot from his revolver. Here it isn't a matter of contradiction:* Oxford English was the chic parlance par excellence. The final warning, von Rauffenstein's entreating his prisoner to turn back – considering what happens earlier in the film – is nothing if not chivalrous'.

'*L'Arte Figurativa e le Altre Arti*', *Parole e Musica*, pp. 161–162.
*See p. 129, n. 1.

Here is Nausicaa (the background is now a soft green),
playing ball with her maidservants in a bright clearing on
the island of the Phaeacians. A threatening dark blue hangs
over Scylla and Charybdis, as Ulysses' ship is tossed like a
wisp of straw on the churning sea. I believe that the scene of
Ulysses' revenge took place in a wash of blood red, while I
am certain that the cave of the Cyclops was immersed in a
reddish-brown light.

Motion pictures, at the time, were in their first stages of
development. The film I am speaking of was naturally silent,
accompanied here and there by subtitles that interrupted
the action for a few seconds. Since it was a silent picture, the
style of acting, needless to say, was excessively declamatory;
yet this overdone pantomime managed to attain a rather
convincing eloquence. Of course, such eloquence if judged
by today's standards would border on the ridiculous, but in
those days it was accepted. Let me give an example.

When Ulysses announces to his terrified comrades, hud-
dled together in a corner of Polyphemus's den, that he has
found a way to get rid of the Cyclops by blinding him, he
touches his right index-finger to his forehead as if struck by
a sudden revelation. A sublime gesture in its own way, which
dwarfs Archimedes' '*eureka*'!

I don't remember Circe at all, nor can I recall whether the
masterpiece of Ulysses's cunning was included in the film.
The fact that Ulysses himself considered it his masterpiece
can be inferred from the self-satisfaction of his comment
after passing one of the hardest tests in the terrible adventure with the Cyclops:

> And I was filled with laughter
> To see how like a charm the name deceived them.[9]

I am referring, as you know, to the passage where Ulysses
tells Poseidon's son, Polyphemus, who is quite drunk, that
his name is 'Nobody':

> 'My name is Nohbdy: mother, father, and friends,
> Everyone calls me Nohbdy'.[10]

[9] Homer, *The Odyssey*, translated by Robert Fitzgerald, Anchor Books,
New York, 1963, p. 157.
[10] *Ibid.*, p. 156.

In 1938 Dr Julius Bahle, lecturer at the University of Constance in Germany, sent me a questionnaire. He wanted to know, in relation to certain studies of his, how a composer works.

It was the first time I had faced such a question. With the aid of memory and my diary, I discovered – much to my surprise at not having observed it before – that there was a *constant* factor in my creative process. By this I mean that the first idea which flashed into my mind, rather than being a germ cell, was the culminating point of the whole composition. When answering Dr Bahle, I cited as examples *Sei Cori di Michelangelo Buonarroti il Giovane* and *Tre Laudi*, two of my major pieces at the time. Today, even my most recent works might be taken to illustrate this observation. But I prefer not to digress.

In a drawer – the most hidden drawer, I think – in my studio at Florence, there is a manuscript that no one has seen or must ever see. It is an opera libretto entitled *Rappresentazione di Anima et di Corpo*, 1932. The date speaks clearly for itself: this libretto was written five years before I began composing my first opera, *Volo di Notte*. And the date and title speak clearly for yet another reason: in those years we were still rediscovering the old Italian masters, and I had always been particularly fond of Emilio de' Cavalieri's oratorio *La Rappresentazione di Anima et di Corpo* [1600].

This libretto was one in which the scenes were linked together by a very thin thread. We must remember that Gian Francesco Malipiero had already given us such masterpieces as *Sette Canzoni* and *Torneo Notturno*. The structure of these works can be accurately described as a series of loosely-related 'panels'. We should also keep in mind a famous letter Ferruccio Busoni wrote to his wife from London in 1913, in which he relates that upon seeing a poster announcing the film *Dante's Hell*, he was seized with the idea for an opera presenting a succession of independent episodes from *The Divine Comedy*.[11] Although it never materi-

---

[11] 'I should not stop with Hell, and not presume as far as Heaven; but end with the meeting with Beatrice.

'Piazza della Signoria, with Dante sitting on the stone on which he was wont to dream; a characteristic street scene depicting the time, perhaps,

alized, Busoni's project is important because it demonstrates how urgently the need for a renovation of opera was
felt even at the time. It reveals too that Busoni, like Malipiero, had in mind a new kind of opera – as distant from
Wagner as from the Italian *verismo*.[12]

My libretto, undoubtedly a monstrosity from a stylistic
viewpoint, consisted of a series of texts from extremely
diverse epochs. There was a fragment from *La Chanson de
Roland* next to an episode from *Don Quixote*; Peer Gynt's
monologue in front of his dying mother; texts from the
macabre masques of the Renaissance alongside a scene from
Più che l'Amore by Gabriele d'Annunzio; and finally, a *lauda* by
Fra Jacopone da Todi. (And this list is far from being

---

too, with Beatrice passing by. And afterwards some six pictures of the
most distinctive episodes: Ugolino, Paolo and Francesca, a couple of
pictures with crowds; finally, the ascent with Beatrice. And, of course, in
Italian'.   Busoni, *Letters to His Wife*, p. 218.

[12] See pp. 109–110. From a lecture given at the Cherubini Conservatory, Florence, on 8 March 1936:

'Mussorgsky instituted the search for psychological truth in opera, and
Ernest Bloch tried to continue it in his early opera *Macbeth* by analyzing
every word, every syllable, every accent. Sometimes, unfortunately, he
neglected the music.

'But already at the beginning of this century, Ferruccio Busoni protested
against Wagnerian drama and against the search for truth on the basis
of declamation. Busoni realized perfectly that the post-Wagnerian theatre
was moribund and that Engelbert Humperdinck was certainly not the
man to resurrect it.

'Busoni desired a return to closed forms, to *parlato*, aria, and ensemble.
In short, he wanted music to regain its ascendancy over words, as in
Mozart's day; or at least, he wished that music, while closely following the
action and the text, should not relinquish logic and structural indepen-
dence. Closed forms have never impeded the precise invention of reality.
[Verdi wrote that the reproduction and interpretation of reality are
excellent things, but that the artist has the task of inventing reality.] In
Leporello's aria "*Ah, Signor, per carità*", Mozart invents fear with strictly
musical means and much more effectively than Bloch, in the scene where
a servant tells Macbeth that Birnam Wood is moving! And in a few bars of
Norma ("*poveri, teneri figli!*"), Bellini invents the drama of maternal love in
such a way that Bloch's scene between Lady Macduff and her son pales by
comparison, despite its sublime text.

'Busoni, then, desired a return to closed forms, and in his operas gave
some notable examples of how his theory could be applied'.

'*Di un Aspetto della Musica Contemporanea*', *Parole e Musica*, pp. 219–220.

complete![13]) If I speak today of such an amorphous and immature endeavour, it is only to emphasize that this libretto presented us the life of man: which means his errors, his questions, his endless struggle. All things considered, the fundamental idea was not astronomically far from that of *Ulisse*.

And now it should be clear why I mentioned the questionnaire sent to me by Dr Bahle. Not only did the initial idea of each composition prove to be the climax of that particular work, but my first attempt at musical theatre already foreshadowed the opera that was to be the culmination of all my intervening efforts, from *Volo di Notte* to the mystery play *Job*.

It has been noted that the central idea of all my works for the musical theatre is always the same: the struggle of man against some force much stronger than he. In *Volo di Notte* we witness the struggle of Rivière, the solitary director of an airline company, who tries despite general opposition to impose night flights; and there is also the ill-fated struggle of the pilot Fabien against the natural elements. The ballet *Marsia* portrays the famous contest between the satyr Marsyas, discoverer of music, and the god Apollo. In *Il Prigioniero*, the Prisoner struggles against the Spanish Inquisition. And finally, the protagonist of *Job* asks God the hardest, most compelling question man has ever dared put to the Divinity. (Not by chance did the idea of *Job* suddenly come to me after I saw Harald Kreutzberg dance a piece entitled *Job Struggles with God*.)

Although Rivière attains a partial victory – only partial, because he clearly feels he is 'bearing his heavy load of victory' – Marsyas is completely vanquished for having dared challenge Apollo. The Prisoner falls into the arms of the Grand Inquisitor, who leads him to the pyre. As for Job, he manages to save himself by virtue of his repentance, just when everything seems to be lost.

Ulysses' struggle is above all a struggle against himself, inasmuch as he aspires to penetrate the mystery of the

[13] See *Parole e Musica*, p. 562.

world. '*Guardare, meravigliarsi, e tornar a guardare*' ('To search, to wonder, and search with greater devotion') seems to be the motto that governs his life. The goddess Calypso has heard him murmur these words in his sleep. Circe, the enchantress, awakens to hear him murmuring these same words.

'Who are you? Whence do you come?' are the first questions the Lotus-eaters ask Ulysses and his comrades. Quite normal questions, as you see. But Ulysses answers evasively. Deep down he no longer knows with certainty who he is. His masterpiece of cunning is turning against him. Here I have departed from Homer, who symbolized Poseidon's vengeance as violent sea storms; in my opera it is Ulysses's sense of lost identity that avenges the god – a revenge less spectacular than the Homeric one, though by no means less painful.[14]

In Hades, Ulysses refuses to give the Shades his name. In Ithaca, just as he begins the massacre of Penelope's suitors, he makes himself known simply by drawing his bow, which in the past only he had been able to subdue.

Just once in the whole opera, and only to grant the request of King Alcinous, does he disclose his name: 'I am . . . Ulysses'. But with what uncertainty! That barely stammered 'I' is surely not an affirmation of personality. (We shall have to wait for his outburst 'I, too, have returned!' – a few moments before the slaughter – to hear him utter a conscious, affirmative 'I'.) But a second later, almost withdrawing into himself, he will ask with a shudder: 'And suppose I am . . . *Nobody*?' He hesitates an instant before pronouncing this last word, and he knows why. Ulysses, insofar as he doubts his identity, is prey to the subtle revenge of Poseidon. In this he decidedly departs from Homer, and from the epos in general, to become a man of

[14] 'To drown at sea, Poseidon's constant threat, is to vanish utterly from the world of men. This is a fate far worse than death in battle, a proper end to a heroic career. More than once Odysseus wishes he had fallen at Troy, for thus at least he could have bequeathed his son a famous name'.
Charles H. Taylor, Jr., 'The Obstacles to Odysseus' Return', *Essays on the Odyssey: Selected Modern Criticism*, ed. C.H. Taylor, Jr., Indiana University Press, Bloomington, 1969, p. 89.

Fernando Farulli's designs for the 1968 première in Berlin of
Ulisse, *here of Penelope and Ulysses. Most of the remaining*
illustrations in this book are taken from Farulli's designs (more of
which are reproduced in F. Farulli, Bühnenbilder und
Kostüme für 'Odysseus' von Luigi Dallapiccola, *STIAV,*
Florence, 1968).

our time – a time of doubt, of perennial inquiry.

Ulysses, followed by Nausicaa, has just entered the hall of
King Alcinous's palace. At that moment Demodocus, the
divine bard, is singing of the hero's great exploits:

> His proud heart was spared the disrespect
> Of returning unacknowledged to his palace,
> And finding his great feats remembered there
> By nobody. . .

Why does the chorus of spectators stress, in an undertone,
the pronoun 'nobody' (*nessuno*), transforming it into a name?
Can this, too, be a sign of the sea god's implacable persecution?

In the scene of Hades, when Ulysses tries to embrace his
mother's Shade and she dissolves 'as a shadow, as a dream',
he realizes that he is alone.

Alone. I am alone. A man
Gazing into the depths of the abyss. . .

Solitude is another element that contributes to the transformation of the mythological hero into a man of our time.[15]

'Who are you? What are you searching for?' the Shades
insistently ask. And here Ulysses, for the first time, poses
the same questions to himself: 'Who am I? What am I
searching for?' Thereupon the Shades, wandering aimlessly
through the infernal regions, repeat like a refrain some
words they had already pronounced at the beginning and
during the course of the scene:

Mourning, lamenting,
Sorrow, repenting, horror. . .

Ulysses has indirectly received his answer – the only possible answer.

In my interpretation, I have tried to reduce the legendary
figure of Ulysses to human proportions. I wanted simply to
make a man, which means a torn and tormented being, as is
every thinking man. Is it possible that, at least up to a
certain point in the action, his stature as a hero seems
diminished? He knows that his encounter with the Lotus-
eaters has been a failure: in fact, several of his comrades
have abandoned him, losing themselves forever. Nor have
his descent into Hades and the meeting with his mother
been victories. Circe reminds him how immature he was
when he landed on the island of Aeaea, and gently but
frankly insists it was she who, 'with patience, with love',
gave him another life and another youth. When she finally
realizes it will be impossible to keep Ulysses for herself, she
takes her revenge – subtly, as is the gods' wont – by giving
him a *conscience* (I am almost tempted to say the sense of sin).

[15] The modern Greek writer Nikos Kazantzakis conceived of Ulysses as
'a being that not only gazes on the abyss without disintegrating, but
which, on the contrary, is filled with coherence, pride, and manliness by
such a vision'.

The Odyssey: A Modern Sequel, transl. Kimon Friar,
Simon and Schuster, New York, 1958, p. xix.
See pp. 101–108 and 273, n. 2.

At this point, I paraphrased some verses from C.P. Cavafy's poem '*Ithaka*':

> Laistrygonians, Cyclops,
> Wild Poseidon – you won't encounter them
> Unless you bring them along inside your soul,
> Unless your soul sets them up in front of you.[16]

From this moment, it appears that Ulysses definitely becomes another person. The days of his daring exploits are forever past. The resolute, almost joyous call to his comrades, spurring them on to the shores of the Lotus-eaters–

> 'Courage!' he said, and pointed toward the land,
> 'This mounting wave will roll us shoreward soon'.[17]

–is the last cry of his youthful boldness. He is no longer young; he knows so much, so very much. His steps will lead him to the kingdom of sorrow, among the Shades of Hades, by now completely conscious of his actions and responsibilities.

One might conclude from all I have said so far that for at least two-thirds of the libretto, the victor is the invisible Poseidon, who, by means of the dread name 'Nobody', holds Ulysses in chains. But, as we know, men accomplish their greatest deeds only in circumstances of extreme necessity. Ulysses met with such a situation in the den of the Cyclops. Now, back at Ithaca, he must rid himself of Penelope's suitors, who are young and numerous while he is alone and no longer young.

On the stage we see Ulysses dressed as a beggar, shabby and miserable. Melantho, the little prostitute who entertains the suitors, is deeply worried by the appearance of this old beggar in the vicinity of the palace, for she has already met him in the mountains near Eumaeus's cabin. But

---

[16] C.P. Cavafy, *Collected Poems*, translated by Edmund Keeley and Philip Sherrard, edited by George Savidis, Princeton University Press, Princeton/Chatto & Windus, London, 1975, p. 35. See Edmund Keeley, *Cavafy's Alexandria: Study of a Myth in Progress*, Harvard University Press, Cambridge (Mass.), 1976, pp. 38–39.

[17] Alfred Tennyson, 'The Lotos-Eaters'.

Antinous, the basest, most cynical of Penelope's suitors, tries to reassure her, saying haughtily: 'That wretch is not a man'. And when Melantho asks '*What* is he?', Antinous replies: '*Who* is he? Nobody'.

Of all his failures, this for Ulysses is the bitterest, the most egregious. Unable to bear this defeat, driven by the weight of its terrible offense, he decides to proceed with his vengeance.

> Let what must be done, be done tonight.
> Ulysses aims high.

This act of vengeance, once completed, liberates him from the obsession of being Nobody. He can now return to the sea.

My Ulysses has probably already impressed you as being quite different from the image presented to us by Homer. Yet, in the course of the Epilogue he moves still farther away from that image to become more and more the man of our time, tormented by all his agonizing questions.

Alone once again on the ocean and – as Tiresias had prophesied – 'Hoary like the sea', he realizes that his long, harsh, incessant struggle to unravel the mystery of his life has come to nothing.

> From such travail, exhausting and inane,
> Mere shards of knowledge, vain
> Babblings, syllables
> Rather than words my recompense.

As he looks at the stars (how often he has observed them under different skies!), he wonders why they now appear to him in a new light, never before imagined. Here, in this silence and absolute solitude, he resembles not so much the Homeric hero as Prince Andrew Bolkonski, who, as he lay wounded at Pratzen, near Austerlitz, looked up at the clouds and realized that, until that moment, he had always seen them with different eyes – that is, with less insight.[18]

The man-Ulysses, the tortured man, feels that he lacks the Word (in the theological meaning of the term), the word

---

[18] Leo Tolstoy, *War and Peace*, Book III, Chapter 13.

| *Circe* | *Tiresias* |

capable of explaining his *raison d'être*.[19] Resigned by now, he continues to tread the path he has followed for so many years, still carrying the burden of his 'To search, to wonder, and search with greater devotion'. He seems to have accepted his destiny. Then, in the very last verse, in a moment of almost unexpected illumination, he feels he has discovered God, and this epiphany delivers him from his solitude.

Recalling the past after Ulysses's departure, Calypso is convinced that the hero did not want to return to Ithaca. She is certain that neither homesickness, nor love for his son, nor devotion to his old father induced him to leave. Nor does Calypso believe that he has forsaken her for Penelope. As we read in Homer, the goddess, on an impulse of moving human femininity, had asked Ulysses some very direct questions about his wife:

Can I be less desirable than she is?
Less interesting? Less beautiful? Can mortals

[19] Compare Schoenberg's *Moses und Aron*, Act II, last verse: '*O Wort, du Wort, das mir fehlt!*' ('O word, thou word, that I lack!'); and Busoni's *Doktor Faust*, last scene: '*Wo die Worte finden?*' ('Where can I find the words?').

Compare with goddesses in grace and form?[20]

In my opera she concludes:

> You were striving
> For something I never could fathom.

In *The Odyssey*, Tiresias prophesies the hero's return to
Ithaca and his reunion with his wife and son, and finally a
last voyage and conclusive landing after Ulysses has
attained wisdom. I have modified the prophecy of Tiresias,
in the sense that he does not speak explicitly of another
voyage but sees Ulysses alone, once again roving the ocean:

> Hoary you shall be, hoary like the sea.
> The waves will cradle you. . .

He pauses. 'All else is obscure. . . .' Then he disappears.

Now it will be clear why Calypso at the beginning of the
opera, and Tiresias in the scene of Hades, spoke as they did.
Both of them still belong to their world and are subject to its
limitations. What my Ulysses has discovered – namely, God
as we define it – transcends the pagan world of mythology.
Consequently, it is beyond the Greek prophet's powers of
foresight and beyond the ken of the goddess.

You will probably ask me why I led Ulysses to this search
and this discovery? May I remind you that in Italy, the figure
of Ulysses came to us through the filter of Dante's interpretation. Dante saw Ulysses as a seeker '*e de li vizi umani e del
valore*' ('of both human vices and virtue'). However, after
bringing him in sight of the mountain of Purgatory, after
bringing him to the threshold of the discovery of God, Dante
has him drown. Nor could the poet go any further. For him,
as for the men of his epoch, only those redeemed by Christ
or touched by Grace could rise into the light.[21]

---

[20] Fitzgerald translation, p. 87.

[21] Dante, *Inferno*, XXVI: 85–142.

'Both in its mythology and in its moral implications this is a revolutionary version of the final voyage of Ulysses. Mythologically its revolutionary feature is that Ulysses never goes home from his Odyssean
wanderings at all. Instead, he goes straight from Circe to pursue his
inordinate desire for knowledge and experience of the unknown world.
Moralistically Ulysses now becomes a symbol of sinful desire for forbidden

A few years after I finished school, I re-read *The Odyssey*, and this time I noticed several aspects my teachers had failed to point out. I was particularly fascinated when I realized that the poem, which is relatively brief (a little more than 12,000 lines in all), presents an admirable characterization of the five possible types of women.[22]

Calypso, who offers Ulysses immortality on the condition that he stay with her forever on the island of Ogygia, impressed me as a symbol of the inspirer.

Nausicaa, whose love is first revealed in a dream, struck me as the most moving character. In so few hours this young girl has understood everything there is to understand, even the very difficult lesson that life is renunciation. Her love for Ulysses is quite real, nor is Ulysses himself insensible to her youthful grace and charm. Nevertheless, their paths run parallel. Nausicaa's farewell is the most extraordinary one could imagine:

> Stranger, you who have seen so much,
> Stranger, you who have suffered so much,
> When you return to your native land
> Think of me sometimes. . .

The daughter of King Alcinous, whose people sail their ships not with oars but with sheer strength of will, asks nothing more than this of the man who has called himself the unhappiest of all mortals.

I recalled Anticleia rather clearly. I was always deeply

---

knowledge. This gives Dante his ultimate reason for condemning him as a false counsellor, because by persuading his comrades to follow him in the quest for knowledge he led them to destruction.'
> W.B. Stanford, *The Ulysses Theme: A Study in the Adaptability of a Traditional Hero*, Basil Blackwell, Oxford, 1968, p. 181.

[22] 'Odysseus' quest for identity is in fact profoundly involved with the feminine. In seeking the wholeness of his being, he passes through intimate experience with various embodiments of archetypal woman, each reflecting some aspect of what he as masculine hero lacks. The majority of these women pose the temptation of a return to the matriarchal order, where a man may be killed or be comfortable, but is dead as a hero in either case. . . . Only Penelope shares Odysseus' intellectual alertness and is yet so alluring that she can represent the feminine counterpart of his heroic individuality.'
Taylor, 'The Obstacles to Odysseus' Return', *Essays on the Odyssey*, p. 98.

moved by this unsurpassed mother figure, who, among the
Shades of Hades, tells her son:

> My longing, my heartache for you, whom destiny
> Drove far over the ocean; the anguish
> Consuming my soul, when I sensed your peril:
> This and my desperate, piercing love
> For you destroyed my body.[23]

I had remembered Circe above all for her carnality, but
the second encounter revealed a woman of extraordinary
intelligence. This is the reason why, as I have said before, I
at first entrusted her with the task of correcting Ulysses's
imperfections and later (also as a revenge), of giving him a
conscience.

My first impression of Penelope must have been a very
superficial one, for it was she who surprised me the most.
Upon reconsidering her, I saw Penelope as a gigantic figure,
the most heroic character in *The Odyssey*.[24]

Although I don't believe a sixth type of woman exists, it is
obvious that several features of the five types I noticed in *The
Odyssey* can be found summed up in the same person.

There are three instances in my opera *Ulisse* where I have
given two roles to the same interpreter. This is the case
when two characters have various points in common.

Calypso has her human parallel in Penelope. The name
'Calypso' means 'the one who hides', with an evident
allusion to the setting sun. In fact, the island of Ogygia is

---

[23] Almost identical words are spoken by the Prisoner's mother in the
Prologue of *Il Prigioniero*:

Once more I'll see you, dear son!
The longing for you
And the anguish for you,
The desperate, piercing love for you
Alone, my precious son,
Consumed my heart all these months!

[24] 'Penelope became a moral heroine for later generations, the embodi-
ment of goodness and chastity, to be contrasted with the faithless,
murdering Clytaemnestra, Agamemnon's wife; but "hero" has no
feminine gender in the age of heroes.'

M.I. Finley, *The World of Odysseus*, Chatto & Windus,
London/Viking Press, New York, 1978, pp. 32–33.

Melantho

Anticleia

Calypso

Nausicaa

supposed to have been situated in the extreme west of the Mediterranean, at the confines of the world as known in Homer's era. Penelope also hides – or at least she tries to hide as much as possible from the attentions of the suitors. That Penelope waits for Ulysses is the element which has rendered her proverbial and immortal. But there is another legend, revived in our century by the Italian poet Giovanni Pascoli in his short narrative poem *L'Ultimo Viaggio*.[25] According to this myth, Calypso also awaits Ulysses's return. Nor are these the only similarities between the goddess and Penelope. There are at least two more: both of them sing and both weave.

Circe finds her human counterpart in Melantho. All differences granted, the sorceress and the little prostitute have the same kind of intelligence – or at least, sensitivity – enabling them to foresee the future. Ulysses, an old beggar in rags, has just arrived in Ithaca. He has hardly exchanged a few words with Eumaeus when Melantho notices him and says to herself, with a vague feeling of uneasiness:

> Nobody have I ever seen
> With such terrible eyes. . .

Does this mean she has recognized him – recognized him even as 'Nobody'? One thing is certain: from the moment she sees the beggar, she is no longer at ease. Antinous tries in vain to reassure her. After repeated refusals, she finally lets him persuade her to dance at the suitors' banquet, but

---

[25] 'Pascoli's intention in his *Ultimo Viaggio* (published in *Poemi Conviviali*, 1904*) is clear. He states in a note that his poem was an attempt to reconcile Dante's and Tennyson's conceptions of Ulysses with Teiresias's prophecy that Ulysses would die "a mild death off the sea". . . .

'Against Dante, he believes with Tennyson's Ulysses that "death closes all", so that Heaven and Hell are irrelevant to his portrait of a hero. But Tennyson's optimistic humanism is equally ineffective for this *fin de siècle* figure. . . .

'Instead of a new heroic adventure outwards, onwards, to new experiences and new glories, his last voyages turn out to be essentially retrograde, a *recherche du temps perdu*. . . . In such an environment Ulysses is No-man, indeed.'   Stanford, *The Ulysses Theme*, pp. 205 and 207–208.
*See Giovanni Pascoli, *Convivial Poems*, Part I, translated and edited by Egidio Lunardi and Robert Nugent, Lake Erie College Press, Painesville, Ohio, 1979.

hers is a dance of death. Later, Melantho will let herself be hanged without uttering a cry or a word of protest.

Melantho's intelligence certainly finds no match among the suitors. The element I have most emphasized in them, especially in Antinous, is their total obtuseness. The word that falls most frequently from the lips of the cynical Antinous, the first word he utters, is 'nothing' (*nulla*).

A correspondence also exists between Demodocus and Tiresias. The divine bard, who offers the flame of his noble inspiration to King Alcinous and his guests,[26] is blind, as poets traditionally were. The prophet is also blind. Demodocus sings about the exploits of the past, while Tiresias knows and reveals the future.

The task of adapting *The Odyssey* for a libretto – since, in my view at least, a presentation of the complete Homeric poem in a single performance was inconceivable – raised the problem of which episodes to choose. Having eliminated Telemachus' search for his father, I planned an opera divided into a prologue and two acts.

There was no particular difficulty in selecting the material for the Prologue; it is composed of three episodes. The first introduces Calypso, by now alone and forlorn, looking out to the sea that has carried Ulysses away. The third depicts Nausicaa (and her subsequent meeting with Ulysses), and begins with the ball-game enacted by the maidservants in a sprightly dance. Between these two episodes, I have inserted an orchestral intermezzo of forceful and threatening character. This intermezzo symbolizes Poseidon, a figure that never actually appears on stage but whose looming presence is often intimated by the music.

My real difficulties arose later, when I was faced with the delicate question of adapting for the libretto books VII to XII of *The Odyssey*: that is, Ulysses's narration of his fabulous adventures to the court of King Alcinous. This narration takes place in the first act, which is divided into five scenes. The curtain rises on a great hall in the King's palace.

---

[26] 'The minstrel stirred, murmuring to the god, and soon/Clear words and notes came one by one. . .' [Fitzgerald translation, p. 140].   –LD

Alcinous

Demodocus

Eumaeus

Antinous

Alcinous asks the divine bard Demodocus to recount what happened after the fall of Troy. At a certain moment of the narration, the hero enters; he is moved to tears at finding himself already become a legend. The King asks his name and then expresses the desire to know where destiny has taken Ulysses over the many years.

'Listen to me,' begins Ulysses. At this moment the past becomes present, and as in a series of flashbacks the episode of the Lotus-eaters (preceded by an attempted rebellion of Ulysses's comrades), the scene of Circe and that of the Cimmerian realm pass before us on the stage. At the end of the Hades episode, the royal hall reappears. The characters are found in exactly the same position as they were at the conclusion of Scene 1. The narration comes to a close. Nausicaa bids Ulysses farewell.

I chose the episodes of the Lotus-eaters, of Circe, and Hades for various reasons, both musical and dramatic. First, they allowed me to organize a kind of 'day': the Lotus-eaters representing the morning, Circe midday, and Hades the evening.[27] But above all, these three episodes – and only these – seemed to give me the opportunity to make occasional, unforced allusions to those I have omitted.

Thus Ulysses's comrades, disappointed that the land they had sighted from afar was not their longed-for Ithaca, rebel when their leader urges them to go ashore. After all I have said about *memory*, it shouldn't be surprising that the first insult they hurl at Ulysses is 'man of short memory'. Then they reproach him with their recent defeats suffered at the hands of the Cicones, the Laistrygonians, and finally the Cyclops; nor do they fail to remind him of the victims lost in each of his past adventures. It is a fact that, in the end, they

---

[27] A similar plan was used in *Cinque Canti* (1956) for baritone and eight instruments, settings of Greek lyrics in Salvatore Quasimodo's translation. The choice and organization of the texts, writes Dallapiccola, 'symbolize man's journey through the day – and, perhaps, through life. Thus, right in the centre, between two songs of morning and two of night, I have placed the song of daytime: "*Acheronte*", the song of suffering. In this way only should one interpret the symbol of the cross, which is delineated five times by the musical notation in the third song'.

LD: Saggi. . . , p. 129.

decide to land – not because Ulysses has commanded it, but because they are already fascinated by the distant, steadily advancing voices of the Lotus-eaters.

So far we have three allusions. The fourth will be made by Circe. At the very last moment, the anger of the enchantress at being abandoned by her lover seems to have subsided. We imagine her sufficiently revenged after she has given him a conscience. And yet, she suddenly turns to him with these words of subtle, perfidious sweetness:

> . . . tell me, can you hear
> The Sirens singing out at sea?[28]

In Scene 5, which closes the first act, allusions are made to Scylla and Charybdis and to the Oxen of the Sun. Thus, to the three *enacted* episodes, six others just as famous are added by way of allusion.

Act II also consists of five episodes. The first three take place in Ithaca: the opening one in the mountains where Eumaeus, the faithful swineherd, lives; the second in front of the palace, where the protagonist decides to proceed with his revenge; the third in the royal hall, where the suitors are banqueting and the slaughter will later take place. Penelope enters a moment before the curtain falls and exclaims a single word: 'Ulysses!'

An orchestral intermezzo brings us to the Epilogue, which I have already described in detail.

*　　　*　　　*

From the diagram (Figure 3, opposite), you can perhaps better understand how I solved the problem of the overall structure of my libretto. The opera is composed of thirteen episodes. Let us see how they are related.

---

[28] 'As Homer describes the incident, the attractions of the Sirens were primarily intellectual. Merely sensual pleasures would not, Homer implies (and Cicero later insists), have allured [Ulysses] so strongly. He had resisted the temptation to taste of the fruit of the Lotus. But one must not overlook, with Cicero, the effect of their melodious song and their unrivalled voices. Music for the Greeks was the most moving of the arts.'
Stanford, *The Ulysses Theme*, pp. 77–78.

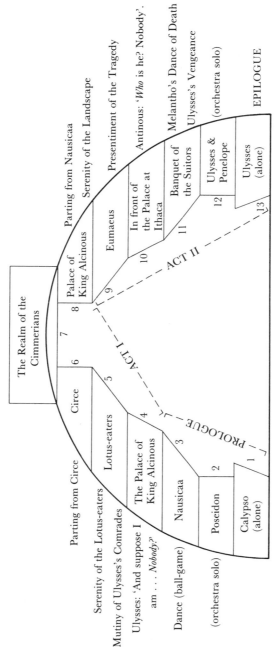

The Realm of the Cimmerians

Parting from Circe
Serenity of the Lotus-eaters
Mutiny of Ulysses's Comrades
Ulysses: 'And suppose I am . . . *Nobody*?'
Dance (ball-game)
(orchestra solo)

Circe — 6 — 7
5 — Lotus-eaters
4 — The Palace of King Alcinous
3 — Nausicaa
2 — Poseidon
1 — Calypso (alone)

ACT I
PROLOGUE

Parting from Nausicaa
Serenity of the Landscape
Presentiment of the Tragedy
Antinous: '*Who* is he? Nobody'.
Melantho's Dance of Death
Ulysses's Vengeance
(orchestra solo)
EPILOGUE

8 — Palace of King Alcinous
9 — Eumaeus
10 — In front of the Palace at Ithaca
11 — Banquet of the Suitors
12 — Ulysses & Penelope
13 — Ulysses (alone)

ACT II

Figure 3

Beginning at the bottom, we have the first and thirteenth episodes. There are two common elements here: in both cases only one character appears on the stage – first Calypso, then Ulysses – and in both, the scene represents the sea.

Moving up to the second and twelfth episodes, we find that they are both for orchestra only.

There is a considerable contrast between the third episode and the eleventh. While Nausicaa participates in the ball-game at the invitation of her maidservants, Melantho dances only on Antinous's command. The ball-game is light and joyous; Melantho's dance, at first mysterious, then sensual, ends violently and dramatically. On one hand, we are presented with the serenity of the beach on the island of the Phaeacians and the sublime dignity of Nausicaa; on the other hand, with the vulgarity and irresponsibility of the suitors during their banquet.

There are also several parallels between these two episodes. Both Nausicaa and Melantho seem emotionally upset: the former by her dream of love, the latter by the nagging questions that the appearance of Ulysses (even while disguised as a beggar) has raised. Nausicaa is called back to reality by her maidservants, Melantho by Antinous. In both scenes, there is a dance. And I shall point out, finally, that for a good part of both, Ulysses remains hidden and appears only near the end of the scene.

Now let's examine the following two episodes. In the fourth, Ulysses is the honoured guest at the palace of King Alcinous. But here, for the first time, he will ask himself: 'And suppose I am . . . *Nobody*?' The parallel episode shows Ulysses in front of *his own* palace, but as a stranger now, disguised and unknown to all. It is here that we find the snatch of dialogue quoted earlier:

Antinous:	That wretch is not a man.
Melantho:	*What* is he?
Antinous:	*Who* is he? Nobody.

This is the last time Ulysses hears his name deformed, a deformation which for him is so full of implications and maledictions.

Next, the fifth and ninth episodes. Contrasting elements

come into play in each: in the former, the rebellion of Ulysses's comrades, as opposed to the happy serenity of the Lotus-eaters; in the latter, the peaceful landscape on the mountains of Ithaca, as opposed to the forewarnings of tragedy that gradually take shape and come to life against this landscape.

Only one analogy can be drawn between the sixth and eighth episodes. In the former, we have the separation of Ulysses and Circe. Her penultimate line shows how confident the sorceress is that she will not be forgotten:

> I shall be the last woman
> You will name.

In the latter, the separation from Nausicaa, we hear her humbly ask Ulysses not to forget her.

At the summit of the vault is the most extensive scene of the opera, 'The Realm of the Cimmerians'.[29] This scene is parallel only to itself. And here, although I had intended to speak only about the libretto, I must make a very brief digression of a musical nature. Often in this episode chords are mirrored, and even considerably long passages are treated in the manner of Bach's mirror fugues, while rigorously adhering to the twelve-tone system.

Since I have never clamorously asserted that 'not even the smallest particle of my work escapes my control', I feel free and independent enough to confess publicly that only when I began preparing this paper did several of the analogies and contrasts I just mentioned come to my notice. Once again I realized how much of artistic creation is due to the unconscious. And being in the vein of public confession, I might add that I only recently discovered that while Calypso, Circe, and Penelope pronounce Ulysses's name, Nausicaa and his mother never do. Nausicaa calls him 'Stranger', even

---

[29] 'It is central to the poem that the journey to the Underworld stands midmost among the thirteen adventures: before it, Cicones, Lotus-eaters, Cyclops, Aeolus, Laestrygonians, and Circe; after it Sirens, Scylla, Cattle of the Sun, Charybdis, Calypso, and Phaeacians. Spatially the Underworld is farthest; mentally it is most diminishing; as regards return it first gives guidance.'

John H. Finley, Jr., *Homer's Odyssey*, Harvard University Press, Cambridge (Mass.), 1978, p. 76.

after she has learned who he is. His mother calls him 'Son'. My instinct, rather than logic or design, dictated this distinction. There *had* to be a difference between the women who had love relationships with Ulysses and those who did not. Thus, once again we witness the reciprocity between the artist and his work, or – if you prefer Nietzsche's image – that glance into the abyss which I called to your attention at the beginning of the lecture.

Very often I have been asked why I write my own librettos. And my answer has always been the same: collaboration with a poet would encumber my work as a composer.

The first draft of a libretto always contains too many words. I remember that the draft of *Il Prigioniero* was eighteen pages long, while the final version – that is, after the music had been completed – was barely twelve. At the time I didn't know this comment of Schoenberg's which today we can all read in the Appendix to *Moses und Aron*: 'The text becomes definitive only during the composing – indeed, sometimes afterwards'. Writing my own librettos allows me to revise them with the greatest freedom; I can organize the play of questions and answers to serve purely musical-constructive functions. Finally, I am able to decide where to take advantage of that power of 'concentration' which so characterizes dramatic music and of which Ferruccio Busoni once spoke with such lucidity.[30] That is, to see where the music allows us to reduce the words to a minimum.

[30] 'Nobody, not even a person of sufficient theatrical experience, can foresee, while writing the libretto, to what extent he can benefit from what Busoni called the power of *concentrazione* of the music – what the music can offer with one chord or two notes. But before having tested that chord or those two notes, we do not know how many words can be eliminated.'

Quoted by Hans Nathan, in 'On Dallapiccola's Working Methods', *Perspectives of New Music*, Spring-Summer 1977, p. 54. This article also contains several excerpts from the manuscript of the *Ulisse* libretto printed, for comparison, opposite the final version of the same passages from the published vocal score. Nathan concludes:

'Changes in the libretto were made constantly (something that the composer did not allow himself with the text of other authors, except for repetitions of words), especially during the preparation of the score, whose events had to become a part of the drama. And to achieve this, he made it a point to visualize the staging, the places at which the singers would stand, their gestures, even the lighting' (p. 56).

Since the language of a libretto is so very different from spoken language and from the idiom of straight theatre, the words must be chosen with great caution. Sometimes problems of this kind are solved easily, but at other times they are a source of enormous difficulties.

For twenty years I have known the opening verse of *Ulisse* – or known at least from where I could paraphrase it. In the Autumn of 1947, to be precise, while crossing a bridge in Venice, I suddenly conceived and jotted down the musical idea for a verse by Machado: '*Señor, ya estámos solos mi corazón y el mar*'.[31.] This verse was both the germ cell and the culminating point of *Quattro Liriche di Antonio Machado* for soprano and piano, finished in September 1948. I have known since then that Calypso, looking out to sea, thinking of Ulysses by now far away, would say: 'Alone once again, your heart and the ocean'.

The sources of the libretto of *Ulisse* are as numerous and diverse in origin as those of the libretto of *Il Prigioniero*. From Aeschylus [the *Oresteia*] I borrowed a few lines in Act I, Scene 1, where Demodocus tells how Clytemnestra persuaded Agamemnon to walk 'on crimson cloths' – something the hero regarded as a bad omen, since it was an honour reserved for the gods.

In the scene of the Lotus-eaters, I used an almost literal translation of some verses by Tennyson, which I have already quoted. The influence of the following lines by Hölderlin–

Schicksallos, wie der schlafende
  Säugling, atmen die Himmlischen;[32]

–is evident in the words of the Lotus-eaters, as they describe their happiness and invite Ulysses and his comrades to share it:

---

[31] From the poem '*Señor, ya me Arrancaste*', in *Campos de Castilla* (1917).

Another brief poem by Machado, '*Noche de Verano*', appears as a preface to the score of *Piccola Musica Notturna* for orchestra (1954, dedicated to Hermann Scherchen).

[32] From '*Hyperions Schicksalslied*', set to music by Brahms in *Schicksalslied*, Op. 54.

Released from destiny,
Free you will feel as in infancy's
Blissful, oblivious slumber.

I have already mentioned my debt to Cavafy's brief poem
'*Ithaka*' for the Circe episode. Now I will add that I derived
several essential lines from it, which govern the entire
structure of the libretto.

I am greatly indebted to James Joyce and particularly, in
the present instance, to *A Portrait of the Artist as a Young Man*.
The '*Sempre! Mai!*' that rings so insistently throughout the
scene of Hades came to mind unexpectedly: another recol-
lection from the most distant past. . . . The episode of the
infernal pendulum which, with its incessant ticking –
evoking the words 'Ever! Never!'[33] – frightened Joyce when
he heard it from a Jesuit as a young pupil at Clongowes
Wood College (Sallins, County Kildare), also frightened me
when another Jesuit told it (in the same words!) to my
high-school class in 1917–18.

I am indebted to Thomas Mann's tetralogy *Joseph and His
Brothers*, specifically the chapter entitled 'Account of Mont-
kaw's Simple Passing', for some of the words Anticleia
speaks in Hades, when she tells Ulysses how she died. I also
borrowed several elements from the play *Der Bogen des
Odysseus* by Gerhard Hauptmann, to delineate the figure of
Melantho.[34] And this is by no means a complete list of my
sources.

But I dimly felt, long before I began drafting the libretto,
that the greatest difficulty lay in finding words befitting the
character of Nausicaa. Three, four, five attempts failed
miserably. How could I find the words that a pure young girl,
the daughter of a king, would use to describe her first dream
of love, to repeat what the unknown mariner had told her

---

[33] Chapter III. In *Requiescant* (1958) for chorus and orchestra, Dallapiccola set Brigid's song 'Dingdong! The Castle Bell!' from *A Portrait of the
Artist*, Chapter I. One of the texts of *Tre Poemi* (1949), for voice and
chamber ensemble, is Joyce's 'A Flower Given to my Daughter' from *Pomes
Penyeach*, in the Italian translation by Eugenio Montale.

[34] For a synopsis of *The Bow of Odysseus* (1914), see Stanford, *The Ulysses
Theme*, pp. 195–199.

while she slept?[35] Then chance came to my rescue.

Around the middle of May 1966, in a side chapel of the Church of Santa Maria Novella in Florence, an inscription caught my eye which I had never noticed before:

Quasi arcus refulgens inter nebulas,
Quasi flos rosarum in diebus vernis[36]
Quasi lilia in transitu aquae.

I realized at once that a paraphrase of these verses would be possible,[37] and that my problem was nearing a solution.

The evening before I finished the libretto of *Ulisse*, I was still uncertain as to what the last verse would be, although I knew very well that it could only be derived from the verse of Machado's paraphrased at the beginning of the opera:

Señor, ya estámos solos mi corazón y el mar.

---

[35] 'With the immortal Circe and Calypso Odysseus had no age, but with Nausicaa he is a mature man. Much of the humour in their encounter stems from this discrepancy of ages which attracts them to each other and yet helps to keep them apart.'

George deF. Lord, 'The Odyssey and the Western World', *Essays on the Odyssey*, pp. 46–47.

[36] In order to emphasize the sense of the miraculous, I wrote '*verno*' [= *inverno*, 'winter'] on a tonal suggestion from the word *ver* ('spring').

–LD

[37] Nausicaa:

Chi era? Che cercava? 'O creatura,'
Mi disse, 'luce sei che squarcia un velo
Di fitte nubi; bianco giglio sei
Sull'acque in furia: vollero gli Dei
Far di te rosa sorta in mezzo al gelo
D'inverno'. Tutto intorno la natura
Taceva. . . .

Nausicaa:

Who was he? What was he searching for?
'O angel of light, you pierce the clouds'
Thick veil, are white as the lily tossed
On swirling waters; a rose amid the frost
Of winter, you bloom to please the gods'.
So he addressed me, then fell silent as nature
All round. . . .

(Prologue: Third Episode)

My pen wrote by itself. Instead of translating–

Signore, ora son soli il mio cuore e il mare

Almighty, now alone are my heart and the ocean

–it wrote:

Signore! Non più soli sono il mio cuore e il mare.

Almighty! No longer alone, my heart and the ocean.

And these, it seemed to me, were the right words.

The first draft of the libretto had been finished for almost a year when, one day in the railroad station of Westport, Connecticut, I saw posted on the wall a quotation from Saint Augustine that wasn't familiar to me:

THOU HAST MADE US FOR THYSELF–AND OUR HEARTS ARE RESTLESS UNTIL THEY FIND THEIR REST IN THEE.[38]

This quotation will be found as a postscript on the last page of the score.

---

[38] '*Fecisti nos ad te et inquietum est cor nostrum, donec requiescat in te*', *Confessions*, Book I, Chapter I.   –LD

Ulisse

at La Scala

Notes for the Italian Première, 13 January 1970

After the world première of *Ulisse* at Berlin,[1] I was pleased to observe how many different things the audience and the critics saw – or thought they saw – in my opera. It's a truism that each of us makes a personal contribution to the enjoyment of a work of art and that, consistent with our sensibility, our tradition, our culture, we are able to see in it things the artist was not fully aware of. On the other hand, sensibility and tradition and culture can themselves blur the exact perception of a work of art. I shall overlook the objection made by certain critics that I demanded an excessive effort of my audience: at least the audience didn't give me that impression.

One of the major difficulties for the Berliners, it seems, was their expectation of an opera based solely on Homer. Dante's interpretation of Ulysses isn't familiar in Germany, as it is in Italy.[2] Indeed, a good many foreign critics spoke of Hamlet and still more of Faust,[3] but none of them – to my

---

[1] Berliner Festwochen, Deutsche Oper, 29 September 1968: Gustav Rudolf Sellner, producer; Fernando Farulli, scene designer; Lorin Maazel, conductor. The same production was given at La Scala, but with Hans Georg Ratjen as conductor.

[2] In his essay '*Ricordo di Wilhelm G. Hertz*' (*Parole e Musica*, pp. 188–192), Dallapiccola pays tribute to a scholar whose German translation of *The Divine Comedy* (1955) deeply impressed him and became the basis of a significant friendship, cut short by Hertz's death in 1965.

[3] See Richard Ellmann, *James Joyce*, Oxford University Press, London and New York, 1982, pp. 435–436.

knowledge – mentioned Dante. And that is probably the reason why the Epilogue came as a shock to certain people. Evidently, the leap between the Homeric hero they expected to see on stage and my Ulysses seemed too great. Faced with the vision of the Supreme Being, the Primal Cause, which my character expresses in the final verse, there were not a few who wondered if I had intended to portray a *Christian* Ulysses. (Others went so far as to write that I set to music the quotation from St Augustine found as a postscript at the end of the score.)

No, that isn't so. *The Odyssey* can be considered – even by very estimable readers – simply an adventure story, albeit the most extraordinary one our western civilization has produced.[4] But if it were only that, it wouldn't have kept for us all its inimitable freshness, its absolute vitality. The poem is imbued with the most ancient myths, and we know that in archaic civilizations the myths expressed what today one might call the philosophy of life, a philosophy which has changed very little across the millennia.

Dante certainly did not fabricate his interpretation, for already in *The Odyssey* the poem of 'the search' is grafted onto the poem of 'the return'. While he chose not to dwell on the proverbial astuteness of Ulysses, Dante did illuminate a side of him too often left in shadow: his hunger for knowledge.

My character starts from Dante's: he is the man in search of himself and the meaning of life. Although Ulysses is the protagonist of the opera, for the most part he may appear

[4] 'The conception of the *Odyssey* as an adventure story is, I am convinced, as great an obstacle to understanding it as to see it simply as moral allegory. The first view removes it from serious consideration as one of the world's greatest poems; the second ignores its status as a poem altogether. A third view is required that will recognize the *Odyssey*'s great spiritual significance at the same time that it recognizes Odysseus as a complex and typically human character. . . . Such a view as this sees the goal of his return as more than a geographical one and recognizes both the established moral order of the *Odyssey*'s universe and the hero's gradual discovery of that order through suffering and error'.

George deF. Lord, 'The Odyssey
and the Western World', *Essays on the Odyssey*, p. 40.

passive in the sense that he never acts provocatively. He is a person who receives rather than gives. We meet him at various stages of life as he questions himself, other men, and nature; we see him descend to Hades to interrogate Tiresias, the Theban prophet. His encounters with the five types of women are symbolic of parting: Calypso, in the Prologue, is already alone, abandoned by Ulysses. Nausicaa takes leave of him with great tenderness. Circe is about to be forsaken. His mother, whom he meets in Hades, vanishes 'as a shadow, as a dream'. And finally, Penelope certainly does not inspire a love duet.[5] (How could there be a love duet when, in Book XXIII of *The Odyssey*, Ulysses tells Penelope at the outset—

> 'My dear, we have not won through to the end.
> One trial – I do not know how long – is left for me
> To see fulfilled. . . .'[6]

—and then relates the prophecy Tiresias had given him in Hades?) The meeting with Penelope accentuates the hero's sense of solitude, that solitude which had already tested him severely upon his return to Ithaca, unknown to everyone.

A few days after the Berlin première, on 11 October 1968, the Hamburg weekly *Die Zeit* published an article by Saul

---

[5] See p. 101, n. 3.
'The suppression of the expected love duet – like the suppression of Homer's opening scenes, which would have added a dramatic symmetry to the work's formal ones – becomes an expressive device in its own intransigent right, and conforms with the moral and intellectual stance of a work that owes much to the example of Busoni, and particularly to his *Doktor Faust*.'

David Drew, 'Dallapiccola's Odyssey',
The Listener, 17 October 1968, p. 514.

[6] Fitzgerald translation, p. 437.
'Homer apparently intended some kind of expiation for Odysseus's offence in blinding Poseidon's son, the Cyclops. But the fact that Homer left this journey still unfulfilled at the end of the *Odyssey* offered scope for writing a sequel, especially when Odysseus had told Penelope after their re-union that he would see "very many cities of men" on this journey. . .'.

Stanford, *The Ulysses Theme*, p. 88.

Bellow on the situation of writers in our time. From this article I should like to quote several passages:

> Public and social events dominate all others. News, rumours, scandals, political campaigns, wars, assassination attempts, youth movements, race riots prevail over religion, philosophy, private sentiments, personal loyalties, love. . . . And so the opinion is widespread that the art of storytelling is now 'irrelevant' and must give way to *reportage*. . . . This attitude implies, therefore, the superiority of action. Its point of departure is that the storyteller possesses no truth of his own, no inner light. Indeed, we admit that no great light emanates from within us. But how much illumination do external sources provide, borrowing their light from daily events? It is the light of billboards, not of Vermeer or Monet.

No doubt it was purely by chance that Bellow's article appeared so soon after the first performance of *Ulisse*, and yet it seems to answer those who judged my opera too little or not at all 'committed'. (There was even one who reminded me that in the past, when writing *Volo di Notte*, I had protested against bureaucracy (*sic*!): an interesting illustration of the point I made at the beginning of this essay, that there are some who see things in a work of art which the artist himself was – or is – not fully aware of.) And, at the same time, it appears to answer those who claimed that *Ulisse* isn't a 'contemporary' opera, since it sets forth purely private and personal convictions and fails to grapple directly with the political and social issues of the moment.

I don't presume to teach, yet one has only to glance at the daily papers to realize that in our shocked and deranged world, large segments of the population of many countries are searching for an *ubi consistam* – they sometimes clamour for it. No one could have imagined this, say, fifty years ago. I did not pursue a subject susceptible to being interpreted in terms of 'current events'. I wrote this opera because I had carried it inside me for long years. And now that it is finished, I have the impression that its theme is *also* contemporary.

Three Scenes from
Ulisse

PROLOGUE: FIRST EPISODE (CALYPSO)

[Seashore on the island of Ogygia. A wide horizon. Calypso
alone on stage, gazing into the distance.]

CALYPSO:

Alone once again, your heart and the ocean.
I mourn for you – I, the goddess Calypso, forsaken,
In whom you confided, sighing before you awaken:
'*To search, to wonder, and search with greater devotion*'.

I sensed the pretence of nostalgia for country
And son and old father, for your wife the contriving
Teardrops that streamed from your eyes to deceive me,
Staining your cheeks and tunic. You were striving
For something I never could fathom: the notion
To search, to wonder, and search with greater devotion.

I would have made you immortal, Ulysses – a fortune
You spurned. And to what was your heart then aspiring,
If not to flee death that is everyman's portion?
Some mystery burns in the spirit always desiring
To search, to wonder, and search with greater devotion.

Alone once again, your heart and the ocean.

*   *   *

ACT I, SCENE 4
(THE REALM OF THE CIMMERIANS[1])

[Loudspeakers transmit the sound of the singing and speaking choirs as if coming from opposite directions.]

THE SHADES [offstage]:

> Lamenting,
> Mourning, repenting, woe unrelenting.
> Mourning, lamenting. . .
> Ever obscurity, never lucidity;
> Ever to agonize, never to hope.
> Oppressed by our history,
> We are a race without destiny.

[Hades. The stage is filled with Shades. It is night; the only illumination is the moon's intermittent reflection in one of the infernal rivers.]

> Ever to agonize, never to hope. . .
> Ever!   Never!

[Ulysses and a few comrades enter and start digging a pit with their swords.]

> Rhythm eternal of rivers Avernal,

---

[1] 'The Cimmerians are living people, not ghosts, but the sun never shines on their land which is always shrouded in mist and cloud. The identification of the Cimmerians was a problem for ancient, as for modern, critics, and the actual reading of the name was in dispute. Among a number of variants in the manuscript tradition is the reading "Cheimerians", and this spelling of the name points to a possible solution. We have it on the authority of Thucydides (I, 46) that the name "Cheimerium" was applied to a harbour and headland in Thesprotia north of the mouth of the Acheron. This suggests that Cheimerium was a district name, possibly derived from a local tribe, and if so we have further confirmation that the region of the lower Acheron furnished the setting for the adventure in the Land of the Dead.'

J.V. Luce, *Homer and the Heroic Age*, Thames and Hudson, London, 1975, pp. 166–167.

Act I, Scene 4: Projection

Stony the coastline, incessant the pounding
Of waves like a voice profound and tremendous:
Ever!   Never!

[Just at this moment, the Shades seem to notice the
presence of Ulysses and his comrades.]

Who are those Shades there?
Pouring libations of milk and honey,
Pouring the sweet votive wine
And last the cool water,
Strewing the wellpit with barley. . .
They are not Shades! They're men! Look–
They slaughter a lamb and sprinkle its blood!
Blood alone can restore our lifelikeness:
Blood, only blood. . .
For us, who witnessed such bloodshed up there on earth,
For us, who committed so much carnage,
Only to perish ourselves in that deluge.

[The Shades now seem to give Ulysses their undivided attention.]

 Who are you, Stranger?
 A mortal here in this realm of torments?
 Who are you? What are you searching for?

ULYSSES:

 I would ask of Tiresias, the seer,
 My destiny: Tiresias,
 Who divines the future. . .

THE SHADES:

 Who are you?

ULYSSES:

     Why should I tell you my name?

[One face in particular, that of a woman, stands out among the Shades: Ulysses does not at first seem to notice her.]

THE MOTHER (ANTICLEIA):

 My son!

[Ulysses turns at once in the direction of her voice.]

     My dear son!

ULYSSES [scarcely breathing]:

     Whose voice is this? Can it
        be. . .?

[Gradually the Shades disappear.]

 No, Mother, I never expected to find you
 Down in this vale of phantoms.

Act I, Scene 4: Projection

I thought you were living still on the rocky island,
That corner of the world most precious to me. . .

THE MOTHER:

Ithaca? No. Death has carried so many away,
Ferried them lightly across to the other shore,
Free from worry, released from anxiety.
No one need close their eyes–
Sleep has shut them so gently. . .

ULYSSES:

Go on, speak further. . .

THE MOTHER:

It wasn't that way, dear child, with me.
My longing, my heartache for you, whom destiny

Drove far over the ocean; the anguish
Consuming my soul when I sensed your peril:
This and my desperate, piercing love
For you destroyed my body.
Now you see how I passed to this realm of Shades,
This desolate landscape
Inhabited only
By a few lone trees and broad rivers.
There, beyond the meadow
Where blow the pale asphodels,
Opens the black and ghastly gate of Hell.

THE SHADES:

Mourning, lamenting, repenting. . .

ULYSSES:

Before I sink forever
Into this dark abode that has never known
The changing seasons – O Mother,
Let me embrace you!

[He moves a few steps towards his Mother; her Shade
withdraws.]

THE MOTHER:

My son!
Little you know of our fate who descend below earth. . .

THE SHADES [very remote]:

Rhythm eternal of rivers Avernal. . .

THE MOTHER:

We're Shades, wavering through the aether like wraiths in
a dream. . .

THE SHADES:

Stony the coastline, incessant the pounding
Of waves. . .

THE MOTHER:

And thus I wafted through your arms, impalpable
As a shadow, as a dream. . .

[with great agitation, terrified]

Do you hear it? There beyond the portal, do you hear
A voice calling. . .

ULYSSES:

You are saying?

THE MOTHER:

. . .the voice whose summons
I must follow. . .

ULYSSES:

Stay with me!

THE MOTHER [desperately]:

My son!

[Her Shade disappears.]

ULYSSES:

Alone. I am alone. A man
Gazing into the depths of the abyss. . .[2]

[2] Compare the words the Prisoner sings after seeing his mother for the last time (*Il Prigioniero*, beginning of Scene 2):

Alone. I am alone again.
Alone with my thoughts. O my Mother! . . .

[The Shades gradually return and fill the stage.]

[bewildered] Who am I? What am I searching for?

THE SHADES:

> Mourning, lamenting,
> Sorrow, repenting, horror. . .

[The Shades become increasingly restless. Tiresias appears, bearing a golden sceptre.[3]]

> Hail, Tiresias!
> Hail, supreme Prophet of Thebes!
> Blind but omniscient Seer, now tell us:
> What has the future in store for this Seeker?
>   Lamenting,
> Mourning, repenting, woe unrelenting. . .

TIRESIAS:

> Monsters from the deep shall rise against you!
> Thunderbolts descend upon your ship!

---

[3] Dallapiccola departs from Homer in having Ulysses consult the prophet only *after* his meeting with Anticleia, which occurs exactly halfway through the central episode of the opera. For the composer, it seems, the personal encounter of mother and son is of paramount interest; the poet may have intended a different emphasis:

'At the sight of his mother's wraith Odysseus bursts into tears. He had not known that she was dead. Yet he does not allow her to come and drink the blood, despite his grief and wonder, until he has first interviewed Teiresias.

'This is a shrewd touch of characterization. Homer makes it clear that Odysseus and his mother were most affectionately attached to each other. Yet here Odysseus purposefully – even callously, some may think – postpones all speech with her until his main purpose is achieved. He knows that the safety of both his comrades and himself depends on what Teiresias predicts. The common weal must take precedence over private affections: prudence must prevail over emotion.'

Stanford, *The Ulysses Theme*, p. 61.

[tenderly]

> You shall kiss the soil of Ithaca again, and your son and
> consort.

[shuddering]

> But then, the bloodbath. . .
> Alone, at last,
> I see you once more roving the ocean—
> Hoary you shall be, hoary like the sea.
> The waves will cradle you. . .

THE SHADES:

> Rhythm eternal of rivers Avernal. . .

TIRESIAS:

> All else is obscure. . .

[he vanishes]

[*Change of Scene*]

THE SHADES:

> Rhythm eternal of rivers Avernal,
> Stony the coastline, incessant the pounding
> Of waves like a voice profound and tremendous:
> Ever!   Never!

*   *   *

ACT II, FINAL SCENE (EPILOGUE)

[Open sea. Ulysses, alone, in a small boat. A starry night.]

ULYSSES:

> No, there are no Furies at my back,
> Exacting vengeance for the men I slayed,
> Reproaching me with the comrades lost:
> These are the monsters Circe first revealed
> That waste my heart within, still unappeased.
> I am a man who watched, who never ceased
> Watching as the world's variety unreeled,
> While all around me rise a speechless host
> With myriad questioning eyes arrayed.
> And in my soul the pack
> Of memories grows sadder and more dense.
> What have I gleaned? How much. . . ? Some fables.
> From such travail, exhausting and inane,
> Mere shards of knowledge, vain
> Babblings, syllables
> Rather than words my recompense.

[looks upwards]

> Stars, how many times I stood entranced
> As under different skies
> Your pure and shimmering lustre passed!
> Stars, how often musingly I glanced
> At your reflective eyes,
> Looking for wisdom in the glance you cast!
> Why do you ill resemble, tonight,
> The stars I once knew? When and how
> Were you fixed in the heavenly frame?
> I fixed my hope upon you in this plight,
> This infinite quest for what I now
> Require: the Word, the Name.

[still more anguished]

> Oh to discover the name, the word how to say it,

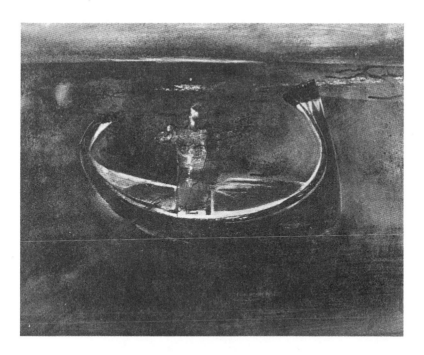

That clarifies all my intense explorations,
That pardons my lifelong peregrinations
And composes the hour – though nothing can stay it.
To search, to wonder, and search with greater devotion.

Once more: tormenting my mind, I try to find what is
true.

[a long pause]

If only a call broke the silence, if only a clue. . .

[another long pause; then, like an epiphany]

Almighty!

[calm]   (No longer alone, my heart and the ocean.

END OF THE OPERA

Opposite, from Ulisse, Act II, Scene 5 (Epilogue): *Ulysses, alone in a small boat, contemplates the stars; the B major chord alludes to* Volo di Notte, Scene 5, *where the pilot Fabien also sees the stars.*

Index

Abbado, Claudio, 180n
Abert, Anna Amalie, 217n
Adler, Friedrich, 40
Adler, Guido, 216, 218
Aeschylus, 259
   Oresteia, 259
Alarcón, Pedro de, 129n
Alcaeus, 36n
Alfieri, Vittorio, 16
Ambros, August Wilhelm, 215,
   216
Amfiparnaso Society, 63–64
Anacreon, 36n
Anderson, Martin, 31
Anderson, William, 18
Ansermet, Ernest, 49n
Aprahamian, Felix, 122n
Aquinas, St Thomas, 156, 157
Aranjuez, 43
Archimedes, 236
Ariosto, Ludovico, 220
   Orlando Furioso, 163
Arndt, Walter, 92n, 102n
Arras, 78
Arrighi, Cletto, 173n
Arrivabene, Count Opprandino,
   174, 175n, 180
Asolo, 18, 115
Atkinson, F.M., 60n
Augustine, St, 262, 264
   Confessions, 262n
Aurore, L', 38
Auschwitz, 40
Austria, 38n, 41, 134

Bach, Johann Sebastian, 20, 90,
   125, 180, 226, 227, 230, 257
   Goldberg Variations (ed.
   Busoni), 227

Musical Offering, A (Ricercare
   II, transcr. Webern), 230
The Well-Tempered Clavier (ed.
   Busoni), 226
Badoaro, Giacomo, 215, 219,
   231
Badoglio, Pietro, 53n
Bahle, Julius, 237, 239
Baker, Theodore, 226n
Ballets Russes, 129n
Ballo, Ferdinando, 225, 226
Bardot, Brigitte, 99
Bartoletti, Bruno, 164n
Basel, 48n
Basevi, Abramo, 178
Baudelaire, Charles, 151, 152,
   173n
   Les Fleurs du Mal, 152
Bayreuth, 96, 174
BBC, 52, 53, 83
Beaumarchais, Pierre-Augustin
   Caron de, 118
Beethoven, Ludwig van, 22n,
   95, 154, 163, 186, 193–194,
   200–201
   Piano Sonata in E minor,
      Op. 90, 154
   Piano Sonata in A major,
      Op. 101, 186
   Symphony No. 5, 163
   Symphony No. 6 (*Pastoral*),
      193–194
Belgium, 49
Bellini, Vincenzo, 113, 133n,
   148, 149, 238n
   Norma, 149, 238n
Bellow, Saul, 265–266
Berenson, Bernard, 36n
Berg, Alban, 13, 23n, 80, 101,

117, 125, 126n, 144n, 153, 171, 176n, 210
Lulu, 125, 144n, 153, 171, 210
Lyrische Suite, 126n
Violin Concerto, 210
Wozzeck, 22n, 80, 101, 117, 144n, 176n
Berlin, 70, 80n, 126, 263, 265
School of Dramatic Art, 70
Berlioz, Hector, 195, 197
Mémoires, 195n
Bischoff, Hans, 226
Blanchard, Pierre, 234n
Bloch, Ernest, 238n
Macbeth, 238n
Bo, Carlo, 20n
Boccaccio, Giovanni, 65n
Boethius, Anicius Manlius Severinus, 47
De Consolatione Philosophiae, 47
Boito, Arrigo, 149, 172–175, 178–180, 182
Bonner, Anthony, 50n
Bonsanti, Alessandro, 21n, 55
Book of Daniel (Bible), 153, 206n
Book of Job (Bible), 20–21n, 61, 65, 67, 68
Boulanger, Nadia, 23n
Borgunto, 53, 54, 55
Brahms, Johannes, 22n, 259n
Bramante, Donato d'Agnolo, 205
Brandeis, Irma, 27, 48n
Brée, Germaine, 50n
Bruckner, Anton, 132n
Brunswick, 112
State Theatre, 77n
Brussels, 50n, 59, 123n
Buchenwald, 40
Büchner, Georg, 94
Budden, Julian, 108n, 127n, 173n, 179n, 188n

Buenos Aires, 84, 85
Busoni, Ferruccio, 13, 18–19, 21, 22n, 31, 57, 91, 95, 101–102, 103, 135, 154n, 163, 164, 166n, 177, 186n, 187n, 199, 220, 226, 227, 231, 237–238, 245n, 258, 265n
Doktor Faust, 95, 101–102, 103, 177, 220, 245n, 265n
Entwurf einer neuen Ästhetik der Tonkunst, 226, 231n
Sarabande und Cortège, 95

Caccini, Guilio, 133, 221
Cairns, David, 195n
Callas, Maria, 64n
Calvin, John, 48n
Calvo, 164n
Campanella, Tommaso, 27, 48
Canada, 48n
Capodistria, 37n
Carducci, Giosuè, 99
Carter, Roy E., 193n
Casanova (de Seingalt), Giovanni Jacopo, 115
Casella, Alfredo, 22n, 23n, 50n, 95n, 109, 111, 193n
Castellion, Sébastien, 48
Cavafy, Constantine P., 243, 260
Cavalieri, Emilio de', 237
La Rappresentazione di Anima e di Corpo, 237
Cervantes Saavedra, Miguel de
The Adventures of Don Quixote, 238
Chanson de Roland, La, 238
Chaplin, Charlie 92
Charlemagne, 43
Charles I (Emperor of Austria-Hungary), 40
Charles V (Emperor), 43, 44, 60n
Chenal, Pierre, 234n–235n

Chotek, Countess Sophie, 40
Chusid, Martin, 26n
Ciano, Galeazzo, 55n
Cione, Edmondo, 225n
Cicero, Marcus Tullius, 17,
    254n
Claudel, Paul, 80n, 113
Coburg, 112
Colette, Sidonie-Gabrielle, 121,
    124
Collaer, Paul, 49
Collodi, Carlo, 91n
Como, 53
Cone, Edward T., 15n
Constance, University of, 237
Cooke, Deryck, 25, 47n
Corrispondenza Politico-Diplomatica,
    44
Coster, Charles de, 51, 60n
    *La Légende d'Ulenspiegel et de
        Lamme Goedzak*, 51, 59–60n
Cot, Pierre, 76
Covigliaio, 34, 48, 49n
Czechoslovakia, 70

Dachau, 40
Dallapiccola, Annalibera
    (daughter), 36, 48n, 116
Dallapiccola, Domitilla Alberti
    (mother), 39, 41–42, 234
Dallapiccola, Laura Coen
    Luzzatto (wife), 27, 48, 50,
    54–55, 61, 63n, 65, 133
Dallapiccola, Luigi, *passim*
    Accademie Straniere in Roma,
        63n
    An Mathilde, 22n
    Canti di Liberazione, 48n
    Canti di Prigionia, 25, 34, 36,
        46–50, 57n
    Cinque Canti, 72n, 210n, 253n
    *Concerto per la Notte di Natale
        dell'Anno 1956*, 72n
    Divertimento in Quattro Esercizi,

        95
Goethe-Lieder, 22n
Job, 17, 65–69, 70, 71, 78, 239
Kohlennot (play), 21n
Liriche Greche, 25, 36, 53, 74
    I. *Cinque Frammenti di Saffo*,
        36n
    II. *Due Liriche di Anacreonte*,
        36n, 74
    III. *Sex Carmina Alcaei*, 25,
        36n, 53
Marsia, 16, 239
Musica per Tre Pianoforti (Inni),
    57n
Piccola Musica Notturna, 259n
Preghiere, 182n
Prigioniero, Il, 9, 14, 17, 20, 23,
    25, 35–36, 37, 45n, 52, 54n,
    55, 56, 57n, 59, 60, 61–63,
    65, 78, 104, 233, 239, 248n,
    258, 259, 273n
Quaderno Musicale di Annalibera,
    48n
*Quattro Liriche di Antonio
    Machado*, 259
*Rappresentazione di Anima et di
    Corpo* (libretto), 237–239
Requiescant, 17, 260n
Segreto, Il (libretto), 21n
*Sei Cori di Michelangelo Buonar-
    roti il Giovane*, 64, 95, 237
Sicut Umbra, 20–21n
Sonatine Canonica, 25, 54, 57n
Tartiniana Seconda, 57n
*Three Questions with Two
    Answers*, 23n
Tre Episodi dal Balletto 'Marsia',
    57n
Tre Laudi, 17, 19–20, 64,
    88–89, 95, 186n, 237
Tre Poemi, 260n
Ulisse, 14, 17–18, 20, 21,
    23–24, 130n, 233, 239–262,
    263–266, 267–279

Volo di Notte, 14, 17, 19–20, 23, 44, 46, 51, 68n, 71, 74–78, 82–90, 92–96, 237, 239, 266, 279

Dallapiccola, Pio (father), 37, 39, 42, 58, 234

d'Amico, Fedele, 16n, 49–50, 54n, 112n,

d'Annunzio, Gabriele, 110n, 216n, 238
  Più che l'Amore, 238

Dante Alighieri, 14, 17, 18n, 20–21, 42, 62n, 117, 151, 207, 219–220, 237–238, 246, 246–247n, 250n, 263–264
  La Divina Commedia (Inferno, Purgatorio, Paradiso), 14, 17, 20–21, 42, 62n, 207, 219–220, 237–238, 246, 246–247n, 250n, 263–264
  Vita Nuova, 117, 151

Da Ponte, Lorenzo, 189, 190, 204, 205, 208

Darmstadt, 111

Debussy, Claude, 13, 22n, 79, 80, 100, 110, 119–121, 124, 144n
  'La Cathédrale Engloutie' (Préludes, Book I), 110n
  Children's Corner, 119–121
  'Clair de Lune' (Fêtes Galantes I), 124n
  'Ibéria' (Images, orch.), 110
  Le Martyre de Saint-Sébastien, 110n
  'Pagodes' (Estampes), 124
  Pelléas et Mélisande, 79, 80, 91, 100, 110n, 119–120, 144n

Dent, Edward J., 50n, 102n, 133n, 144, 188n, 231n

de' Paoli, Domenico, 36n, 74, 78

Devoto, Giacomo, 54

Diaghilev, Sergei, 129n

Diane de Poitiers, 136n

d'Indy, Vincent, 216, 217, 227, 228

Disney, Walt, 124

Donizetti, Gaetano, 133n, 148, 154, 155
  Lucia di Lammermoor, 154, 155
  Lucrezia Borgia, 117

Doráti, Antal, 9–11

Douglas, Lord (Alfred), 127n

Drew, David, 14n, 265n

Dreyfus, Alfred, 38

Edizione Suvini Zerboni, 16n, 21, 28, 54n, 62n

Ellmann, Richard, 263n

Epstein, Jacob, 63n

Escorial, 43

Europe, 38, 40, 41, 63n, 84

Faber, Marion, 42n

Faccio, Franco, 172–173, 174, 175
  I Profughi Fiamminghi, 172–173

Falla, Manuel de, 129n
  El Sombrero de Tres Picos, 129n

Farulli, Fernando, 28, 241, 263n

Fauré, Gabriel, 22n

Fehring, 41

Feldbach, 41

Fiesole, 53

Finley, John H., 257n

Finley, M. I., 248n

Fitzgerald, Robert, 24, 236n

Florence, 9, 36, 49n, 50n, 52, 54, 57, 61, 63, 70, 78, 96, 115, 165, 237
  Cherubini Conservatoire, 238n
  Maggio Musicale, 35n, 37n, 77, 94, 117n, 217, 234
  Santa Maria Novella, 261
  Teatro Comunale, 164n

Florimo, Francesco, 108n

Forte, Allen, 103n
France, 77, 78
Franz Ferdinand (Archduke of Austria), 40
Franz Joseph (Emperor of Austria-Hungary), 40, 43
Frazzi, Vito, 22n
Frescobaldi, Girolamo, 230
Friar, Kimon, 242n
Fusinato, Arnaldo, 137

Gagliano, Marco da, 133
Galassi, Jonathan, 136n
Gallico, Claudio, 217n
Gallimard, Gaston, 76
Gasco, Alberto, 91n
Gatti, Guido M., 63–65, 69n
Gavazzeni, Gianandrea, 22
Germany, 44n, 57, 77n, 263
Gesualdo, Carlo (Prince of Venosa), 219
Ghent, 60
Ghislanzoni, Antonio, 136
Gide, André, 76n, 83n, 191, 199
    Journal 1939–1942, 191, 199
Gielen, Michael, 103n
Gilbert, Stuart, 76n, 78n
Giordani, Paolo, 54
Giorgione da Castelfranco, 218
'*Giovinezza*' (Fascist anthem), 113
Gluck, Christoph Willibald, 80, 91
    Alceste, 80
    Iphigénie en Aulide, 91
Goebbels, Joseph, 77
Goethe, Johann Wolfgang von, 19, 22n, 38n, 79, 84, 92n, 101n, 218n, 263
    Faust, 19, 84, 92, 101n, 218, 263
    Iphigenie in Tauris, 79
    Torquato Tasso, 79
Goldman, Richard F., 13n, 47n

Goldoni, Carlo, 205n
Goldschmidt, Hugo, 216, 218
Gotta, Salvatore, 113n
Graves, Robert, 65n
Graz, 37, 41, 45, 58, 131
Grazebrook, Alvary E., 26n
Great Britain, 49
Greenberg, Noah, 153n
Gregor, Joseph, 81
    Weltgeschichte des Theaters, 81
Grevenberg, Julius, 132
Grieg, Edvard, 225
    'To the Spring' (*Lyric Pieces*), 225
Grossi, Pietro, 128
Guerrini, Guido, 91n
Gui, Vittorio, 54
Guillaumet, Henri, 78

Haas, Robert, 216
Hammond, Arthur, 28
Handel, George Frederick, 16
Harden, E., 91n
Hartmann, Karl Amadeus, 22n
Hauptmann, Gerhard, 260
    Der Bogen des Odysseus, 260
Hayakawa, Sessue, 124
Haydn, Franz Joseph, 132n
Heine, Heinrich, 22n
Hertz, Wilhelm G., 263n
Hildesheimer, Wolfgang, 42n, 201n
Hindemith, Paul, 22n, 23n
Hines, Robert S., 19n
Hitler, Adolf, 44, 48, 49, 50, 57, 59, 77n
Hoare, Sir Samuel, 49
Hoffmann, E.T.A., 220–221
    Don Juan, 221n
Hofmannsthal, Hugo von, 81n
Hölderlin, Friedrich, 259n
    Hyperions Schicksalslied, 259–260
Homer, 14n, 17, 24, 143–144, 219–220, 228, 234–236,

239–258, 261n, 263–265,
268n, 274n
The Odyssey, 14, 17, 24,
219–220, 234–236,
239–258, 261n, 263–265,
268n, 274n
Honegger, Arthur, 22n,
167–168, 234n
Horowicz, Bronislaw, 37n, 63
Hughes, H. Stuart, 44n
Hugo, Victor, 43–44, 136n, 152,
173n
La Légende des Siècles, 43–44,
152
Le Roi s'Amuse, 136n
Hull, R.F.C., 61n
Humperdinck, Engelbert, 121,
238n

Ibsen, Henrik, 79, 219, 238
Peer Gynt, 238
International Society for
Contemporary Music
(ISCM), 36n, 50, 59n, 111n,
187n
Istria, 38, 40
Italian Radio, 128
Italian Society for Contem-
porary Music, 114
Italy, 38, 44n, 47, 134, 263

Jacopone da Todi, 72n, 238
Jalowetz, Heinrich, 111n,
186–187, 192
Jiménez, Juan Ramón, 20n
Joyce, James, 22n, 233, 260,
263n
Pomes Penyeach, 260n
*A Portrait of the Artist as a
Young Man*, 260
Ulysses, 213
Jung, Carl, 61
Antwort auf Hiob (*Answer to
Job*), 61

Kazantzakis, Nikos, 242n
The Odyssey: A Modern Sequel,
242n
Kaufmann, Walter, 233n
Keeley, Edmund, 243n
Kerman, Joseph, 80n, 100n,
166n
Kerrigan, Anthony, 51n
Kierkegaard, Søren, 194, 197,
200
Kiesewetter, Raphael Georg,
215
Kimbell, David R.B., 134n
Kleiber, Erich, 23n
Knox, Bernard, 71n
Kreutzberg, Harald, 61, 239

Labroca, Mario, 217, 234
László, Magda, 36n
Leibnitz, 40
Leipzig, 123n
Letteratura, 21n
Ley, Rosamund, 18n, 102n
Liguoro, Giuseppe di, 234n
Lindbergh, Charles, 90
Listener, The, 14n, 25n, 265n
Liszt, Franz, 54n, 57, 166, 193n,
200
Années de Pèlerinage, 193n
Réminiscences de Don Juan, 166n,
193n, 200
Lodi, 53
Lombardy, 134
London, 50, 59, 63n
Lord, George deF., 261n, 264n
Lowe-Porter, H.T., 215n
Luce, J.V., 268n
Ludwig II (King of Bavaria), 91
Lunardi, Emilio, 250n
Lyons, 45n

Maazel, Lorin, 263n
Machado, Antonio, 259, 261
Noche de Verano, 259n

Señor, ya me Arrancaste, 259,
    261
Machiavelli, Nicolò, 65n, 180
Mack Smith, Denis, 38n, 44n,
    45n, 52n, 55n, 65n, 113n
Maderna, Bruno, 23n
Maeterlinck, Maurice, 100n
Maffei, Countess Clarina, 172,
    173
Mahler, Gustav, 22n, 42n, 105,
    113, 131n, 176
    Symphony No. 1, 131n
Mainz, 112
Malipiero, Francesco, 169n
Malipiero, Gian Francesco, 13,
    22n, 23n, 104, 109–116, 168–
    169n, 216, 230n, 237, 238
    La Favola del Figlio Cambiato,
        112
    Filomela e l'Infatuato, 111
    Iscariota, L', 115
    Mistero di Venezia, Il, 111–112
        I. *Le Aquile di Aquileia*, 112n
        II. *Il Finto Arlecchino*, 112n
        III. *I Corvi di San Marco*, 112
    Omaggio a Belmonte, 115
    Orfeide, L', 109n
        I. *La Morte delle Maschere*,
            109n
        II. *Sette Canzoni*, 109–110,
            111, 169n, 237
        III. *Orfeo, ovvero l'Ottava
            Canzone*, 109n, 111
    Pause del Silenzio I, 114
    Poemi Asolani, 109
    Stagioni Italiche, Le, 109
    Torneo Notturno, 104, 109, 110,
        111, 112–114, 237
    Tre Commedie Goldoniane, 111
    Uno dei Dieci, 115
Mallarmé, Stéphane, 22n, 219
Mann, Thomas, 13, 22n, 37,
    184n, 215, 260
    Confessions of Felix Krull,

    Confidence Man, 184n
    Doktor Faustus, 184n
    Joseph and His Brothers, 13,
        184n, 215, 260
    The Magic Mountain, 37
Mantelli, G. Alberto, 226n
Manzoni, Alessandro, 16,
    173–174
    I Promessi Sposi, 173–174
Marcello, Benedetto, 173n
Maria Theresa (Empress of
    Austria), 43
Maria Antoinette (Queen of
    France), 91
Markevitch, Igor, 16n, 23n,
    35–36, 53, 129
    Psaume, 36n
Martinique, 81–82
Martin y Soler, Vicente, 205
    *Una Cosa Rara, ossia Bellezza ed
        Onestà*, 205
Mary Stuart (Queen of Scots),
    46
Mascagni, Pietro, 81
    Cavalleria Rusticana, 81n
Mason, Colin, 25
Massimo, Leone, 53n
Massine, Léonide, 23, 129–130,
    220, 234
Materassi, Leaura, 24
Materassi, Mario, 24
Materassi, Sandro, 49n, 57
Matisse, Henri, 23n, 234n
Mayor, Andreas, 192n
Melles, Carl, 52n
Melville, Herman, 14n
Messiaen, Olivier, 22n, 23n
Mexico, 48n
Michelangelo Buonarroti, 205
    'The Last Judgement', 205
Michelangelo Buonarroti the
    Younger, 64n
Michelet, Jules, 45n
Michigan, University of, 24

Mila, Massimo, 19, 35, 52n,
167–168, 180, 233
Milan, 53, 64n, 173, 174, 233
La Scala, 172, 233, 263
Milhaud, Darius, 23n, 45, 80,
144n, 210–211
Christophe Colomb, 80, 144n
David, 211n
La Mort d'un Tyran, 45
Millay, Edna St Vincent, 152n
Milloss, Aurel M., 16
Mittergraben, 40
Moissi, Alexander, 70–73
Momigny, Joseph-Jérôme de,
154n
Mondo, Il, 21
Monet, Claude, 266
Montale, Eugenio, 135–136n,
260n
Monte Carlo, 123
Monteverdi, Claudio, 13–14,
133, 215–231, 234
Incoronazione di Poppea, L', 218
Ritorno di Ulisse in Patria, Il,
13–14, 215–224, 227–231,
234
Mordden, Ethan, 104n
Moscow, 62n
Mozart, Wolfgang Amadeus,
13, 16, 19, 24–25, 42, 87, 117,
118, 126, 127, 154, 187–211,
220–221, 238n
Così fan tutte, 126
Don Giovanni, 16, 24–25, 42,
117, 118, 127, 189–192,
194–211, 220–221, 238n
Dorfmusikantensextett, 193n
Entführung aus dem Serail, Die,
187, 220
Nozze di Figaro, Le, 87, 118,
205–206, 220
String Quartet in D minor,
K.421, 154n
Symphony No. 40 in G

minor, K.550, 187
Violin Concerto No. 5 in A
major, K.219, 154
Zauberflöte, Die, 19
Mugnone, L., 81n
Mulè, Giuseppe, 91n
Munich, 59, 112
Munthe, Axel, 65n
Music Review, The, 13n
Music Survey, 25, 47n
Musical Quarterly, The, 25, 186
Mussolini, Benito, 44, 45, 49,
53, 55n, 112, 115n
Mussorgsky, Modest, 119, 120,
121, 180, 238n
Boris Godunov, 119, 121, 180
The Nursery, 119, 120, 121

Naples, 64n
Napoli, Gennaro, 91n
Nathan, Hans, 13n, 18n, 22n,
72n, 258n
New York, 155
Newlin, Dika, 105n
News Chronicle, 59n
Nicolodi, Fiamma, 16n, 18, 21,
22, 25, 27
Nietzsche, Friedrich, 233, 258
Beyond Good and Evil, 233n
NIR (Belgian radio), 49
Nono, Luigi, 23n
Nugent, Robert, 250n

Oakland, 210n
Oberhollabrun, 40
Osthoff, Wolfgang, 178, 180,
217n
Ovid, 17
Ozeray, Madeleine, 234n

Padua, 115
Paganini, Niccolò, 25, 54
Palestrina, Giovanni Pierluigi
da, 226

Paragone, 25
Parente, Alfredo, 225, 226
Paris, 50, 74, 76, 82, 111, 123n,
    172, 234
  Opéra, 129n, 168, 169n
  Petite Scène, 216
Pascoli, Giovanni, 250
  L'Ultimo Viaggio, 250
Pattay, Ezio, 43
Pavlova, Tatiana, 164n
Pergolesi, Giovanni Battista,
    173n
Peri, Jacopo, 133, 221
Petrarch (Francesco Petrarca),
    138–139, 151–152, 179
Petrassi, Goffredo, 64
Petrobelli, Pierluigi, 23–24
Philip II (King of Spain),
    43–44, 50, 51, 59
Piacenza, 53n
Piave, Francesco Maria, 136n,
    178, 180
Picasso, Pablo, 129n
Pick-Mangiagalli, Riccardo, 91n
Pirandello, Luigi, 79, 112n
Pisino, 37, 42n
Pistoia, 54n
Pizzetti, Ildebrando, 91n, 111n
Pola, 37
Poliziano, Angelo, 111, 112,
    113–114
Polyphonie, 24
Ponte, Il, 62n
Popolo d'Italia, Il, 96
Poulenc, Francis, 23n
Praga, Emilio, 173n
Prague, 111, 123n
Predappio, 53n
Previn, André, 122n
Previtali, Fernando, 49n, 117n
Princip, Gavrilo, 40
Proust, Marcel, 17, 22n, 37,
    192, 233, 250n
  À la Recherche du Temps Perdu,
    17, 192
Prunières, Henry, 216
Puccini, Giacomo, 42n, 81,
    110n, 233
  Tabarro, Il, 81
  Tosca, 99–100

Quasimodo, Salvatore, 36n,
    253n

Racine, Jean Baptiste, *Phèdre*,
    191–192
Radio Audizioni Italiane (RAI),
    17n, 35
Rassegna Musicale, La, 24, 211n
Ratjen, Hans Georg, 263n
Ravel, Maurice, 13, 22n, 101,
    117n, 120–125
  L'Enfant et les Sortilèges, 101,
    121–125
  Ma Mère l'Oye, 120–121, 125
  Valses Nobles et Sentimentales,
    22n
Regresso di Maiano, 54
Reinhardt, Max, 71n, 81n
Renoir, Jean, 235n
  La Grand Illusion, 235n
Respighi, Ottorino, 22n, 90,
    91n
  La Fiamma, 90
Reynolds, Barbara, 134n, 151n
Ribbentrop, Joachim von, 50
Ricordi, Giulio, 94n, 136n, 173,
    174, 179
Ricordi, Tito, 172
Riemann, Hugo, 226
Risorgimento, 40, 134, 179
Rome, 17n, 49, 63, 64, 65n, 68,
    112, 114, 231n
Rossi, Enzo, 37n
Rossi, Mario, 138n, 217n
Rossini, Gioacchino, 42n, 64n,
    118, 133n, 138, 148–149,
    188–189

Barbiere di Siviglia, Il, 118, 188–189
Guillaume Tell, 138, 148–149
Turco in Italia, Il, 64n
Royal Air Force, 52
Rubinstein, Ida, 83n, 110n
Rufer, Josef, 16n

Sachs, Maurice, 76
Sacrati, Francesco, 219
Ulisse Errante, 219
Saggiatore, Il, 21, 28
Saint-Exupéry, Antoine de, 74–78, 83–86, 87
Pilote de Guerre, 76–77, 78
Terre des Hommes, 75, 76, 78
Vol de Nuit, 74, 75, 76n, 78, 83–86, 87
San Domenico, 54, 55,
San Francisco, 211
Sappho, 36n
Sarajevo, 40
Sardanapalus, 10
Sarti, Giuseppe, 205
Fra i Due Litiganti il Terzo Gode, 205
Savidis, George, 243n
Savinio, Alberto (Andrea de Chirico), 64, 219–220
Savonarola, Girolamo, 49
Sayers, Dorothy L., 207n
Scapigliatura, 173–174
Scarlatti, Domenico, 94, 192–193, 194
Scarpini, Pietro, 54n, 57
Scheldt, River, 59
Scherchen, Hermann, 23n, 35–36n, 37n, 63, 103n, 259n
Schiller, Jonathan, 25n, 26
Schindler, Anton Felix, 154
Schlee, Alfred, 77n
Schneider, Louis, 216
Schoenberg, Arnold, 13, 14, 23n, 45, 57, 103, 103–104n,

105, 110, 115, 126n, 186, 187, 193, 245n, 258
Erwartung, 103
Harmonielehre, 187, 193
Moses und Aron, 22n, 103–104n, 245n, 258
Ode to Napoleon Buonaparte, 46
Pierrot Lunaire, 110
Suite, Op. 29, 186
Survivor from Warsaw, A, 46
Schrade, Leo, 217n
Schubert, Franz, 132n, 153
Nacht und Träume, 153
Schumann, Robert, 22n, 119
Album für die Jugend, 119
Kinderszenen, 119
Searle, Humphrey, 16n
Sessions, Roger, 14–15, 19, 23n, 25, 26, 26–27n, 210
Settignano, 36n
Shackelford, Louise, 27
Shackelford, Rudy, 30, 31
Shakespeare, William, 22n, 135–136n, 165n, 174–175, 263
Hamlet, 263
Julius Caesar, 174
King Lear, 22n, 165n
Othello, 174–175
Sherrard, Philip, 243n
Shostakovich, Dmitri, 22n
Siciliani, Francesco, 61–63
Siena, 115
Singleton, Charles S., 20n
Slezak, Leo, 58
Smith, Madeleine M., 19n
Società, 50n
Socrates, 48, 225
Solaria, 21n
Somma, Antonio, 155, 165n
Sonzogno, Edoardo, 81n
Sophocles,
Oedipus Rex, 71–72
Spanish Civil War, 64
Stadeler, Herr, 77n

Stanford, W.B., 247n, 250n, 254n, 260n, 265n, 274n

Strauss, Richard, 13, 81n, 118, 126–128
  Der Rosenkavalier, 118
  Salome, 126–128

Stravinsky, Igor, 83, 90
  Les Noces, 47n
  Perséphone, 83

Stroheim, Erich von, 235n

Stuckenschmidt, H.H., 186, 193n

Stürgkh, Count Karl von, 40

Sudetenland, 59

Swenson, David F. and Lilian M., 194n

Tanglewood, 210n

Tausig, Karl, 226

Taylor, Charles H., Jr., 240n, 247n

Tempo, 23n

Tennyson, Alfred, 243, 250n, 259
  'The Lotos-Eaters', 243, 259
  'Ulysses', 250n

Thucydides, 268n

Titian, 218

Tognelli, J., 112n

Tolstoy, Leo, 244n
  War and Peace, 244n

Tommasini, Vincenzo, 64

Toni, Alceo, 91n

Toscanini, Arturo, 23n, 110n, 155, 170–171, 198, 226

Trentino, 38n, 234

Treviso, 116

Trieste, 37, 40

Unamuno, Miguel de, 51, 225
  The Tragic Sense of Life, 51n, 225

Universal Edition, 77n

USA, 48n, 49, 107

Van den Borren, Charles, 216, 218, 223

Varèse, Edgard, 22n, 23n, 47n
  Ionisation, 47n

Vecchi, Orazio, 64n
  L'Amfiparnaso, 64n

Venice, 16n, 18, 77, 115, 186, 231, 259
  Teatro di San Cassiano, 227, 231

Verdi, Giuseppe, 13, 16, 26, 27, 42n, 58, 63, 87, 90, 93–94, 108, 110, 111n, 113, 127n, 133n, 134–151, 154–163, 164–171, 172–181, 182–185, 188n, 201–202, 223, 238n
  Aida, 136, 172, 174
  Alzira, 178
  Attila, 169n, 178
  Ballo in Maschera, Un, 16, 26, 90, 133n, 135, 143, 147–148, 154–163
  Falstaff, 94, 182–185, 223
  Giovanna d'Arco, 178
  Luisa Miller, 94
  Macbeth, 142
  Nabucco, 140
  Otello, 58, 93, 127n, 134–135, 140, 147, 149, 174–175, 179, 181, 184, 185
  Re Lear, 165n
  Requiem, 174
  Rigoletto, 94, 136, 137, 140, 145–146, 150, 164–171, 188n, 201–202
  Simon Boccanegra, 93n, 94, 117–118, 138–139, 175–181
  Traviata, La, 87, 137, 144–145
  Trovatore, Il, 94, 141, 147, 148, 150–151

Verdi, Giuseppina (Strepponi), 174

Verlaine, Paul, 51
  La Mort de Philippe II, 51n

Vermeer, Jan, 266
Verona, 55n
Vienna, 81, 132n
National Library, 215, 217
Neue Freie Presse, 81
Villiers de l'Isle-Adam, Count
Philippe Auguste, 21n, 50–51,
52, 55
L'Enjeu, 21n
La Torture par l'Espérance,
50–51, 52, 55
Virgil, 17, 228
Vogel, Emil, 216
Vogel, Wladimir, 22n, 45, 51,
114
Thyl Claes, 45, 51n
Voltaire, François Marie
Arouet, 77

Wagner, Richard, 13, 22n, 38n,
41, 42, 91, 110, 129n, 130,
131–132, 137, 163, 172, 174,
176, 238
Fliegende Holländer, Der, 42,
110, 131, 176
Lohengrin, 91
Meistersinger von Nürnberg, Die,
41, 131–132
Parsifal, 129n, 130, 131
Ring des Nibelungen, Der, 41,
137
II. *Die Walküre*, 137

Tristan und Isolde, 91, 130n,
132
Wagner, Wolfgang, 22–23,
131–132
Walker, Frank, 172n, 180n
Weaver, William, 26n, 87n,
93n, 108n, 165n
Webern, Anton, 21, 22n, 23n,
36n, 111, 230–231
Concerto, Op. 24, 111n
Wedekind, Frank, 171
Wellesz, Egon, 45n
Wilde, Oscar, 127n
Salome, 127n
Wilson, Woodrow, 42
World War I, 37, 38, 40, 41, 42,
235n
World War II, 49, 51, 63n, 64,
77, 78

Xenophon, 225

Zandonai, Riccardo, 91n
Zeit, Die, 265–266
Zemlinsky, Alexander von, 126
Zlotnik, Asher G., 182n
Zola, Emile, 38
Zuffellato, Guido, 91n
Zurich, 35
Zurletti, Michelangelo, 17n
Zweig, Stefan, 46

HAVERGAL BRIAN ON MUSIC
Volume One: British Music
Edited by
Malcolm MacDonald

Havergal Brian (1876–1972) is best known as a prolific composer of symphonies – among them the enormous *Gothic* – who is gradually becoming recognised as an important and individual voice in 20th-century British music. It is far less widely realised that for a period of nearly 45 years (1904–1949) Brian was a comparably productive musical journalist.

Malcolm MacDonald has been investigating Brian's vast journalistic output, using his letters and other evidence to trace many of his unsigned contributions, and has selected enough material to fill a projected series of six volumes, each grouped around a common theme. In this first volume of selections he has brought together many of Brian's principal writings on the composers and events of the British Musical Renaissance – from polemical articles written when actively campaigning for his fellow-composers in the Midlands before World War I, to more considered appraisals of the inter-war period. Brian's heroes Elgar and Delius and his close friend Granville Bantock are generously represented – but we also find him discussing figures as diverse as Bax, Britten, Foulds, Goossens, Holbrooke, Holst, Billy Mayerl, Cyril Scott and Vaughan Williams.

In a substantial introduction, Malcolm MacDonald outlines Brian's journalistic career; and he has annotated the articles to elucidate Brian's copious contemporary references. The result is both a work of scholarship and an important historical source for an understanding of the British music of the early 20th century.

'Brian was an intelligent, broad-minded and perceptive writer, and gives a fair, if unorthodox, picture of British musical life in the first 40 years of this century.'   Clifford Bartlett, *BRIO*

'Brian is compulsive reading, serious, perceptive, bias, wrong, prescient, and always stylish and literate. [. . .] I can't wait for Volume 2.'
John Cox, *Southern Evening Echo*

Musicians on Music No. 3
438pp; index
£19.50 (hardcover): ISBN 0 907689 19 1
£9.50 (softcover): ISBN 0 907689 20 5

KLEMPERER ON MUSIC
Shavings from a Musician's Workbench
OTTO KLEMPERER
With a Preface by
Pierre Boulez
Edited by
Martin Anderson

Otto Klemperer's conducting career covered nearly three-quarters of this century. Although he was not chiefly a man of words, he wrote frequently on music during the course of his long life, and the writings assembled in this book date from 1906 until 1971. Klemperer writes here about musicians he knew and worked with, dwelling with especial interest and respect on Gustav Mahler, whose personal recommendation was vital in the early successes of Klemperer's career. His long association with Beethoven is documented in several articles. He writes on Bach, Berg, Bruckner, Hindemith, Mendelssohn, Mozart, Pfitzner, Schoenberg, Shostakovich, Sibelius, Strauss, Stravinsky, Tchaikovsky, Wagner, and others. He talks of colleagues such as Beecham and Toscanini, Ewald Dülberg and Max Reinhardt. He documents his own career, discussing conducting as far apart as Argentina and Russia, his return to Germany, his compositions, his battle to save Berlin's Kroll Opera.

Klemperer on Music also features, in print for the first time ever, a complete list of Klemperer's own compositions. He composed throughout his long life and his list of works is substantial, including symphonies, works for voice and orchestra, chamber and instrumental music, operas and many songs.

'Not only do his topics possess intrinsic historical interest [. . .] his view acquire historic importance in their own right'
Arthur Jacobs, *The Musical Times*

'such an enjoyable read'   *Hampstead and Highgate Express*

Musicians on Music No. 2
246pp; index
£12.95 (hardcover): ISBN 0 907689 13 2
£5.95 (softcover): ISBN 0 907689 14 0

BOULT ON MUSIC
Words from a Lifetime's Communication
SIR ADRIAN BOULT
With a Foreword by
Bernard Shore
and an Introduction by
Vernon Handley

One of this century's best-loved conductors, Sir Adrian Boult often wrote and broadcast on music during the course of his long life. His style of expression, whether writing, speaking or conducting, was always concerned with directness of communication. *Boult on Music* assembles the most important of Sir Adrian's broadcast essays and talks, exploring many aspects of his art. He discusses composers he knew and worked with, like Elgar and Vaughan Williams, as well as such figures as Schubert and Bach. He examines the craft of his conductor colleagues, like Toscanini, Wood, Nikisch and Beecham, and of fellow musicians like Menuhin and Casals. He also turns his attention to the problems and practicalities of the conductor's task.

Bernard Shore, for many years Sir Adrian's Principal Viola in the BBC Symphony Orchestra and a distinguished writer on music, contributed a Foreword on 'The Art of Sir Adrian'; and Vernon Handley, whom many regard as Sir Adrian's successor as the most important conductor of British music, introduces *Boult on Music*, assembled as a tribute to this great and modest man.

'There is no doubt that this was a collection worth making . . . . here are wisdom and kindness – two qualities which all who knew Sir Adrian will instantly recognise'
Jerrold Northrop Moore, *Times Literary Supplement*

'Never dull, often illuminating' *Southern Evening Echo*

'wisdoms worth long pondering' Michael Oliver, *The Gramophone*

Musicians on Music No. 1
196pp; index
£9.95 (hardcover): ISBN 0 907689 03 5
£4.95 (softcover): ISBN 0 907689 04 3